T0319691

Advances in Evolutionary Institutional Economics

STUDIES IN EVOLUTIONARY POLITICAL ECONOMY

Titles in the series include:

Understanding the Dynamics of a Knowledge Economy
Edited by Wilfred Dolfsma and Luc Soete

Advances in Evolutionary Institutional Economics
Edited by Hardy Hanappi and Wolfram Elsner

Varieties of Capitalism and New Institutional Deals
Edited by Wolfram Elsner and Hardy Hanappi

Advances in Evolutionary Institutional Economics

Evolutionary Mechanisms, Non-Knowledge and Strategy

Edited by

Hardy Hanappi

University of Technology, Institute for Mathematical Methods in Economics, Research Group Economics, Vienna, Austria

and

Wolfram Elsner

University of Bremen, Faculty of Economics and Business Studies, Institute for Institutional and Innovation Economics, Bremen, Germany

STUDIES IN EVOLUTIONARY POLITICAL ECONOMY

Edward Elgar
Cheltenham, UK • Northampton, MA, USA

© Hardy Hanappi and Wolfram Elsner 2008

All rights reserved. No part of this publication may be reproduced, stored in a retrieval system or transmitted in any form or by any means, electronic, mechanical or photocopying, recording, or otherwise without the prior permission of the publisher.

Published by
Edward Elgar Publishing Limited
The Lypiatts
15 Lansdown Road
Cheltenham
Glos GL50 2JA
UK

Edward Elgar Publishing, Inc.
William Pratt House
9 Dewey Court
Northampton
Massachusetts 01060
USA

A catalogue record for this book
is available from the British Library

Library of Congress Control Number: 2008927981

ISBN 978 1 84720 908 5

Printed and bound in Great Britain by MPG Books Ltd, Bodmin, Cornwall

Contents

Contributors

Sebastian Berger has a PhD in Economics (Bremen University) and is currently Lecturer at the University of Missouri Kansas City. Specialization: Social Costs of Business Enterprise; Development Economics; Ecological Economics; Political Institutionalism.

Martin Binder is a research fellow at the Max Planck Institute of Economics in Jena where he is working on welfare theoretic problems from an evolutionary perspective. Other research interests include institutional economics and the philosophy of economics.

Guido Buenstorf is a senior researcher at the Evolutionary Economics Group of the Max Planck Institute of Economics in Jena (Germany). His research interests center on industry evolution, entrepreneurship, and technology transfer.

Paul Davidson is a Visiting Scholar at the New School for Social Research. He is editor of the *Journal of Post Keynesian Economics*.

John B. Davis is Professor of History and Philosophy of Economics at the University of Amsterdam and Professor of Economics at Marquette University. He is author of *Keynes' Philosophical Development* and *The Theory of the Individual in Economics*, and co-editor of the *Journal of Economic Methodology*.

Wolfram Elsner is Professor of Economics, Faculty of Economics and Business Studies, Institute for Institutional and Innovation Economics (iino), University of Bremen. He worked outside academia from 1986 to 1995, as Director of the Planning Division of the Ministry of Economic Affairs of the State of Bremen, among others.

Hardy Hanappi is Professor of Economics and Head of the Research Group 'Economics' at the University of Technology in Vienna. He is also Jean Monnet Professor for Political Economy of European Integration.

Stavros Ioannides is Professor of Economics at Panteion University, Athens, Greece. His research focuses on Austrian Economics, evolutionary and institutional economics and the theory of the firm. He is the author of *The Market, Competition and Democracy: A Critique of Neo-Austrian Economics* (1992) and has co-edited *Evolution and Path Dependence in Economic Ideas: Past and Present* (2001) with Pierre Garrouste, and *European Collaboration in Research and Development: Public Policy and Business Strategy* (2003), with Yannis Caloghirou and Nicholas Vonortas, all published by Edward Elgar.

Oliver Kessler is Assistant Professor for International Relations at Bielefeld University. His research focuses on social constructivism, social theory of non-knowledge, and interdisciplinary research. He serves as one of the research coordinator of the Economic Sociology Research Network of the European Sociology Association.

Sascha Kraus is Assistant Professor at the University of Oldenburg, Germany, Lecturer at the University of Klagenfurt, Austria and the European University Viadrina Campus Slubice, Poland. His main research interests are entrepreneurship, strategy, and evolutionary economics.

Uta-Maria Niederle is Research Associate at the Max Planck Institute of Economics in Jena. Her major fields of interest are a general theory of institutional change, the evolution of property rights and the law, economic history and social anthropology, endogenous preferences, concepts and models of dynamics and systems.

Carl Henning Reschke holds a doctorate from the University of Witten/Herdecke, Germany. He is a founding member of the Institute for Management Research Cologne. His research interests center around strategy, innovation, cognition and evolution of social systems.

J.W. Stoelhorst is assistant professor at the Amsterdam Business School of the University of Amsterdam, where he teaches strategy and organization. He is one of the coordinators of the EAEPE research area 'The Ontological Foundations of Evolutionary Economics'. His research interests are on the intersection of theories of competitive advantage, theories of the firm and theories of technological change.

Ulrich Witt is Professor of Economics and Director at Max Planck Institute of Economics in Jena, Germany. His research fields are 'Economic Behavior' and its biological and psychological foundations, 'Long-term Economic

Growth', 'Institutional Change', 'Consumption and Production Theory', 'Industry Dynamics' and 'Firm Development', 'Methodological and Conceptual Problems of Theories of Evolution'.

Introduction: Evolutionary Economics in the Making

Hardy Hanappi and Wolfram Elsner

This book is concerned with evolutionary economics. Most of the contributors consider themselves more or less as members of this scientific community, and the sample of chapters presented is a good example of the evolutionary process of theory development as envisaged by evolutionary economics. From an evolutionary perspective theory advances by a continuous reshuffling of a variety of research approaches: new elements, i.e. innovative research papers, are continuously added while old ones are shifted into the background, either due to their increasing irrelevance for pressing research questions or due to new research results that prove them to be misleading special cases. As a matter of fact the recent renaissance of evolutionary economics owes much to the unifying force of the common goal to show that neoclassical economic theory has committed both crimes – it is useless with respect to policy advice and its assumptions make it an inadequate special case that therefore produces only inadequate theorems. Since the early 1980s more and more evolutionary economists thus have put the bugaboo of neoclassical economic theory to the test and proved that it failed – even if it always was hard to identify what the core of neoclassical thought really was. But to weed out bad theory from the variety of proposed theories is just one part of the evolutionary research process; the other part consists of adding new elements, of proposing more promising routes of research. And it is this new agenda that became more prominent in the most recent decade of research in evolutionary economics – and as a consequence in this book.

As Herbert Simon once compellingly coined it, the evolutionary process in principle consists of two elements: [1] a generator of variety sometimes called *mutation*, and a process of *testing*. Since received neoclassical economics does not pass the test, evolutionary economists are now left with the difficult task of developing a new variety by mutations. With respect to the mysterious concept of mutation no direct import from biology, where randomness plays the central role for this concept, is advisable.[2] What seems to be clear is that the process of mutation needs two parts: a set of old, inherited structures, and some kind of original new glue that binds them to a newly emerging quality, a novelty. By the interaction of these two elements random mutation is transformed into directed mutation.[3] As noted above, after showing that the dominating competing theory, the core of neoclassical economics, failed the test to provide adequate insight for understanding the political economy, evolutionary economics now is turning to produce a new theory – a new directed mutation – out of given theory fragments and original intuition.

Several routes to guide the quest for this new approach can be identified. Four of them are particularly important, and the chapters in this volume provide an impressive account of how successfully they can be followed.

Route 1 works on the concept of theory-guiding visions. This idea has been emphasized by Joseph Schumpeter and in essence holds that to understand as well as to develop an approach a general vision of how the object of investigation seems to work is mandatory.[4] Chapter 1 by Ulrich Witt thus provides an interesting framework of visions held by evolutionary economists and even tries to give some empirical quantitative estimation of how important they currently are. Another, somewhat competing contribution to this route can be found in Chapter 2, written by J.W. Stoelhorst, who – following Geoff Hodgson – proposes Universal Darwinism as a guiding vision.

Route 2 also puts visions in its focus, but instead of working on contemporary held visions it tries to rediscover and to resurrect grand theories produced by past scholars. This route earns special attention since it explicitly considers theoretical knowledge as an historically changing stock variable. Parts are added, parts are discarded, and parts are forgotten due to circumstances that should not necessarily have devalued them. As the history of thought shows in many cases it proved easier to rediscover things than to reinvent them. In Chapter 4 of this volume Sebastian Berger and Wolfram Elsner revive two concepts – the 'Open Systems Approach' and the 'Cumulative Circular Causation' – closely linked to such eminent theorists as Veblen, Kaldor, Kapp, Myrdal and Georgescu-Roegen. Another important contribution in this vein comes from Paul Davidson in Chapter 8. He presents his view on a resurrected Keynes, with a strong emphasis on the methodological innovation to be found there – but also sharing Keynes's own emphasis on pressing questions of economic policy, an aspect too often missing in evolutionary approaches. A third, extremely appealing chapter along these lines is provided by Stavros Ioannides in Chapter 10. The arguments of this chapter center on the treatment of the concept of knowledge during important debates in the history of economic thought.

Ioannidis covers a wide range – from Mises and Hayek via Stigler and Arrow to Grossman and Helpman – to present an illuminating survey.

Route 3 for the emergence of the new theory proposes turning attention to empirical findings. Following this route has produced tremendous success for the natural sciences and certainly is an indispensable ingredient for every scientific project. Guido Buenstdorf in Chapter 3 concentrates on industry evolution, in particular on the case of the US farm tractor industry, to show how empirical findings can inform a general theory of economic evolution. The second example of a bottom-up development of an evolutionary perspective comes from Carl Henning Reschke and Sascha Kraus in Chapter 9. They start with the empirically observed needs of strategic management to give management science an evolutionary twist. Both chapters not only make clear how important it is to scrutinize the processes that actually take place, they should also convince economists that there is still an enormous territory not yet explored.

Finally route 4 towards innovative theory paves its way by the use of methodological innovation. Three chapters in this volume are particularly concerned with this topic. In Chapter 5 Martin Binder and Uta-Maria Niederle present their view on the interdependence between institutions and preference change. Indeed they are representative of a large group of evolutionary economists, which launches new concepts as being central to economic theory – hence the label methodological innovation. While the preference structures of individuals in mainstream theory usually are assumed to be exogenously fixed, the authors consider their change in relation to institutions, a phenomenon not even explicitly modeled in most standard models though omnipresent in real economic life. Institutions, understood as temporary solutions to social contradictions,[5] certainly play an overwhelming role in the understanding of contemporary economics. And it is not surprising that the heated scientific debate on the nature and essence of these meso-economic phenomena is one of the major innovative sources of evolutionary economics.[6] In Chapter 6 John B. Davis proposes agent-based modeling to model what he calls 'complex individuals', i.e. individuals based on a relational conception. He critically discusses recent approaches to this problem, e.g. Jason Potts's work, and poses them in an epistemological context. Another original methodological innovation then comes from Oliver Kessler in Chapter 7, who emphasizes the importance of ignorance for the development of knowledge. He proves how useful it is to start with standard Bayesian concepts to arrive finally at rather unconventional conclusions.

As the little tour de force covering received theory – from Frank Ramsey via Leonard Savage to Ludwig Wittgenstein – of Oliver Kessler's contribution shows, the chapters always contain a certain amount of overlapping areas with respect to the proposed four routes. Paul Davidson covers institutions important for international finance; Sebastian Berger and Wolfram Elsner underline methodological innovations initiated by Erwin Schrödinger, and so on. It is exactly this cross-fertilization that seems to be one of the more important characteristics of evolutionary economics. Returning to the argument in the beginning of this introduction, all these efforts to provide theory for further theory evolution contained in this book are to be seen as elements for a future evolutionary economics – a new combination in status nascendi.

The work presented in this volume owes a lot to the scientific community of evolutionary economists, and in particular to the European Association for Evolutionary Political Economy (EAEPE). For more than 20 years the vivid intellectual exchange within this community, e.g. at the EAEPE conference in Bremen 2005 where the first versions of the chapters of this book were presented, has stimulated research and has generated a continuous flow of new ideas. Our special thanks of course go to the contributing authors – it is their work, which we edit. Manuel Wäckerle's pivotal organizational and editorial help in the production process has to be emphasized as well as the good cooperation with the publishing team at Edward Elgar, in particular with Matthew Pitman. Cooperation has been a pleasure – and we hope that reading it will be a pleasure too.

NOTES

[1] 'The simplest scheme of evolution is one that depends on two processes; a generator and a test. The task of the generator is to produce variety, new forms that have not existed previously, whereas the task of the test is to cull out the newly generated forms so that only those that are well fitted to the environment will survive. In modern biological Darwinism genetic mutation is the generator, natural selection the test' (Simon, 1969, p. 52).

[2] Stephen Jay Gould in his monumental book on evolutionary theory advises an adverse move for biology '... to reset the balance of structure and function, or constraint and selection, in evolutionary theory – so that structure and constraint, the formerly disfavored and neglected first terms of each pairing, can achieve the same attention and respect that we properly accord to the proven potency of Darwinian forces represented by the second term in each pairing' (Gould, 2002, p. 1155). The interdependence of testing environments and variety generating vital forces thus always should be kept in mind.

[3] In (Hanappi 1994, pp. 7-21) the stepwise advancement of directed mutation has been used to distinguish different stages of evolution.

[4] 'Obviously, in order to be able to posit ourselves any problems at all, we should first have to visualize a distinct set of coherent phenomena as a worth-while object of our analytic efforts. In other words, analytic effort is of necessity preceded by a preanalytic cognitive act that supplies the raw material for the analytic effort. ... , this preanalytic cognitive act will be called Vision' (Schumpeter, 1954, p. 41).

[5] Compare (Hanappi and Egger 1995) for a summary of the productive role of contradictions and (Hanappi 2002) for an approach to model emergence and vanishing of institutions.

[6] Interesting recent contributions to this topic come from (Dopfer, Foster and Potts 2004) and (Elsner 2007).

REFERENCES

Dopfer Kurt, John Foster and Jason Potts (2004), 'Micro-meso-macro', *Journal of Evolutionary Economics*, 14(3).

Egger Edeltraud and Hanappi Hardy (1995), *Modelling Creative Contradictions for Organizational Change*, Proceedings of the Hawaii International Conference on Systems Science − 28 'Modelling the Dynamics of Organizations and Information Systems', IEEE, Maui, Hawaii.

Elsner Wolfram (2007), 'Why Meso? On "Aggregation" and "Emergence", and Why and How the Meso Level is Essential in Social Economics', *Forum for Social Economics*, 36(2), pp. 1-16.

Gould S.J. (2002), *The Structure of Evolutionary Theory*, Belknapp Press of Harvard University Press, Cambridge, MA and London.

Hanappi H. (1994), *Evolutionary Economics*, Avebury Publishing, Aldershot.

Hanappi H. (2002), *Endogenisierung von Institutionen*, in M. Lehmann-Waffenschmidt (ed.), *Studien zur Evolutorischen Ökonomik*, *V*, Duncker & Humblot, Berlin, pp. 113-132.

Schumpeter J. (1954), *History of Economic Analysis*, Oxford University Press, London.

Simon H.A. (1969), *The Sciences of the Artificial*, MIT Press, Cambridge, MA.

PART ONE

EVOLUTIONARY MECHANISMS

1. Heuristic Twists and Ontological Creeds: A Road Map for Evolutionary Economics

Ulrich Witt

INTRODUCTION

By the end of the 1980s, interest in, and arguments based on, evolutionary concepts had become characteristic of a new heterodoxy in economics. It was formed by a group of economists so heterogeneous that one could write: 'The difficulties involved in trying to identify the common elements in ... "evolutionary approaches" would seem to be matched only by the diversity of their theoretical backgrounds. Indeed, with the exception of cases based on an analogy with biological evolutionary theory, similar diversity also appears in the attempts made over the past few years to identify the essential features of an evolutionary approach in economics' (Witt 1992, p. 3). Since those times the use of the label 'evolutionary' in the economic literature has heavily increased. In their bibliometric analysis of the EconLit database, Silva and Teixeira (2006) document that, of all articles with the term 'evolutionary' among their keywords that were published in economic journals up to 2005, less than 2 percent appeared in 1990. The yearly share increases steadily to almost 12 percent in 2004. The development looks pretty much like an exponential growth path that fills a growing niche that, in 2005, represents roughly 1 percent of all EconLit covered journal articles published in economics. Yet, as the authors explain, there is still neither a common methodology nor a consensus on the relevant topics in the articles – not to speak of a 'hard core' of assumptions as it underlies, for example, the equilibrium-cum-optimization framework of canonical economic theory.

One particular cluster of contributions can, however, be singled out: that of evolutionary game theory. Authors in this field differ in their background and interests from those contributing to what can broadly be characterized as evolutionary economics. In fact, the two communities seem to take little notice of each other (see, for example, the statements in Nelson and Winter 2002 and in Samuelson 2002). The distinct features of evolutionary game theory, as compared to rational game theory, are special assumptions and solution algorithms originally designed to meet explanatory demands in evolutionary biology, particularly sociobiology (see Trivers 1971; Maynard Smith 1982). After the big success of rational game theory some authors also developed an interest in evolutionary game theory – though its application to economic phenomena did not seem to have been the primary motive (see, for example, Weibull 1995). Indeed, while evolutionary game theory makes a lot of sense in sociobiology in explaining how certain forms of genetically determined social behavior can be fostered by natural selection, the theory still seeks a similarly convincing application in the economic domain (see Friedman 1998; Dosi and Winter 2002).

Applications of evolutionary game theory in economics follow basically two interpretations. One interpretation borrows from evolutionary biology the notion of a selection mechanism and the corresponding algorithms (usually some form of replicator dynamics, see Schuster and Sigmund 1983) for modeling human learning processes in an economic context. Since learning is a non-genetic adaptation process, the idea is not to claim that the biological mechanisms directly apply to economic behavior. The idea rather is to construct analogies between genetic adaptation mechanisms and non-genetic ones. Constructing analogies between different disciplinary domains is a frequent *heuristic* device, that is guidance in framing problems and setting up hypotheses. A question to be distinguished from this is the *ontological* claims that theories make (often implicitly) regarding the connection between the disciplinary domains involved. In ontological terms, that is with respect to the basic assumptions about the structure of reality, analogy constructions typically treat the economic problems as disconnected from, and independent of, the biological ones.

In the other interpretation of evolutionary game theory the specific biological context of evolutionary game theory is declared directly relevant to economics. It is claimed that certain very basic features of human economic behavior like altruism, moral behavior, fairness, and other rules of conduct are genetically determined and therefore best explained as a result of natural selection (see, for example, Binmore 2001). Often the existence of such features of human behavior is traced back to their conjectured emergence at the times of early human phylogeny when natural selection pressure on the human species was still high enough to shape behavior according to what can be speculated to have raised genetic fitness. Unlike in the former interpretation, such a view obviously presumes a monistic, naturalistic ontology.

In contrast to the research focusing on applications of evolutionary game theory, the contributions to evolutionary economics are much more diverse in interpretation and origin. In part, this reflects different views of evolution as they were held at different times. The very notion of evolution is an offspring of the philosophy and social philosophy of the late 18th and early 19th centuries that has later been adopted into the biological thought of the late 19th and 20th centuries. Early philosophical writings on evolution thus anteceded Darwin (and seem to have influenced him). These earlier writings had, and still have, an impact on evolutionary economics independent of, and in addition to, more recent ideas that were borrowed from emerging evolutionary biology. A particularly significant case is the pre-Darwinian evolutionary thought developed by Scottish moral philosophers like Hume and Adam Smith. In view of this fact it is not surprising that the background of, and the interpretations offered by, different strands of thought in evolutionary economics vary considerably.

As will turn out, with respect to the heuristic twists and the ontological creeds there is a similar divide between the different strands of thought in evolutionary economics as has been diagnosed for evolutionary game theory. As in the case of evolutionary game theory, the authors often do not seem aware of what assumptions they implicitly make. In view of the influence of methodological instrumentalism in economics (claiming to evaluate hypotheses exclusively by their predictive power) it may not be surprising that, unlike in other disciplines, there is no culture of discussing why and how one arrives at one's hypotheses (the heuristic problem). Similarly, there is no tradition of laying open the ontological assumptions – evolutionary economics being no exception. However, a discussion of these points is very helpful for understanding where, and why, different authors have developed such different, partly incommensurable views on what evolutionary economics is all about as well as what distinguishes evolutionary economics from the more canonical economic theory.

In some contributions, selection metaphors or formal analogies, borrowed from evolutionary biology, are used as heuristic devices to model processes of economic change. If the ontological question of how economic change relates to change in nature is not entirely ignored, a kind of two-tier ontology is usually assumed. This means that economic and biological evolutionary processes are considered independent and disconnected elements of reality. In contrast, other contributions follow a monistic, naturalistic approach in which evolutionary change in the economy and in nature represent one sphere of reality and are therefore considered mutually dependent processes. (An ontological continuity assumption like this does not exclude, of course, that evolution in the economy and in nature take place by different means, in different forms, and on different time scales and therefore require quite different explanatory hypotheses, see Witt 2004.)

Given the diversity of the contributions, an attempt to take stocks of the development of evolutionary economics in general is out of reach here. What will be offered instead is a more expanded inquiry into how heuristic twists and ontological creeds lead to the different, partly incommensurable approaches in evolutionary economics and how they influence recent research trends. Accordingly, the second section starts a reflection on what is an evolutionary approach and shows how the different answers to this question indeed correspond with the particular heuristic twist and ontological creed of the corresponding authors. By distinguishing between heuristic attitudes and ontology assumptions two different dimensions of the problem become visible that are used in the third section for drawing up a road map for evolutionary economics. Of the various competing interpretations of evolutionary economics that are discussed, all have their strengths and weaknesses. For this reason it is difficult to decide on a priori grounds which one to favor. In order to rely not only on an own appraisal here, the fourth section reports on the results of an opinion poll among evolutionary economists who were asked to evaluate the progress that has been made in the field and, thus, to indirectly assess the different heuristic twists and ontological creeds. The fifth section offers the conclusions.

WHAT DOES AN EVOLUTIONARY APPROACH MEAN?

The question of what an evolutionary approach to economics means has been discussed for two decades now, but there is still no general agreement on the answer. But the issues on which the opinions differ have become clearer. One issue is the differences in ontological creeds which are rarely explicitly stated. As already mentioned in the introduction, some contributions to evolutionary economics presume something like a two-tier ontology. This means that evolution in nature and evolution in the economy are treated as belonging to different, disconnected spheres of reality. Such a non-monistic ontology is often vindicated by recourse to the fundamental Cartesian divide between humanities – where economics belongs – and the sciences (see, for example, Herrmann-Pillath 2001). Other contributions presume a monistic ontology. This means that they see the two spheres of evolution as connected and, hence, favor a naturalistic, but not necessarily reductionist, approach to economic changes (see, for example, Dopfer and Potts 2004 who explicitly reject the Cartesian dualism). Let us use the labels 'monistic' vs. 'two-tier' as short-hand notation for the two alternative creeds (Table 1.1).

Another issue, to be distinguished from the ontological controversy, is the differences in heuristic attitudes. These attitudes determine how problems are framed and hypotheses are formed in developing a theory. At this level, the only general agreement seems to be the understanding that evolution means systematic change over time. There is no agreement as to what the systematic features are. The answer differs according to whether or not one's frame of reference for the concept of 'evolution' is the Darwinian theory of natural selection. In many disciplinary domains, not just evolutionary economics alone, attempts at conceptualizing evolution are orientated today by, or have their heuristic basis in, the Darwinian theory of natural selection. Its success has made evolutionary biology for many writers the ideal of an evolutionary science. Whether it is the evolution of technology, of science, of language, of human society, or of the economy, the systematic elements of change are identified with the working of three principles: blind variation, selection, and retention (see Ziman 2000; Hull 2001; Hashimoto 2006; Hallpike 1985, 1986; Nelson 1995, respectively). These principles are abstract, but still domain-specific, reductions of some key elements of the Darwinian theory of natural selection (Campbell 1965).

It cannot be denied that the Darwinian theory is a very attractive heuristic reference frame. However, borrowing its concepts – even in a very abstract form – in order to conceptualize evolution in other disciplinary domains means to draw on analogy constructions. As discussed elsewhere (Witt 2003a), this implies a considerable risk of misrepresentations. There are other ways of framing evolution in generic terms that do not rely on a heuristic inspired by evolutionary biology and, consequently, lead to different concepts. To explain this consider an entity that evolves, for example, a population of living organisms, the production and consumption activities of the agents in an economy, a language spoken in a human community, or the set of ideas produced by the human mind. These entities are obviously capable of transforming themselves over time 'from within'. (Their change over time can be, but does not have to be, triggered by external, unexplained forces or 'shocks' affecting them.) As argued elsewhere (Witt 1993), the ultimate cause of why they can change endogenously is their capacity to create novelty, where novelty is defined as something that alters a pre-existing structure, context, functioning, or meaning. The processes by which this is done can vary greatly from one scientific domain to another.[1]

However, where novelty emerges locally in a system (for example in a species, in languages, or in the economy), recognizing the endogenous generation of novelty alone is a necessary, but not sufficient, condition for understanding the self-transformation process of that system. The self-transformation process then also hinges on whether and how novelty disseminates in the corresponding system. The dissemination is usually contingent on many factors. It may be a matter of complex, competitive diffusion processes like in natural selection. Or it may be anything between

simple imitation and complex cascading and chain reactions as in the
dissemination of human thought, practices, and artifacts. 'Evolution' can thus
be characterized generically – in a way that is not domain-specific – as a
process of change whose systematic elements are the endogenous generation
of novelty and its subsequent dissemination. Obviously, Campbell's
conceptualization of evolution as a process driven by the principles of blind
variation, selection, and retention, is a special, domain-specific case, since
the emergence of novelty can, but does not have to, result from blind
variation, and the dissemination can, but does not have to, be subject to
selection and retention.[2] If the alternative heuristic twists, to be dubbed here
'Darwinian concepts' vs. 'generic concepts', are cross-tabulated against the
two alternative creeds at the ontological level, four different combinations
result as in Table 1.1.

Table 1.1: Combinations of Alternative Heuristic and Ontological Positions

		Ontological creed	
		monistic	*two-tier*
Heuristic twist	*Darwinian concepts* (variation, selection, retention)	'Universal Darwinism'	'neo-Schumpeterians'
	generic concepts (novelty emergence and dissemination)	'Continuity Hypothesis'	'Schumpeter's development'

In order to briefly explain the different combinations consider the first row
in Table 1.1 representing a heuristic twist in which the evolution is
conceptualized in terms of the Darwinian theory of natural selection. Such a
heuristic position is compatible with a monistic ontology. In fact, that
combination corresponds to the approach suggested by the proponents of
'Universal Darwinism'. Their interpretation claims equal validity of the
abstract principles of variation, selection, and retention for evolutionary
processes at any layer of reality, including economics (see Hodgson 2002;
Hodgson and Knudsen 2006; for a criticism see Buenstorf 2006; Cordes
2006). However, a heuristic conceptualization of evolution by means of the
Darwinian principles is also compatible with a two-tier ontology, that is with

rejecting the monistic claims of the naturalistic Darwinian world view. Indeed, this seems to be a frequent position in evolutionary economics (though it is sometimes difficult to distinguish from ambivalence towards, or ignorance of, the relevance of the naturalistic stratum for economic theorizing). Many contributions, most prominently the neo-Schumpeterian synthesis proposed by Nelson and Winter (1982), construct analogies between competitive economic processes and natural selection or use selection algorithms as formal metaphors for describing organizational change and industrial dynamics. But they refrain from taking a naturalistic perspective on the changes in the economy they explore.

The second row of Table 1.1 represents a heuristic position whose concept of evolution is derived from a generic (domain-transcending) characterization. A heuristic position like that is again compatible with both a monistic and a non-monistic, two-tier ontology. In fact, the combination of a non-Darwinian concept of evolution and a non-monistic ontology corresponds to Schumpeter's understanding of economic 'development intrinsically generated from within itself'.[3] Here 'development' is a synonym for 'evolution', the term that Schumpeter avoided precisely because he did not want to be associated with a monistic, Darwinian perspective. In his portrayal of economic development, the economy is pushed forward by entrepreneurial innovations. If successful they are imitated many times over and thus disseminate in, and change the structure of, the industries. With the endogenous emergence of novelty and its dissemination, Schumpeter (1912) thus postulated general principles of evolutionary change (independent of any Darwinian analogies) long before the recent debate on generic, trans-disciplinary features of evolution.

The combination of a generic heuristic position and a monistic ontology can be given a reductionist interpretation, but this is neither necessary nor does it seem appropriate for the domain of evolutionary economics. As explained elsewhere (Witt 2003b, Chap. 1) a non-reductionist alternative can be based on an ontological 'continuity hypothesis'. The rationale of this hypothesis can perhaps best be understood by setting the economic evolutionary process in historical perspective with evolution in nature. Consider the processes by which the species have evolved in nature, and still change, under natural selection pressure. In the monistic view this is a form of evolution that, in historical time, antecedes all man-made, cultural forms of evolution, including economic evolution. In fact, it has shaped the ground for, and still influences the constraints of, cultural evolution. But – and this makes the continuity hypothesis a non-trivial claim – the mechanisms and regularities of cultural evolution that have emerged on that ground differ substantially from those of natural selection and descent. Human intelligent learning, creativity, and understanding have generated mechanisms of intragenerational adaptation that, for their high pace alone, cannot reasonably be reduced to the mechanisms and regularities of evolution in nature.

Like Universal Darwinism, the continuity hypothesis thus rests on an ontological monism. Unlike Universal Darwinism it does not claim, however, that evolution in nature and cultural evolution in the economy can identically be reduced to the abstract Darwinian principles of variation, selection, and retention (see Vromen 2004). The heuristic that is characteristic of the continuity hypothesis is more sophisticated. For the times where evolution in nature overlapped with economic change – as was likely the case in early phases of human phylogeny – it suggests to investigate the interactions between genetically based natural selection processes on the one hand and cultural learning on the other.[4] Where – as in present times – economic change results exclusively from cultural evolution, however, the continuity hypothesis suggests to focus on how novelty emerges, under what conditions, and whether and how novelty diffuses through imitation and adoption processes.

A ROAD MAP FOR EVOLUTIONARY ECONOMICS

Each of the four combinations denoted in Table 1.1 implies different answers to the question of what is special about the evolutionary approach and leads to different ways of theorizing about evolutionary change in the economy. Table 1.1 therefore offers a convenient grid for drawing up a road map for evolutionary economics. An attempt will now be undertaken to outline in brief such a map and to locate on that map selected contributions. At the end of the 19th century, several prominent economists were impressed by Darwin's theory of evolution and the way it changed the scientific understanding of the world. Some, like Alfred Marshall, toyed with evolutionary ideas, but did not break with the contemporary approach of 'pure' economics that rejected any naturalistic, monistic ontology.

The exception is Veblen who not only introduced the term 'evolutionary economics' to the discipline (Veblen 1898), he also gave it a programmatic interpretation that was clearly informed by a monistic Darwinian world view (see Hodgson 1998). Moreover, he showed a remarkable awareness of the role of heuristic frames when he criticized his fellow economists' use of *mechanic* metaphors like 'tendencies', 'controlling principles', 'equilibria', 'disturbing factors' etc. His monistic, Darwinian view of the descent of man notwithstanding, he resisted the idea of replacing these mechanical metaphors by biological ones, for example the selection metaphor. Instead, he suggested tracing the historical record of human economic activities that, he submitted, evolve according to the changing habits, including habits of thought, and institutions in their cumulative adaptations to the self-generated new conditions. In his books (Veblen 1899, 1914) he reconstructed in detail the history of particular attitudes and habits of thought that he considered significant for the 'cumulative causation' of the present-day appearance of the economy including its technology and institutions. In doing so he insisted that man-made institutional evolution unfolds by its own rules. With the latter claim he can be argued to come close to the continuity hypothesis (see Cordes 2007). Although he did not consider any generic characterization of evolution, Veblen's position may thus be inferred to be closer to the lower left cell in Table 1.1 than to the position of Universal Darwinism in the upper left cell.[5]

While Veblen is considered the father of evolutionary economics by some, others see the intellectual roots of evolutionary economics in Schumpeter (1912, 1934). As already mentioned, Schumpeter avoided the term 'evolution' just because of its Darwinian connotations (possibly also because he did not wish to be associated with Veblen's 'evolutionary economics'). He seems to have seen his theory of economic development as supplementing the existing pure theory of economics (see Schumpeter 1912, Chap. 7) and apparently also as having the same – non-monistic – ontological status. His heuristic inspiration seems to have come at least in part from another major intellectual controversy of his time, namely the debate on the Marxist teachings of a crisis-prone capitalist development of the economy. Not a Marxist himself, Schumpeter realized, however, that the uneven growth process in the period of 'promoterism' in Europe in the late 19th and early 20th centuries had created previously unknown forms of industrialism and wealth. For him, capitalist development therefore meant first of all entrepreneurship and innovations or, in more abstract terms, the emergence of novelty and its dissemination. As mentioned, in identifying these driving forces of change generated 'from within' the economy, Schumpeter thus recognized the generic features of evolution independent of Darwinian concepts. (Combined with non-monistic ontology this explains his place in the lower right cell of Table 1.1.)

However, Schumpeter did not exploit the potential of his ingenious heuristic twist. With an artificial distinction between invention and innovation and the claim that it is not the conceiving of new ideas, but the 'doing the thing', the carrying out of innovative ventures, that drives development, he stopped the analysis halfway. Important as this step is for a breakthrough in explaining what drives economic evolution, some crucial problems of how the economic evolutionary process works are excluded. To mention some: How is new knowledge being created? What does a possible feedback between search, discovery, experimentation, and adoption of innovations look like? By what motivations may those feedbacks be governed? Furthermore, by insisting on making the connection to the theory of unsteady capitalist development, that is to business cycle theory, Schumpeter was able to make himself a name as a contributor to what was the cutting edge research in economics at the time.[6] But he missed the opportunity to set the stage for what could have become a Schumpeterian school focusing on the evolution of the economy.

When Schumpeter (1942) later modified important parts of his theory, this was not conducive either to strengthening the evolutionary focus. Asserting that the promoter-entrepreneur has become increasingly obsolete, he abandoned even those (psychological, motivational) underpinnings of his theory that had been difficult to reconcile with the equilibrium-cum-optimization paradigm (Schumpeter 1942, p. 132). In the bureaucratic organization of the large corporations and trusts, he claimed, the carrying out of innovations had been taken over by teams of trained specialists. But he did not explain how these teams operate in their innovative activities, how the search for, and the pursuit of, novel strategies is achieved and affects performance. He remained reluctant to address the problem of how novelty emerges in the economy. Instead, he focused on what he considered the significant implications of an incessant, routine-like, industrial innovativeness. Monopolistic practices are portrayed as characteristic of the process of 'creative destruction' (ibid., Chap. 8) and a necessary concomitant of the economic growth that the process generates. Such an interpretation challenges the static model of perfect competition and has therefore attracted a great deal of attention among economists.[7]

At the beginning of the 1950s, in the debate on 'economic natural selection' (Alchian 1950; Penrose 1952), a new combination of heuristic orientations and ontological assumptions – the selection analogies and metaphors belonging to the upper right cell of Table 1.1 – made their appearance. The controversy revolved around the question of whether, in a competitive market, firm behavior (and its underlying objectives) can survive, if it is not profit-maximizing. The motivation of some participants in the debate was to rectify profit-maximizing behavior (Friedman 1953). But, on closer inspection, the profit level that suffices to ensure survival at a particular time and in a particular market turns out to vary with so many factors that no unique profit maximum can be determined (Winter 1964; Metcalfe 2002). Its limited constructive value notwithstanding, the debate was instrumental in establishing an approach to evolutionary economics characterized by a heuristic analogies to Darwinian concepts combined with a non-naturalistic (non-monistic) ontology. In the form outlined by Nelson and Winter's (1982) neo-Schumpeterian synthesis, this approach seems in the meantime to have become something like the 'dominant design' in evolutionary theorizing.

The neo-Schumpeterian synthesis combines Schumpeter's (1942) broad views of industrial innovativeness, structural change, and growth with a conceptualization of the evolutionary process in terms of a selection metaphor. This means that, while Nelson and Winter took over Schumpeter's non-monistic ontological position, they followed a different heuristic twist. (Hence the place in the upper right cell of Table 1.1.) The point of departure for the synthesis can be argued to be Schumpeter's assertion that the role of the entrepreneur as an innovator was taken over by teams and departments in corporate organizations. Where Schumpeter lacked a notion of how those corporate divisions operate, Nelson and Winter entered the organizational and behavioral theories of the firm that had been developed in the meantime by the Carnegie school (March and Simon 1958; Cyert and March 1963).

Informed by the notion of bounded rationality, Nelson and Winter (1982, Chap. 5) argue that organizations are based in their internal interactions on behavioral routines, rules of thumb, and regular interaction patterns. Production planning, calculation, price setting, and even the allocation of R&D funds, are all seen as following routine and rule-bound behavior. Based on the selection metaphor, the firms' routines are then interpreted as 'genotypes' and the specific decisions resulting from the applied routines as 'phenotypes'. The latter are supposed to affect the firms' overall performance. Different routines and different decisions lead to differences in the firms' growth. On the assumption that routines which successfully contribute to growth are not changed, the actual expansion can be understood as an increase in relative frequency of those 'genes-routines', while routines causing a deteriorating performance are unlikely to expand. Their relative frequency therefore declines.

Nelson and Winter's conceptualization of economic evolution allows the exploration of the implications of the fairly realistic scenario by running simulation experiments. They achieve in this way a powerful reinterpretation of economic growth as being driven by technological search and market selection. This reinterpretation sets the stage for a great number of inquiries done later into the role of technological innovations, their competitive market penetration, and their effects on productivity increases (see, for example, Dosi et al. 1988). Another important result is the reinterpretation of innovativeness and the market structure emerging from innovation competition. Nelson and Winter (1982, Chap. 14) show that instead of the original version of the Schumpeter hypothesis on the relationship between market structure and innovativeness, their simulation results suggest the inverse causal relationship. This means that the degree of concentration within an industry, taken as a measure for the degree to which monopolistic practices are pursued, is itself a consequence of, rather than a prerequisite for, a high rate of innovativeness in the industry.

Nelson and Winter's simulation-based analysis succeeds in demonstrating that evolutionary economic processes can be modeled in a way that challenges the canonical equilibrium-cum-optimization approach in economics. The simulation-based modeling of selection processes operating on populations of firm routines and of competitive innovativeness has become a major tool in evolutionary economics since for investigating the consequences of innovative activities in the markets (see Malerba and Orsenigo 1995). Other authors took up, varied, and extended Nelson and Winter's simulation approach. Gerybadze (1982) introduced product innovations. Andersen (1994) extended the program to include game-theoretic simulations and tried to generalize the approach into what he called 'artificial economic evolution'. Kwasnicki (1996) elaborated on innovation-driven industrial dynamics by allowing firm routines to be recombined.

The introduction of analytical models based on diffusion and replicator dynamics by Metcalfe (1988, 1994) allowed the rigor of the analogy constructions to be increased. In his thorough restatement of Schumpeter's notion of creative destruction, Metcalfe (1998) puts the competitive process center stage. In his model, a principle is reproduced which was originally stated by the biologist R.A. Fisher (who merged Darwinian theory with population genetics in the 1920s). That principle relates the variance in terms of behavior within a given population to the speed with which selection eliminates inferior traits from that population. In Metcalfe's economic framework, the variety of behavioral traits within a population of firms in an industry is defined by comparison with the current best practice in technology. Under certain assumptions this translates into corresponding production cost differentials. Fisher's principle then states that competition within the industry will be fiercer, the greater the variety of firms and their technologies. Entering the Schumpeterian notion of an entrepreneurial innovation process, which always increases the variety in an industry, the dynamics of the competitive capitalist engine of growth is elegantly exposed as an interplay of variety-increasing and variety-reducing processes.

All these further developments have essentially maintained the specific combination of a Darwinian inspired heuristic (selection metaphor) with a non-monistic ontology that is characteristic of the neo-Schumpeterian synthesis. Indeed, the central role of the selection metaphor as the distinguishing principle of evolutionary economics has repeatedly been emphasized (see, for example, Dosi and Nelson 1994; Nelson 1995; Zollo and Winter 2002) and a reinterpretation in terms of the position of 'Universal Darwinism' has recently been rejected (Nelson 2006). But it has also been suggested that the focus of evolutionary economics be extended to the institutional side of the economy and the co-evolution of technology and institutions (Nelson and Sampat 2001). The problem then is that the heuristic use of the selection principle, characteristic of the neo-Schumpeterian synthesis, cannot easily be extended to an analysis of institutional evolution, not to speak of other facets of economic evolution occurring, for example, in consumer behavior, in forms of non-market coordination, or in the changing role of nature and natural constraints for human living. Some doubts may therefore be raised as to whether the heuristic underlying the neo-Schumpeterian synthesis is indeed appropriate to cover the entire range of evolving economic phenomena.

Contrary to such doubts, the popularity of the selection metaphor seems to be unbroken, if not even growing, not least also as a result of increasing utilization of the genetic algorithms and, more generally, evolution algorithms (see Schwefel 1992) that were developed in artificial intelligence. These simulation devices merge a numerically emulated recombination (mutation) process with the simulated selection processes. It is not clear, however, what economic processes can be represented by these formal metaphors and analogies. Marimon et al. (1989) demonstrate that a spontaneous emergence of a medium of exchange in a decentralized exchange economy can be simulated on this basis – confirming Menger's (1963) old conjecture. Yet, unlike in the competing game-theoretic explanations for the same phenomenon based on analytical models (for example Wärneryd 1990), it is not entirely evident whose behavior is actually supposed to be described by the variant of the genetic algorithm applied by Marimon et al. (1989). Something similar holds for the explanation of norms emerging from adaptive learning given by Dosi et al. (1999) on the basis of a model using genetic programs.

Sometimes it is argued that evolution algorithms are good for modeling individual learning (Ebersberger and Pyka 2004). Yet there are both theoretical and empirical arguments raising doubts about this claim (see Chattoe 1994; Brenner 1998). When focusing on aggregate market dynamics resulting from the actions of large numbers of agents, it may be useful and acceptable to approximate their behavior by a rough trial-and-error learning hypothesis and to model this by genetic algorithms or programs massively operating in parallel and interacting. This has been shown by Markose et al. (2005) who simulate the evolution of a population of successful investment strategies in a competitive environment that, at the aggregate market level, reproduces the stylized facts of financial markets (power law distribution of investors' income and market efficiency). Again this modeling strategy competes, of course, with analytical models, this time of the replicator dynamics type in evolutionary finance (see Blume and Easley 1992).

The neo-Schumpeterians (as well as other adherents of selection metaphors and analogies) differ from Schumpeter in their heuristic orientation but not in their ontological assumptions. More recently there have also been some theoretical works that differ from Schumpeter neither in their ontological assumptions nor in their heuristic orientation on the generic features of evolution, that is on the emergence and diffusion of novelty (the combination in the lower right cell in Table 1.1). These works covered by the catchwords 'path-dependence' and 'lock-in' of technological developments (see David 1993; Arthur 1994), do not use selection algorithms, but model more or less complex, competitive diffusion processes. The relevance of these contributions becomes apparent when one tries to assess the role of dynamic models in evolutionary economics.

The notion of dynamics originates from Newtonian physics and its selective interest in patterns of convergence to unique equilibria, that is states of rest, of gravitating systems. Evolutionary processes – undergoing an incessant change – cannot be grasped in terms of a convergence to a unique equilibrium. If incessant change is interpreted as an unending series of transitions, what is minimally needed to account for this series are higher order dynamical systems in which multiple equilibria or attractors exist that are either locally asymptotically-stable or unstable. This minimal requirement is addressed by the concept of 'path-dependence' of evolutionary processes. It refers to the fact that, in these higher order dynamical systems, their initial conditions and the trajectory they realize under random influences jointly determine which of the multiple equilibria the process is attracted to.[8] Even with multiple equilibria, however, a crucial question remains: how does the evolutionary process come to leave a local equilibrium that has temporarily been attained?[9] This question is not addressed by the contributions discussed here. Like Schumpeter, these authors do not deal with the emergence of novelty that may, or may not, diffuse in the economy.

Unlike Schumpeter, the neo-Schumpeterians, and much of the diffusion literature (but similar to Veblen), the contributions that remain to be discussed now take a monistic ontological position. Depending on what heuristic twist that ontological creed is combined with, it is characteristic either of 'Universal Darwinism' or the 'continuity hypothesis'. While there has not yet been much work demonstrating in what way 'Universal Darwinism' can be made fruitful in concrete economic research (but see Hodgson and Knudsen 2004), the position of the continuity hypothesis is well established in contributions from quite different strands of thought.

A first, important representative of this combination is Georgescu-Roegen (1971), an author who is more often associated today with ecological economics than with evolutionary economics. This situation is not due to a lack of explicit statements on Georgescu-Roegen's part. It rather reflects a lack of attention paid to his writings in evolutionary economics, presumably precisely because of his strong naturalistic ontological creed. Georgescu-Roegen's major themes are the role of novelty in driving evolution and the role of entropy in constraining evolution (see Georgescu-Roegen 1971, 1979). Both issues are given a broad methodological and conceptual discussion and are finally applied to reformulating economic production theory. In reflecting on the conditions and the evolution of production he strongly conveys the gist of what has been called here the continuity hypothesis. This is perhaps even more true for his inquiry into the technology and institutions of peasant economies in contrast to modern industrial economies (see also Georgescu-Roegen 1976, Chapters 6 and 8). His concern with the fact that natural resources represent finite stocks that are degraded by human production activities induced him to criticize the abstract logic of canonical production theories and their basis in subjective value accounting that tend to play down these concerns. This criticism meets with core positions of the later emerging ecological economics movement.

A similar blend of positive, evolutionary theorizing and normative, environmental concerns is also indicative of other contributions belonging to this version of evolutionary economics. Among them are Georgescu-Roegen's student John Gowdy (1994) and Faber and Proops (1998). Gowdy and Faber and Proops both emphasize the role of the emergence of novelty, and they focus in a naturalistic perspective on production processes, their time structure, and their impact on natural resources and the environment. In doing so they continue and extend Georgescu-Roegen's work. Both also add to it a discussion of policy implications that is indeed revolving around core issues in ecological economics, thus explicitly connecting the agenda of evolutionary and ecological economics.

An author of a very different stance whose heuristic and ontological position comes close to the continuity hypotheses is Hayek (1971, 1979, 1988, Chap. 1). Focusing on the relationship between socio-economic evolution on the one hand and the Darwinian theory of natural selection on the other, Hayek distinguishes between three different levels at which human society evolves. The first level is that of biological evolution during human phylogeny. At this level, he argues, primitive forms of social behavior, values, and attitudes become genetically fixed as a result of selection processes. This implies an order of social interactions for which sociobiology provides the explanatory model. Once genetically fixed, these attitudes and values continue to be part of the genetic endowment of modern humans, even though biological selection pressure has now been largely relaxed. The second level of evolution, Hayek explains, is that of human intelligence and its products, that is knowledge and the numerous ways of recording, transmitting and processing it. Evolution at this level is driven by intention, understanding and human creativity resulting in new knowledge and its diffusion.

Between these two levels of evolution – 'instinct and reason' – Hayek (1971) claims, there is a third level of evolution, whose identification he considers the genuine contribution of his theory of societal evolution. It is at this level that those rules of conduct, morals, and traditions emerged, and still emerge, that shape human interactions into the orderly forms of civilization. As rules of conduct they are learnt and passed on, Hayek argues, in cultural, not genetic, transmission. The establishment of, and changes in, such norms are not deliberately planned or controled. This is rather the result of spontaneous processes in which historical accidents figure large. In the longer run, however, the chances that rules are transmitted and maintained within groups are correlated with the groups' success in terms of their economic prosperity and their population growth (either by successful procreation or by integration of outsiders). A growing population fosters specialization and division of labor which favor, in turn, groups with superior rules. By the same logic, groups not adopting appropriate rules are likely to decline. Through this group selection process, the rules of conduct, norms, and morals which eventually prevail are suited for the survival of an increasing number of members of the group. In short, Hayek interprets natural selection to operate not only on competing species but also on competing human groups defined by common cultural norms. His three layers theory of evolution goes beyond the continuity hypothesis as stated above by invoking a group selection argument. Yet it is not evident that the additional argument is indeed empirically significant for modern societies. Even if it is, it is not clear what systematically shaping effect this would have. Group selection would likely operate today on such a broad bundle of rules of conduct, knowledge elements and capabilities, physical habitat conditions, and other factors relevant at the level of culturally distinguishable human groups that it is difficult to see what precisely will be selected for.

Even without an additional group selection argument the continuity hypothesis allows a naturalistic account of the influence of the human genetic endowment and the natural constraints on human economic behavior that, taken by itself, promises important new insights on how consumption, production, and institutions have systematically changed in the long run (see Witt 2001, 2004, 2006 respectively). Modern humans can indeed be conjectured to have innate dispositions and adaptation mechanisms or programs that date from, and have been shaped by, fierce natural selection pressure earlier in human phylogeny. It is also likely that the inherited features still define the basic behavioral repertoire because, with the rise of human intelligence and the achievements of the collective, cultural, evolutionary process, selection pressure on humans has ceased to generate much genetic change. Assume in addition that the economic conditions of the early humans under which our innate behavioral repertoire has been shaped are in many respects similar to the present living conditions of other species in the higher animal kingdom that have been unchanged since. Then it may be argued that the equivalent of preferences, production techniques, and institutions today observable in the higher animal kingdom can give an indication of what the economy of early humans may have looked like before cultural evolution took off. Likewise, what, in comparison, has changed successively in human history can give an indication of the relative pace of, and the specific achievements in, man-made economic evolution.

ACHIEVEMENTS OF EVOLUTIONARY ECONOMICS – SOME RESULTS OF AN OPINION POLL

The road map outlined in the previous sections can be read as an orientation about the role that Darwinism plays in evolutionary economics both at the heuristic and the ontological level. As it turned out, the various contributions considered are associated in one way or another with one of the four combinations of heuristic twists and ontological creeds in Table 1.1. What seems currently most frequent in evolutionary economics is the neo-Schumpeterian combination of Darwinian concepts at the heuristic level and a rejection, or at least neglect, of a naturalistic monism at the ontological level (upper right cell). There is some research related also to the other three combinations, but it seems less frequent. However, the frequency with which certain heuristic and ontological positions are pursued is at best an indirect indicator of their scientific value. The question to be discussed in this section is therefore how fruitful research based on the different combinations has been in the past in advancing the understanding of economic evolution. In order to answer the question it is necessary first to identify the achievements of evolutionary economics and then to associate them with the alternative heuristic twists and ontological creeds. Instead of presenting here the author's own views, the results of an opinion poll will be reported that has been conducted in 2004 among 149 academic scholars all over the world.

To obtain qualified answers it seemed essential to approach scholars with sufficient expertise, that is familiarity with the problems and developments in evolutionary economics. The addressees were therefore selected according to whether they had adopted an evolutionary approach in their own published work. The 149 scholars who had been identified were sent a questionnaire in a rather informal way by e-mail that posed the question:[10]

> 'Summarizing evolutionary economics' achievements, what would you consider the most significant insights that have so far been gained? Please give 4 or 5 keywords or names of contributors.'

The questionnaire was returned by 53 addressees (36 percent), 43 from Europe and 10 non-Europeans. By professional status, 37 of the responses came from professors and 16 from non-professors (post-docs, lecturers, researchers, etc. with an average age younger than that of the professors). The keywords nominated by the respondents for each of the two questions were classified into keyword categories with synonyms or near-synonyms being subsumed to one category. Since some of the keywords given by single respondents could be associated with only very few, or even no, keywords given by somebody else, a rather large number of 48 different keyword categories resulted.

In order to concentrate on the more broadly supported keyword categories, the results given below report only those categories for which at least five (that is roughly 10 percent of all) respondents had nominated a keyword. Under this restriction, 16 keyword categories resulted. The categories and the number of times the keywords in the respective categories were nominated in the returned questionnaires are given in Table 1.2.

Judging by the frequencies of the keywords, research on 'innovations and endogenous technological change' is mentioned most as an achievement of evolutionary economics together with 'evolution of institutions and norms'. While the first rank for the neo-Schumpeterian topics does not seem very surprising, what may be a surprise is the share of respondents who have nominated these topics which, with only 26 percent of all respondents, seems fairly small. In the case of the keyword category 'evolution of institutions and norms' it is not clear whether this refers to the agenda of 'old' (American) institutionalism or that of 'new' institutionalism with its game-theoretic background. The evolutionary version of game theory as such is only among the less frequently (10 percent) mentioned achievements.[11]

Achievements of research into the micro foundations of evolutionary economics are represented by the two keyword categories 'learning' (21 percent) and 'bounded rationality' (12 percent). This is not a very strong representation, but it indeed highlights the topics that seem most significant in an evolutionary approach to economic behavior. As it seems, the coincidence of recognizing progress in the micro foundations of evolutionary economics *and* rating it as significant insights is not very frequent. This may be interpreted as indicating that the micro foundations have not been very high on the agenda of evolutionary economics so far. Something similar certainly holds for the Hayekian evolutionary agenda represented by the keyword category 'spontaneous order' and the conceptual reflections represented by 'generic features of economic evolution' (both reaching just 10 percent).

Table 1.2: Research Rated 'Most Significant Insights'

Keyword categories	Nominated by respondents		Nominations by professional status			
	Number	%	Profs	Rank	Non-profs	Rank
Innovation and technological change	14	26	11	I	3	III
Evolution of institutions and norms	14	26	11	I	3	III
Learning behavior	11	21	7	III	4	II
Knowledge creation and use	10	19	5	V	5	I
Variation and selection mechanism	9	17	8	II	1	V
Diversity and population thinking	9	17	7	III	2	IV
Industry evolution and life cycles	9	17	4	VI	5	I
Path dependence	9	17	7	III	2	IV
Non-equilibrium market dynamics	8	15	6	IV	2	IV
Novelty and invention	7	13	3	VII	4	II
Bounded rationality	6	11	5	V	1	V
Co-evolution institutions/technology	6	11	4	VI	2	IV
General features of evolution	5	9	4	VI	1	V
Routines	5	9	4	VI	1	V
Spontaneous order	5	9	3	VII	2	IV
Evolutionary game theory	5	9	3	VII	2	IV

Concerning the association of keyword categories in Table 1.2 with the combinations of heuristic twists and ontological creeds in Table 1.1 the following seems quite obvious. The five keyword categories 'innovation and endogenous technological change', 'variation and selection mechanism', 'diversity and population thinking', 'industry evolution and life cycles', and 'routines' are closely related to the neo-Schumpeterian combination. For the other keyword categories, except perhaps 'spontaneous order', an association with at least two of the four combinations seems possible. It cannot be excluded therefore that, in the mind of the respondents, even more of the keywords they nominated are actually associated with a position as that of the neo-Schumpeterian (the non-naturalistic, selection-metaphor-based position). In contrast, none of keyword categories can be exclusively associated with any of the other combinations in Table 1.1.[12] In the overall ranking of achievements expressed in the opinion poll, the neo-Schumpeterian position thus clearly stands out.

This assessment does not change substantially when the sample is split according to professional status and when the rankings of professors and (on average younger) non-professors are counted separately. According to a Spearman rank correlation test conducted on the two ranking lists, the hypothesis that the two rankings are independent cannot be rejected at a 1 percent significance level. However, the keyword categories in which the ranking differs most strongly between professors and non-professors do not point to a systematic deviation between the two groups in the assessment of the alternative approaches. The keyword category 'industry evolution and life cycles' associated with the neo-Schumpeterian approach ranks first among non-professors, but has only rank six among professors. On the other hand, the similarly associated keyword category 'variation and selection mechanism' ranks second among professors, but has only rank five among non-professors. The other two keyword categories 'knowledge creation and use' and 'novelty and invention' which non-professors clearly rank higher than professors (rank I and II vs. rank V and VI respectively) were among those that could not be identified as uniquely associated with either of the two approaches.

CONCLUSION

In this chapter an attempt has been made to trace out the influence that heuristic twists and ontological creeds have on the framing of problems and the way in which hypotheses are formulated in evolutionary economics. What different authors consider special about the evolutionary approach turned out to hinge on how they conceptualize evolution in the economy. Likewise, their definitions of the agenda of evolutionary economics vary with their monistic or dualistic ontology. It also turned out that much of the debate, particularly regarding the heuristic problems, is a quarrel about the role that Darwinism should play for evolutionary economics. Ironically, many of the authors strongly endorse Darwinian concepts at the heuristic level – where they are most problematic. At the same time, they explicitly reject, or completely ignore, the challenge of a naturalistic, Darwinian world view on what happens in the economy – where, in the understanding of modern sciences, it might be quite appropriate to adopt such a view.

It may be argued that this imbalance is a response to a misinterpretation of what it means to take a Darwinian world view on the economy. As explained, adopting such a view does not necessarily mean ending up with Universal Darwinism (that is classified here as a heuristic twist in which analogies are still borrowed from evolutionary biology, albeit disguised in abstract formulations). Instead, it has been claimed that such a view leads to what has been called here the continuity hypothesis. Once a monistic ontology is accepted, the postulate of an ontological continuity between evolution in nature and cultural and economic evolution is trivial. The non-trivial part of the hypothesis is that the form in which evolution continues is different. Cultural evolution follows its own regularities that differ from those of evolution in nature precisely because, with human intelligence, new forms of systematic change have become feasible.

The different combinations of heuristic twists and ontological creeds provide a grid for drawing up a road map for the still very heterogenous field of evolutionary economics. Contributions from the various strands of thought can in this way be located into four different clusters. The development of evolutionary economics over the past hundred years does not follow any particular path on the map, nor did the different clusters all find equal attention. In recent years a combination of Darwinian concepts at the heuristic level and a rejection of a naturalistic monism at the ontological level is frequently pursued, the combination characteristic of the neo-Schumpeterian approach. As was shown, this has not always been so and, even today, some contributions to evolutionary economics favor other combinations. However, it is not the frequency with which a certain combination of heuristic twists and ontological creeds is chosen that determines its scientific value. It rather is the fruitfulness in terms of generating important insights on the economy and its evolutionary transformation that matters.

In order to assess the fruitfulness of the alternatives, opinions about achievements in past research in evolutionary economics have been polled by means of a questionnaire sent out to academic researchers actively publishing in the field of evolutionary economics. Where possible the achievements nominated were then associated with one of the four different heuristic and ontological positions. In the overall ranking of past achievements expressed in the opinion poll, the neo-Schumpeterian position was found to stand out, while a revival of a naturalistic Darwinian world view on the economy – as it had been advocated by eminent scholars like Veblen, Georgescu-Roegen, and the late Hayek – still has to be awaited.

NOTES

[1] In the biological domain, for instance, genetic recombination and mutation follow regularities much different from those of the creation of, say, new grammatical habits and the coining of new idioms in the evolution of language. Both these cases differ, in turn, from the invention and adoption of new production techniques or new consumer goods in the evolving economy.

[2] Note that when applied to the domain of evolutionary biology, the notions of emergence and dissemination of novelty are compatible with, and can be expressed in terms of, the Darwinian notions of genetic recombination, mutation, gene flow, genetic drift, and natural selection.

[3] Schumpeter (1912, p. 75, my translation, UW); the quote is from the appendix to chapter 1 in the German 1st edition of the *Theory of Economic Development*. The appendix has been omitted from the later editions on which the English translation (Schumpeter 1934) was based.

[4] This is the topic of the literature on co-evolution, see Boyd and Richerson (1985), Henrich (2004).

[5] The richness of the historical material Veblen was able to organize with his focus on the role of habits and institutions in the evolution of the economy established him as the founder of American institutionalism. Yet, as Hodgson (2001) has shown, his successors in this school quickly lost Veblen's naturalistic, Darwinian world view and the corresponding ontological assumptions out of sight.

[6] In elaborating on how entrepreneurs accomplish innovations and, by doing so, induce development 'from within the economy', the upshot of his discussion is that these innovative activities occur in a regular cyclical pattern. The latter, in turn, causes an unsteady economic growth process which passes through 'prosperity and depression'.

[7] As an isolated conjecture, the hypothesized relationship between market structure and innovativeness has been discussed under the label 'Schumpeterian competition' in innumerable empirical and theoretical investigations (see, for example, Baldwin and Scott 1987 for a survey). However, from the point of view of evolutionary economics the debate on Schumpeterian competition went astray. It became dominated by notions of optimal innovation race strategies and equilibrium investments into innovative activities (Reinganum 1989). What once had started with the young Schumpeter's concern with the inadequacies of the neoclassical tools for explaining economic change thus ended with a vindication of precisely those tools.

[8] See Arthur et al. (1984). If a unique, globally asymptotically-stable equilibrium exists for an autonomous dynamical system, then each solution of the system is bound to converge to the equilibrium independent of the initial condition and independent of the particular path that is taken. Unique equilibria are therefore incompatible with the notion of path-dependence of a process.

[9] Because of a special assumption in Arthur et al. (1984) concerning the stochastic features of the competitive diffusion process, the equilibrium to which the process is eventually attracted cannot be left anymore. This is called a 'lock-in' of the process. However, as argued elsewhere (Witt 1997), this may be considered a rather unconvincing construct since evolution does, of course, overcome temporarily prevailing stasis.

[10] The selection procedure for the addressees of the questionnaire inevitably implied some subjective discretion. Moreover the lack of anonymity in the email-based response mode cannot be excluded to have had an impact on who was inclined to respond and in which way. These circumstances may have caused selection biases. For this reason alone, the results to be reported cannot claim to be based on a statistically representative sample of the opinions of all academic researchers actively contributing to evolutionary economics.

[11] This result reflects the fact that, in selecting the addressees of the questionnaire, researchers working exclusively on evolutionary game theory without applications relevant to evolutionary economics have not been included in the sample.

[12] Even among all 53 keyword categories that emerged from the opinion poll there was not a single one that was, for example, associated with either the combination represented by the lower left cell itself or any ecological–environmental correlates in the spirit of Georgescu-Roegen that it may be argued to have.

REFERENCES

Alchian, A.A. (1950), 'Uncertainty, Evolution, and Economic Theory', *Journal of Political Economy*, Vol. 58, 211-221.

Andersen, E.S. (1994), *Evolutionary Economics – Post-Schumpeterian Contributions*, London: Pinter.

Arthur, W.B. (1994), *Increasing Returns and Path Dependence in the Economy*, Ann Arbor: Michigan University Press.

Arthur, W.B., Ermoliev, Y.M. and Kaniovski, Y.M. (1984), 'Strong Laws for a Class of Path-dependent Stochastic Processes with Applications', *Proceedings of the International Conference on Stochastic Optimization*, Berlin: Springer, 287-300.

Baldwin, W.L. and Scott, J.T. (1987), *Market Structure and Technological Change*, Chur: Harwood Academic Publishers.

Binmore, K. (2001), 'Natural Justice and Political Stability', *Journal of Institutional and Theoretical Economics*, Vol. 157, 133-151.

Blume, L. and Easley, D. (1992), 'Evolution and Market Behavior', *Journal of Economic Theory*, Vol. 58, 9-40.

Boyd, R. and Richerson, P.J. (1985), *Culture and the Evolutionary Process*, Chicago: Chicago University Press.

Brenner, T. (1998), 'Can Evolutionary Algorithms Describe Learning Processes?', *Journal of Evolutionary Economics*, Vol. 8, 271-283.

Buenstorf, G. (2006), 'How Useful is Generalized Darwinism as a Framework to Study Competition and Industrial Evolution?', *Journal of Evolutionary Economics*, Vol. 16, 511-541.

Campbell, D.T. (1965), 'Variation and Selective Retention in Socio-cultural Evolution', in: H.R. Barringer, G.I. Blankstein and R.W. Mack (eds), *Social Change in Developing Areas: A Re-interpretation of Evolutionary Theory*, Cambridge, MA: Schenkman, 19-49.

Chattoe, E. (1994), 'The Use of Evolutionary Algorithms in Economics: Metaphors or Models for Social Interaction?', in: E. Hillebrand and J. Stender (eds), *Many-Agent Simulation and Artificial Life*, Amsterdam: IOS Press, 48-83.

Cordes, C. (2006), 'Darwinism in Economics: From Analogy to Continuity', *Journal of Evolutionary Economics*, Vol. 16, 529-541.

Cordes, C. (2007), 'Turning Economics into an Evolutionary Science: Veblen, the Selection Metaphor, and Analogy Thinking', *Journal of Economic Issues*, Vol. 41, 135-154.

Cyert, R.M. and March, J.G. (1963), *A Behavioral Theory of the Firm*, Englewood Cliffs, NJ: Prentice Hall.

David, P.A. (1993), 'Path-Dependence and Predictability in Dynamical Systems with Local Network Externalities: A Paradigm for Historical Economics', in: D.G. Foray and C. Freeman (eds), *Technology and the Wealth of Nations*, London: Pinter, 208-231.

Dopfer, K. and Potts. J. (2004), 'Evolutionary Realism: A New Ontology for Economics', *Journal of Economic Methodology*, Vol. 11, 195-212.

Dosi, G. and Nelson, R.R. (1994), 'An Introduction to Evolutionary Theories in Economics', *Journal of Evolutionary Economics*, Vol. 4, 153-172.

Dosi, G. and Winter, S.G. (2002), 'Interpreting Economic Change: Evolution, Structures and Games', in: M. Augier and J.G. March (eds), *The Economics of Choice, Change and Organization*, Cheltenham, UK and Northampton, MA, USA: Edward Elgar, 337-353.

Dosi, G., Freeman, C., Nelson, R., Silverberg, G. and Soete, L. (eds) (1988), *Technical Change and Economic Theory*, London: Pinter Publishers.

Dosi, G., Marengo, L., Bassanini A. and Valente, M. (1999), 'Norms as Emergent Properties of Adaptive Learning: The Case of Economic Routines', *Journal of Evolutionary Economics*, Vol. 9, 5-26.

Ebersberger, B. and Pyka, A. (2004), 'The Use of Genetic Programming in Evolutionary Economics', in: J. Foster and W. Hölzl (eds), *Applied Evolutionary Economics and Complex Systems*, Cheltenham, UK and Northampton, MA, USA: Edward Elgar, 78-94.

Faber, M, and Proops, J.L.R. (1998), *Evolution, Time, Production and the Environment*, Berlin: Springer.

Friedman, D. (1998), 'On Economic Applications of Evolutionary Game Theory', *Journal of Evolutionary Economics*, Vol. 8, 15-43.

Friedman, M. (1953), 'The Methodology of Positive Economics', in: M. Friedman, *Essays in Positive Economics*, Chicago: University of Chicago Press, 3-43.

Gerybadze, A. (1982), *Innovation, Wettbewerb und Evolution*, Tuebingen: Mohr.

Georgescu-Roegen, N. (1971), *The Entropy Law and the Economic Process*, Cambridge, MA: Harvard University Press.

Georgescu-Roegen, N. (1976), *Energy and Economic Myths – Institutional and Analytical Economic Essays*, New York: Pergamon.

Georgescu-Roegen, N. (1979), 'Methods in Economic Science', *Journal of Economic Issues*, Vol. 8, 317-328.

Gowdy, J. (1994), *Coevolutionary Economics: The Economy, Society and the Environment*, Boston: Kluwer Academic Publishers.

Hallpike, C.R. (1985), 'Social and Biological Evolution I. Darwinism and Social Evolution', *Journal of Social and Biological Structures*, Vol. 8, 129-146.

Hallpike, C.R. (1986), 'Social and Biological Evolution II. Some Basic Principles of Social Evolution', *Journal of Social and Biological Structures*, Vol. 9, 5-31.

Hashimoto, T. (2006), 'Evolutionary Linguistics and Evolutionary Economics', *Evolutionary and Institutional Economics Review*, Vol. 3, No. 1, 27-46.

Hayek, F.A. (1971) 'Nature vs. Nurture Once Again', *Encounter*, Vol. 36, 81-83.

Hayek, F.A. (1979), *Law, Legislation and Liberty. Vol. 3, The Political Order of a Free People*, London: Routledge & Kegan Paul.

Hayek, F.A. (1988), *The Fatal Conceit*, London: Routledge.

Henrich, J. (2004), 'Cultural Group Selection, Coevolutionary Processes and Large-scale Cooperation', *Journal of Economic Behavior and Organization*, Vol. 53, 3-35.

Herrmann-Pillath, C. (2001), 'On the Ontological Foundations of Evolutionary Economics', in: K. Dopfer (ed.), *Evolutionary Economics – Program and Scope*, Boston: Kluwer, 89-139.

Hodgson, G.M. (1998), 'On the Evolution of Thorstein Veblen's Evolutionary Economics', *Cambridge Journal of Economics*, Vol. 22, 415-431.

Hodgson, G.M. (2001), *How Economics Forgot History: The Problem of Historical Specificity in Social Sciences*, London: Routledge.

Hodgson, G.M. (2002), 'Darwinism in Economics: From Analogy to Ontology', *Journal of Evolutionary Economics*, Vol. 12, 259-281.

Hodgson, G.M. and Knudsen, T. (2004), 'The Firm as Interactor: Firms as Vehicles for Habits and Routines', *Journal of Evolutionary Economics*, Vol. 14, 281-307.

Hodgson, G.M. and Knudsen, T. (2006), 'Why We Need a Generalized Darwinism, and Why Generalized Darwinism is not Enough', *Journal of Economic Behavior and Organization*, Vol. 61, No. 1, 1-19.

Hull, D.L. (2001), *Science and Selection: Essays on Biological Evolution and the Philosophy of Science*, Cambridge: Cambridge University Press.

Kwasnicki, W. (1996), *Knowledge, Innovation and Economy – An Evolutionary Exploration*, Aldershot, UK and Brookfield, US: Edward Elgar.

Malerba, F. and Orsenigo, L. (1995), 'Schumpeterian Patterns of Innovation', *Cambridge Journal of Economics*, Vol. 19, 47-66.

March, J.G. and Simon, H.A. (1958), *Organizations*, New York: Wiley.

Marimon, R., McGratton, E. and Sargent, T.J. (1989), 'Money as a Medium of Exchange in an Economy with Artifically Intelligent Agents', *Journal of Economic Dynamics and Control*, Vol. 14, 329-373.

Markose, S., Tsang, E. and Martinez Jaramillo, S. (2005), 'The Red Queen Principle and the Emergence of Efficient Financial Markets: An Agent Based Approach', in: T. Lux, S. Reitz and E. Samanidou (eds), *Nonlinear Dynamics and Heterogeneous Interacting Agents*, Berlin: Springer, 287-299.

Maynard Smith, J. (1982), *Evolution and the Theory of Games*, Cambridge: Cambridge University Press.

Menger, C. (1963), *Problems of Economics and Sociology*, Urbana: University of Illinois Press (first edition in German 1883).

Metcalfe, J.S. (1988), 'The Diffusion of Innovations: an Interpretative Survey', in G. Dosi, C. Freeman, R.R. Nelson, G. Silverberg and L. Soete (eds), *Technical Change and Economic Theory*, London: Pinter Publishers, 560-589.

Metcalfe, J.S. (1994), 'Competition, Fisher's Principle and Increasing Returns in the Selection Process', *Journal of Evolutionary Economics*, Vol. 4, 327-346.

Metcalfe, J.S. (1998), *Evolutionary Economics and Creative Destruction*, London: Routledge.

Metcalfe, S. (2002), 'On the Optimality of the Competitive Process: Kimura's Theorem and Market Dynamics', *Journal of Bioeconomics*, Vol. 4, 109-133.

Nelson, R.R. (1995), 'Recent Evolutionary Theorizing About Economic Change', *Journal of Economic Literature*, Vol. 33, 48-90.

Nelson, R.R. (2006), 'Evolutionary Social Science and Universal Darwinism', *Journal of Evolutionary Economics*, Vol. 16, 491-510.

Nelson, R.R. and Sampat, B. (2001), 'Making Sense of Institutions as a Factor Shaping Economic Performance', *Journal of Economic Behavior and Organization*, Vol. 44, 3-54.

Nelson, R.R. and Winter, S.G. (1982), *An Evolutionary Theory of Economic Change*, Cambridge, MA: Harvard University Press.

Nelson, R.R. and Winter, S.G. (2002), 'Evolutionary Theorizing in Economics', *Journal of Economic Perspectives*, Vol. 16, 23-46.

Penrose, E.T. (1952), 'Biological Analogies in the Theory of the Firm', *American Economic Review*, Vol. 42, 804-819.

Reinganum, J.F. (1989), 'The Timing of Innovation: Research, Development, and Diffusion', in: R. Schmalensee and R.D. Willig (eds), *Handbook of Industrial Organization*, Vol. I, Amsterdam: North-Holland, 849-908.

Samuelson, L. (2002), 'Evolution and Game Theory', *Journal of Economic Perspectives*, Vol. 16, 47-66.

Schumpeter, J.A. (1912), *Theorie der wirtschaftlichen Entwicklung*, 1st edition, Leipzig: Duncker & Humblot.

Schumpeter, J.A. (1934), *Theory of Economic Development*, English translation of Schumpeter (1912), Cambridge, MA: Harvard University Press.

Schumpeter, J.A. (1942), *Capitalism, Socialism and Democracy*, New York: Harper.

Schuster, P. and Sigmund, K. (1983), 'Replicator Dynamics', *Journal of Theoretical Biology*, Vol. 100, 533-538.

Schwefel, H.-P. (1992), 'Imitating Evolution: Collective Two-Level Learning Processes', in: U.Witt (ed.), *Explaining Process and Change: Approaches to Evolutionary Economics*, Ann Arbor: Michigan University Press, 49-63.

Silva, S.T. and Teixeira A.A.C. (2006), 'On the Divergence of Evolutionary Research Paths in the Past Fifty Years: A Comprehensive Bibliometric Account', *Papers on Economics and Evolution*, #0624, Jena: Max Planck Institute of Economics.

Trivers, R.L. (1971), 'The Evolution of Reciprocal Altruism', *Quarterly Review of Biology*, Vol. 46, 35-57.

Veblen, T. (1898), 'Why Is Economics Not an Evolutionary Science?' *Quarterly Journal of Economics*, Vol. 12, 373-397.

Veblen, T. (1899), *The Theory of theLeisure Class – An Economic Study of Institutions*, New York: MacMillan.

Veblen, T. (1914), *The Instinct of Worksmanship and the State of the Industrial Arts*, New York: MacMillan.

Vromen, J. (2004), 'Conjectural Revisionary Economic Ontology: Outline of an Ambitious Research Agenda for Evolutionary Economics', *Journal of Economic Methodology*, Vol. 11, 213-274.

Wärneryd, K. (1990), *Economic Institutions – Essays in Institutional Evolution*, Stockholm: Gotab.

Weibull, J.W. (1995), *Evolutionary Game Theory*, Cambridge, MA: MIT Press.

Winter, S.G. (1964), 'Economic "Natural Selection" and the Theory of the Firm', *Yale Economic Essays*, Vol. 4, 225-272.

Witt, U. (1992), 'Evolution as the Theme of a New Heterodoxy in Economics', in: U. Witt (ed.), *Explaining Process and Change – Approaches to Evolutionary Economics*, Ann Arbor: Michigan University Press, 3-20.

Witt, U. (1993), 'Emergence and Dissemination of Innovations', in: R. Day and P. Chen (eds), *Nonlinear Dynamics and Evolutionary Economics*, Oxford: Oxford University Press, 91-100.

Witt, U. (1997), '"Lock-in" vs. "Critical Masses" – Industrial Change Under Network Externalities', *International Journal of Industrial Organization*, Vol. 15, 753-773.

Witt, U. (2001), 'Learning to Consume – A Theory of Wants and Growth of Demand', *Journal of Evolutionary Economics*, Vol. 11, 23-36.

Witt, U. (2003a), 'Generic Features of Evolution and Its Continuity: A Transdisciplinary Perspective', *Theoria*, Vol.18, 273-288.

Witt, U. (2003b), *The Evolving Economy*, Cheltenham, UK and Northampton, MA, USA: Edward Elgar.

Witt, U. (2004), 'On the Proper Interpretation of "Evolution" in Economics and its Implications for Production Theory', *Journal of Economic Methodology*, Vol. 11, 125-146.

Witt, U. (2006), 'Animal Instincts and Human Sentiments – On the Origin and Evolution of Economic Institutions', Paper presented at the AFEE Meetings Boston 2006.

Ziman, J. (2000), *Technological Innovation as an Evolutionary Process*, Cambridge: Cambridge University Press.

Zollo, M. and Winter, S.G. (2002), 'Deliberate Learning and the Evolution of Dynamic Capabilities', *Organization Science*, Vol. 13, 339-351.

2. Generalized Darwinism from the Bottom Up: An Evolutionary View of Socio-Economic Behavior and Organization

J.W. Stoelhorst

INTRODUCTION

Institutional and evolutionary economists have recognized that organizations are social as well as economic entities, but in modern evolutionary theories of the firm the social dimension of economic organization is typically lost. This is a result of the fact that these theories take the existence of firms as given, focus on the explanation of market and industry level phenomena, and in doing so use notions such as routines to abstract from individual behavior within the firm. This chapter takes another approach and reasons from the bottom up. It is argued that for both historical and ontological reasons, individual behavior should be seen as the starting point of theorizing about socio-economic organization. Organizations are a social solution to the individual problem of survival, and while they introduce an additional level of analysis with its own emergent properties, any theory of economic organization should both acknowledge and be consistent with the nature of individual behavior.

Making individual behavior central to evolutionary theories of socio-economic organization raises a number of fundamental questions. An evolutionary view of individual behavior that recognizes the social aspect of economic organization would see individuals as competing in a socio-economic environment, with their success depending on their socio-economic fitness. But what is socio-economic fitness? While an evolutionary analysis of socio-economic behavior necessarily involves such a concept, its nature is not at all clear. A concept of socio-economic fitness implies social as well as economic selection pressures, but what is the nature of these pressures? And is adaptation to socio-economic pressures not an ontogenetic rather than a phylogenetic process that defies explanation in terms of the population logic of evolutionary theories?

The purpose of this chapter is to answer these questions by applying Generalized Darwinism to the analysis of socio-economic behavior and organization. Its intended contributions are threefold. First, the chapter presents an argument for the importance of building theories of socio-economic organization on an evolutionary understanding of what drives individual behavior. Second, it demonstrates how Darwinism can be used to understand the evolution of individual behaviors in socio-economic contexts. Third, it shows how such an understanding can be used to advance evolutionary theories of economic organization.

The chapter proceeds as follows. It asks how Generalized Darwinism can ground theories of economic organization and argues that the historical and ontological primacy of individual behavior calls for theories of economic organization that are grounded in an evolutionary understanding of human behavior. It takes Nelson and Winter's (1982) seminal contribution to modern evolutionary economics as its starting point and shows how their treatment of the firm abstracts from individual behavior. It is furthermore argued that this treatment of individual behavior goes against their own research agenda, and it is shown that Generalized Darwinism can help develop an evolutionary theory of economic organization in which individual behavior has the place that Nelson and Winter originally envisaged. The chapter demonstrates how the ontogenetic nature of individual learning in socio-economic contexts can be understood in Darwinian terms by modeling the evolution of individual behavior in terms of the selective retention of successful behaviors in an individual's behavioral repertoire. It asks what socio-economic selection pressures shape individual behavior and develops a typology of four selection mechanisms (market, hierarchy, social network, expert) that may operate in socio-economic contexts. The firm is discussed as an example of a socio-economic selection environment, and implications for an evolutionary theory of the firm are derived. The chapter concludes by developing the contours of a Darwinian theory of socio-economic organization that links the traditional concern for selection between firms with an additional concern for the selection of individual behaviors within them.

EVOLUTIONARY ECONOMICS AND DARWINISM

It has recently been argued that there is both a need and a possibility to move beyond the truism of survivor selection that is characteristic of much evolutionary theorizing in economics (Knudsen 2002). There is a need for more rigorous explanations of economic evolution that go beyond the use of biological metaphors (Hodgson 2002), and there is the possibility to develop such explanations by building on the premises of what has become known as 'Generalized Darwinism' (Hodgson 2002, 2003; Hodgson and Knudsen 2006; Stoelhorst 2005a, in press; Stoelhorst and Hensgens 2006).[1]

Economists use the term evolution in a variety of ways. Some theories are called evolutionary simply because they deal with change over time, while others are specifically based on biological metaphors and analogies. Nelson and Winter's (1982) evolutionary economics belongs to the latter category. One of their achievements is that they ground their evolutionary theory more firmly in Darwinian principles than their predecessors in economics (Hodgson 1993). This is illustrated in the way in which Nelson (1995) describes the general principles of evolutionary theory:

'The general concept of evolutionary theory ... involves the following elements. The focus of attention is on a variable or set of them that is changing over time and the theoretical quest is for understanding of the dynamic process behind the observed change ... The theory proposes that the variable or system in question is subject to somewhat random variation or perturbation, and also that there are mechanisms that systematically winnow on that variation. Much of the predictive power of that theory rests with its specification of the systematic selection forces. It is presumed that there are strong inertial tendencies preserving what has survived the selection process' (p. 54)

But there is the possibility of a third category of evolutionary theory in economics. Such theory would go beyond the analogical use of evolutionary principles and start from the recognition of ontological similarities between all complex open systems. The label 'Generalized Darwinism' captures the notion that the development over time of any open complex system can be understood in terms of the same principles that are at the core of Darwin's theory of natural selection (for example Plotkin 1994; Cziko 1995; Dennett 1995). The universality of Darwin's theory stems from its specification of a general, substrate neutral, algorithm to explain evolution (Dennett 1995). This algorithm consists of three meta-mechanisms: variation, selection and retention (Campbell 1965, 1974; Plotkin 1994), and a Darwinian explanation of evolution consists of specifying the nature of these three mechanisms for the domain that is being studied (see Hodgson and Knudsen 2006; Stoelhorst in press).

The triumvirate of variation, selection and retention is implicit in Nelson's specification of the general concept of evolutionary theory above, yet Nelson and Winter have been reluctant to admit to more than the use of a Darwinian analogy (Hodgson 2003; Nelson 2006). This reluctance seems to stem from an understandable fear to get stuck in 'notions that, while salient in biological evolution, seem irrelevant or wrong-headed when applied to economics' (Nelson 1995, p. 54).[2] Therefore, it 'seems more fruitful to start with a general notion of evolution' (ibid.). But this is exactly what Generalized Darwinism is about: to abstract from the specific mechanisms of biological evolution, and specify the general principles of evolution as they apply across entirely different domains.

This chapter is premised on the idea that something can be gained from developing more fully specified Darwinian accounts of economic phenomena.[3] While Nelson's general concept of evolution above goes some way towards specifying what the general principles of evolution are, his description does not qualify as a fully developed Darwinian framework. First, whereas he puts emphasis on the need to specify 'systematic selection forces', he makes allowance for the mere assumption of the existence of mechanisms for variation and retention. Generalized Darwinism calls for the specification of all three mechanisms. The second way in which Nelson steers clear of an explicitly Darwinian account is by not specifying what evolution is about. From the vantage point of Generalized Darwinism, his phrase 'understanding the dynamic process behind the observed change' is unnecessarily vague. Darwinism is about explaining adaptive change, variety, and the accumulation of design (Stoelhorst in press). To say that when mechanisms of variation, selection and retention are present 'evolution will occur', means to say that (1) the systems in question will become adapted to their local environment, (2) that variety between systems will develop from common origins, and (3) that design, or adaptive complexity, will accumulate without the necessary interference of an (omniscient) designer. It is by explicitly recognizing these *explananda* that evolutionary theory can move beyond the truism of survivor selection.

DARWINISM AND THE EVOLUTIONARY THEORY OF THE FIRM

Evolutionary theories of economic organization typically focus on how markets select efficient firms. While not perfect (Knudsen 2002), our understanding of how such economic selection works is fairly well developed (Nelson and Winter 1982). But a firm is both an economic and a social entity and merely asking how economic selection works would deny the inherently social nature of economic organization. The idea that a firm is both an economic and a social entity has a long history in management studies (Barnard 1938), but most economic theory abstracts from the social dimension of economic organization. Nelson and Winter's (1982) work is an exception in the sense that part II of their book (chapters 3-5) offers an elaborate discussion of the behavioral principles on which firms operate. However, they do not offer a fully developed theory of the firm.

There is an interesting parallel between the work of Nelson and Winter and that of Darwin. In his book on the universal applicability of Darwinian principles, Dennett (1995) points out that Darwin developed his theory by 'starting in the middle'. Despite choosing the title 'The Origin of Species', Darwin *assumed* the existence of many different species, and from that mid-stage point in biological evolution proposed that natural selection could explain both the variety of these species and their adaptation to their specific natural environments. Nelson and Winter's evolutionary theory similarly starts in the middle. Their primary concern is to account for economic change, and their way of addressing this phenomenon is to assume the existence of firms and competitive markets. But a theory of the firm should ideally explain the existence of firms, as well as their internal organization and the differences between them (Holmstrom and Tirole 1989; Foss 1996). Nelson and Winter's theory of economic change offers an elegant theory of why firms are different (see also Nelson 1991), but it does not explain why firms exist and gives a rather simplified account of their internal organization.

It is with respect to this last point, the way in which the internal organization of the firm is treated, that we find a fundamental tension in Nelson and Winter's work. In *An Evolutionary Theory of Economic Change* they explicitly state that it is their aim to develop a theory of economic change that is based on realistic behavioral assumptions. And part II of their book not only sets out to present a behaviorally realistic view of what goes on inside firms, but also succeeds in doing so. Unfortunately, this realism is lost in the rest of the book, which is aimed at modeling different aspects of economic growth. In parts III-VI of the book, the elaborate discussions of the inner workings of the firm in part II are essentially collapsed into the notion of routines.[4] This is shorthand for the idea that firms routinize their behavior in the quest for economic success, and an essential part of an explanation of economic growth in terms of a variation-selection-retention algorithm operating on a population of firms. However, in putting so much of the explanatory burden of their models on this notion, Nelson and Winter veer away from their own agenda with respect to building theory on realistic behavioral assumptions. In essence, the notion of routines abstracts from individual behavior. This is most obvious when considering how Nelson and Winter model variation. In their models variation results from higher-level search routines that induce change in lower-level operating routines. In such a conceptualization, the individual is absent from any consideration of organizational change, and variations in individual behavior as a source of variation within firms are lost in an infinite regress of different levels of routines operating on each other (see Winter 2003).

In his review of evolutionary theorizing, Nelson quite rightly takes the position that theories of socio-cultural evolution have 'not as yet tried to come to grips with the dynamics of change in modern industrial societies' (1995, p. 60).[5] He goes on to argue that evolutionary theorists that work in these traditions 'have by and large assumed that selection mechanisms are individualistic, transmission mechanisms are person to person, and that "memes" like genes are carried by individuals. Yet these perceptions seem quite inadequate for analysis of how science or modern technology evolves, or forms of business organization, or law' (1995, p. 61). It is with this latter position that this chapter takes issue.

The position that is taken here is that there is a need to build theories of economic organization from the bottom up. There are three reasons for doing so that will be further developed in the remaining sections of the chapter. First, the behavior of individuals is the historical linking pin between biological and cultural evolution. Individual behavior is therefore an essential part of any explanation for why socio-economic institutions such as the firm exist in the first place. Second, abstracting from individual behavior is an unfortunate way of circumventing the problem of agency. Firms do not behave as such, only their employees do. In other words, in addition to being the historical linking pin in an explanation of why firms exist, individual behavior is also the ontological linking pin in explanations of how the internal organization of firms affects their performance in the market. It follows from the two previous points that a theory of the firm that wants to explain why firms exist, why they are different and how they are organized, needs to build on an understanding of how individual behavior relates to the nature and performance of firms. Note also that such an understanding is in line with Nelson and Winter's own insistence on theories that take a behaviorally realistic view of economic organization. The third reason for advocating the development of a theory of economic organization that reasons from the bottom up is simply that it can now be done. As will be demonstrated below, Generalized Darwinism offers a general framework that can make the necessary connections between selection of individual behaviors within socio-economic contexts such as the firm, on one hand, and selection between socio-economic groups such as the firm, on the other. Our current understanding of Darwinism makes it possible to take up the legacy of Nelson and Winter's view of the firm and develop it in ways that are consistent with their original agenda.

INDIVIDUAL BEHAVIOR AS HISTORICAL LINKING PIN

Evolutionary theories of biological, social, economic, and cultural phenomena abound. But what is often lost in this melee of theorizing is that there is an undeniable historical connection between the different phenomena that these theories address. In addition to teasing out the general principles of evolution, Generalized Darwinism also posits that all design in our world is the result of an evolutionary process, and that the common origins of all adaptive complexity can be traced back along evolutionary pathways, all the way to the emergence of life in the primeval soup (see Dennett 1995). Witt (2003, 2004) has suggested a similar idea in evolutionary economics. His 'ontological continuity hypothesis' states that there are historical links and ontological similarities between production in nature and in the economy.[6] These historical links are lost in theories of economic organization that start in the middle by assuming the existence of firms, and while this may not be much of a sacrifice when explaining industrial change or economic growth, a theory of the firm as a socio-economic institution has much to gain from taking them seriously.

Dennett's (1995) discussion of evolution as a cumulative design process shows how Darwin's theory of natural selection does away with the necessity to invoke an omniscient designer to explain adaptive complexity. Darwin's theory explains how the complex designs of living organisms could arise from simple beginnings through a mindless algorithm of variation, selection and retention. In the case of biological evolution, this algorithm works through random variation in the genotype (which codes for the design of organisms), and selective retention of phenotypic behavior that is successful in securing scarce resources from the environment. This selective retention takes place through a generational filter: the genes of organisms that are unsuccessful in the competition for survival and mates are lost for the next round. Dennett goes on to show that, when suitably abstracted from their specific manifestation in biology, the principles of variation, selection and retention can also explain cultural evolution. But he also makes another point: that biological and cultural evolution can not only both be understood as processes in which useful design variations accumulate from the bottom up, but that they should ultimately be seen as part of one and the same process.

This view of evolution as a process in which change percolates from the bottom up through selective filters and results in ever increasing forms of adaptive complexity is as much a part of Generalized Darwinism as the variation-selection-retention algorithm itself. It establishes the historical primacy of selection at the level of individual organisms over the evolution of such cultural entities as the modern firm. In doing so, it also raises some fundamental questions. How is it that one and the same evolutionary process has produced both living organisms and cultural phenomena? Or, in terms of what concerns us here: how has the selection of individuals pursuing their own interest resulted in the existence of such social entities as the firm? In other words, how are biological and cultural evolution related, and how does the existence and nature of the firm fit within this scheme?

This brings us to the notion of 'major transitions' in the evolutionary process (Maynard-Smith and Szathmary 1997). Biological evolution is essentially the result of differential success in two separate biological realms. Organisms engage in matter-energy transfer processes to survive and they reproduce. The evolutionary biologist and paleontologist Eldredge (1995) refers to the behavior of organisms related to matter-energy transfer as 'economic'. Biological evolution thus hinges on two types of behavior: 'economic' and 'reproductive'. During the billions of years of biological evolution, the process of variation, selection and retention has hit on many viable designs to exploit the available matter and energy, as well as on different ways to reproduce these designs. Some of the designs that the process of biological evolution has hit on have been particularly 'good tricks' that have fundamentally transformed the process of evolution itself. These particular design tricks are the so-called major transitions in the evolutionary process.[7] Dennett (1995) calls them 'cranes' to illustrate how the mindless process of evolution can lift itself to new levels of complexity.

The nature of such major transitions can help us understand the place of the firm in the overall process of the evolution of adaptive complexity. All major transitions share three features: they (1) involve an increased division of labor, that (2) is made possible by a new way of transmitting information, and (3) they result in the emergence of an additional level of selection (Maynard Smith and Szathmary, 1997). For instance, in the case of the transition from single-celled life to multi-cellular organisms, the division of labor takes the form of cell differentiation. This can only work if there is a way to coordinate the behavior of the specialized cells for the benefit of the whole organism, as well as a way of passing on the information about how to do this to the next generation. The solution of this problem in biological evolution needs to be understood in terms of a multi-level selection logic that explains how a viable multi-cellular system can emerge in the face of competition for scarce resources among individual cells that pursue their own interest (Maynard Smith and Szathmary 1997; Sober and Wilson 1998). As soon as multi-cellular organisms emerge, there is an additional level of selection to consider: selection between organisms. But the emergence of this new level of selection depends on the way in which the design of the organism overcomes the problem of the competition between individual cells. In all major transitions, there is the real problem that selection at the lower level of organization will disrupt integration at the higher level. Any increase in adaptive complexity must therefore be understood in terms of how it solves the conflict of interest at the level of selection that preceded it.

This logic also needs to be applied to explain the transition to social organization. While in multi-cellular life there is division of labor between the cells within an organism, social organization makes use of division of labor between organisms within a group. Social organization thus takes the principle of coordinating specialist tasks to a higher level of complexity and introduces an additional level of selection: that of the group. We have here a very general principle in the design of adaptive complexity that was introduced to economics by Adam Smith's discussion of the pin factory. The division of labor enables specialization and efficiency gains, but comes with a problem of coordination that needs to be overcome by the design of the system. Note that social organization can emerge through genetic mechanisms alone, as it has done in social insects such as ants and bees. But it can take on yet another level of complexity if cultural transmission systems that make use of (symbolic) language to pass down information about successful designs are in place. Learning by imitation and language allowed humans to pass on information through time by way of another mechanism than genetic reproduction. This has resulted in a level of social organization that is unique in the animal kingdom: we are the only species that is able to sustain cooperation in large groups of individuals that are not genetically related (Bowles and Gintis 2003; Fehr and Fischbacher 2003). Note that this unique human ability has all the characteristics of a major transition. There is a marked increase in the division of labor that is made possible by a new way of transmitting information (symbolic language) and that gives rise to additional levels of selection.

Modern firms are an example of these new levels of selection. In essence, firms are a social solution to the economic problem of securing scarce resources that individuals face. This solution is made possible by cultural transmission mechanisms that allow individuals to coordinate their behaviors and keep competition between them from undermining the functional integrity of the firm as a whole. In so doing, the existence of firms introduces an additional level of selection in terms of the competition for scarce resources between them. This between-group level of selection has its own emergent properties and is a bona fide target for the development of theories about what happens at this additional level of analysis. But a view that takes the ontological continuity of all evolutionary processes seriously would call for an understanding of what happens at this level of analysis in terms of how firms are able to coordinate the behavior of individuals in ways that channel within-group competition to the benefit of their performance in between-group competition (see Campbell 1994).

INDIVIDUAL BEHAVIOR AS ONTOLOGICAL PIN

The previous section made a point of the historical primacy of individual selection over group selection and pointed out that the functional integrity of a system at a level above the individual needs to be explained in terms of how it channels competition between individuals for the benefit of the group as a whole. This section develops a second reason for the need to explicitly build theories of socio-economic organization on an understanding of how they channel individual behaviors. This second reason is that a proper treatment of agency would see individual behaviors as the ontological linking pin in an evolutionary explanation of how the behavior of groups evolves.[8]

Problems with agency in evolutionary theory come in two forms: one that is general to all evolutionary theory and another that is specific to theories at the level of groups such as the firm. As Nelson (1995) states, much of the predictive power of an evolutionary theory rests with its specification of systematic selection forces. The archetypal examples are the ways in which the natural environment selects organisms in biology and the ways in which markets select firms in economics. But what do we mean when we say that 'the environment selects'? This phrase seems to impute agency to the environment. This directs our attention away from the agency that really matters in understanding selection. To understand selection, we need to recognize that the relevant agents are the systems competing for scarce resources. What is selected is the system's relative ability to secure scarce resources from the environment. Selection, then, is about winnowing the ways in which systems interact with their environments.

Selection works on open systems that need resources from their environment to survive. Living organisms need energy to overcome the second law of thermodynamics, and firms need to generate income to pay their suppliers, employees and owners. If these resources are not secured, the system simply cannot maintain its functional integrity. Selection pressure exists to the degree that the resources that the system needs for survival are scarce. It follows that what is selected is the system's relative ability to secure scarce resources from the environment. That the relevant agency is not in the environment but in the system that is being selected can be seen when considering natural selection. In the case of natural selection, the environment does not actively promote successful behaviors. Instead, the less successful organisms are weeded out. This does not happen by any positive act from the environment, but simply as the result of the organisms coming up short in the competition for resources. In that sense, the term 'natural selection' is a misleading metaphor. Darwin adopted the term to show how natural selection could have similar effects as artificial selection, but in doing so gave us a term that can be easily misinterpreted. While the nature of artificial selection shows that agency can be part of the selection mechanism, this is not necessarily the case and is secondary to the logic of evolution.

To be able to specify the agency around which evolution revolves, let us refer to the way in which a system interacts with its environment as the system's *behavior*. Underlying a system's behavior is the way in which the components of a system interact. Let us refer to this as the system's *design*. The design of a system underwrites its behavioral repertoire in the sense that it both enables and constrains the possible ways in which the system can interact with its environment. The notions of an open complex system's 'behavior' and 'design' allow us to specify more fully how selection works. Selection weeds out the designs of systems that are unsuccessful in securing sufficient scarce resources from the environment to survive. Or in shorthand, selection propagates designs that allow for successful behavior. As a corollary, evolution can be understood as a process in which the ways in which systems interact with their environment change over time so that (1) individual systems become adapted to their local environment, (2) variety between systems increases, and (3) design principles that underlie behavior that works accumulate. The mechanisms that drive this process are the introduction of variation in the behavior of individual systems, selective pressure from scarce resources, and retention of the principles of successful behavior in the systems' design.

The central role of interaction with the environment, or 'behavior', in the evolutionary logic points to a further problem with the notion of agency in evolutionary theories at levels above the individual. A social group such as the firm does not behave as such. It is the firm's employees that behave, and the 'behavior' of a firm can only be understood as the coordinated behavior of its employees. The way in which social entities such as the firm interact with their environments is simply an extension of the behavior of their members, and the notion of agency should therefore be reserved for the level of analysis where it belongs: that of the individual. We can, of course, use the notion of 'the behavior of the firm' as shorthand in analyses at the level of competition between firms. But, and this is essential, we cannot say anything that is empirically meaningful about how the behaviors of firms change over time without explicitly referring to individual behavior. To explain how firms change the way they interact with their environment and how they adapt to changing circumstances (or fail to do so), the evolutionary algorithm requires a specification of the mechanism of variation. And individual agency is quite simply the only source of variation in how firms behave. It is the new CEO, the enterprising manager, the innovative engineer, or the pro-active employee that are the sources of behavioral variations on which selection works.

SOCIO-ECONOMIC FITNESS AND THE EVOLUTION OF INDIVIDUAL BEHAVIOR

The previous two sections each developed a fundamental reason to develop evolutionary theories of socio-economic organization from the bottom up. The historical and ontological primacy of individual behavior calls for the development of theories of economic organization that build on an evolutionary understanding of individual behavior. But can the evolution of individual behavior be understood in Darwinian terms? Evolutionary theory in biology distinguishes between phylogenetic (evolutionary) and ontogenetic (developmental) processes. Darwinism is generally seen as pertinent to phylogenetic processes only. The reason for this is that it is not clear how the population logic that is at the heart of the Darwinian algorithm applies to ontogenetic processes. In phylogenetic processes, the generational filter of natural selection weeds out the genes of those individuals in the population that come up short in the competition for resources and mates. In biology, individual behaviors are selected, the genes that code for successful behaviors are retained, and populations evolve. It would indeed seem that this population logic is lost when we consider how individuals adapt their behavior during their lifetime. But this is not necessarily so.

The result of the Darwinian algorithm is that organisms become adapted to their environment. Fitness is a measure of how well an individual organism is adapted to its local environment. The fitness of all organisms is in large part the result of the accumulation of adaptations that have been passed on through genetic mechanisms. In other words, their level of fitness is the result of an evolutionary process that has taken place before their lifetime. But many organisms also have an ability to adapt during their lifetime. While obviously constrained by the adaptations that have been passed down through genetic mechanisms, they have an additional ability to evolve successful ways of interacting with their environments through what we call learning. There are different types of learning, which range in sophistication from such simple forms as operant learning, through learning by imitation, to conscious reasoning and formal instruction. Organisms that possess the ability to learn thus have a second type of mechanism at their disposal to increase their fitness.

In essence, learning is an ontogenetic process, but in modeling its nature the population logic of Darwinism can nevertheless be preserved. This can be seen when we consider how learning leads to an increase in adaptive fit. For this to happen, organisms need to be able to vary their behavior and selectively retain the behaviors that work. Consider the genetic endowment of an organism as an enabler of, and constraint on, its possible behaviors. Seen in this way, each organism has a set of possible behaviors. Learning during an organism's lifetime can then be understood as a way of selecting those behaviors that work under specific environmental conditions. At the most rudimentary level, this may take the form of selecting from a given set of behaviors. But in higher animals with more complex behaviors, it may also involve adding possible behaviors during the organism's lifetime. In each case the Darwinian logic still applies.[9] Learning can be understood as the selective retention of specific behaviors in an individual's set of possible behaviors.

Let us refer to an organism's set of possible behaviors as its 'behavioral repertoire'. With this notion the population logic is preserved. To flesh out a Darwinian explanation of learning we furthermore need to specify mechanisms of variation, selection and retention. Let us start by retention. The central question here is where the learned behaviors of an organism are encoded. The answer must be found in the neural system, where behavioral dispositions are stored. Next, consider variation. Here the question is how variations in behaviors are introduced. Again, the answer must be found in the neural system where behavioral reactions to environmental stimuli are triggered.[10] On this interpretation, it is easy to render learning in Darwinian terms similar to those that apply to phylogenetic evolution: individual behaviors are selected, the neural connections that code for successful behaviors are retained, and the repertoire of behaviors evolves. In Darwinian terms, learning is the differential propagation of behavioral dispositions.

This leaves us with the task to specify mechanisms of selection. Selection refers to what leads to the differential propagation of behaviors, so that the fitness of individual organisms is increased. This brings us back to our main concern of understanding the evolution of socio-economic behavior. Such an understanding requires a definition of socio-economic fitness. Such a definition is most easily given by separating social from economic fitness. Let us define economic fitness as the ability to secure the resources necessary for survival from the natural environment. Let us define reproductive fitness as the organism's ability to pass on its genes in the reproductive game. Together, these two types of fitness are what drive biological evolution. But when social organization emerges as a solution to the economic problem, and especially when such social organization hinges on more advanced forms of learning, a third form of fitness becomes relevant that we may refer to as social fitness. Let us define social fitness as the organism's ability to secure resources from the social environment. This third type of fitness is especially relevant when the social environment involves scarce resources other than food and mating opportunities. A Darwinian explanation of individual learning needs to show that such socially scarce resources exist.

THE MECHANISMS OF SOCIO-ECONOMIC SELECTION

The previous section has shown how individual learning can be understood in a way that preserves the population logic needed for the Darwinian algorithm to apply. But a Darwinian explanation of changes in socio-economic behavior also needs to be clear about the nature of socio-economic selection pressures, and this in turn requires the specification of socio-economic resources that may be scarce. In modern society, money and status are obvious examples of such resources. Modern humans still face the economic and reproductive problem, but the selection pressures of the natural environment have in large part been replaced by selection pressures from our socio-cultural environment that put a premium on an individual's ability to secure money and status. Even though there may be a strong relationship between a person's ability to earn money and achieve social status, on one hand, and his or her ability to secure food resources and create mating opportunities, on the other, the type of behavior that leads to success in a socio-economic environment is in many ways different from the type of behavior that would lead to success in the natural world. Complex forms of social organization and highly developed learning abilities thus give rise to a type of selection environment that is fundamentally different from the natural environment that shaped the behavior of our early ancestors.

Positing money and social status as the scarce resources in socio-economic environments opens up the possibility to unravel the nature of the selection pressures that individuals face in such environments. Table 2 presents a first attempt at this essential task for an evolutionary theory of socio-economic change.

Table 2.1: The Sources of Socio-Economic Selection Pressure

	Economic		Social	
Scarce	Money		Status	
resource		Group membership	Power	Authority
Selection pressure	Market	Social network	Dominance hierarchy	Expert opinion
Selection mechanism	Price	Peer pressure	Enforcement	Rules
Instinct	Survival Status	Belonging	Submission	Docility

The table proposes that the coordination of individual behavior involves four types of socio-economic selection pressure. The sources of these pressures are markets, social networks, dominance hierarchies, and expert opinions. These four selection mechanisms should be understood as *Idealtypen*, in the sense that the specific ways in which social institutions such as the firm coordinate individual behavior will typically involve a mix of the selection pressures associated with each of them.

Let us consider each of the elements of this table in turn. In keeping with the point of departure of the chapter, the first distinction in the table is between the 'economic' and 'social' dimensions of socio-economic organization. The second column of the table captures the traditional concern of economic theory in Darwinian terms by summarizing how market exchange leads to selection pressures on behavior. Money is the scarce resource, and the market exerts selection pressures through the price mechanism. Individuals respond to these selection pressures because of two evolved genetic dispositions, or instincts: their survival instincts and their status consciousness make them look for ways to secure the necessary resources from the environment to survive and establish their status and in modern environments securing money has become a proxy for meeting both these needs.

But individuals meet their needs in a social context, and economic selection by the market is not the only selection pressure they face. The rest of the table presents an attempt to capture the way in which the social aspect of socio-economic organization leads to selection pressures on individual behavior. The pertinent 'resource' in social contexts is status, and money is not the only source of status. The table distinguishes between three additional sources of status: group membership, power, and authority. Status can become a source of selection pressure when it is scarce. For instance, individuals can derive status from their membership of a group, especially when such membership is exclusive. But group membership also comes with selection pressures on individual behavior from the group as a social network. Within a social network, peer pressure will make certain behaviors more successful than others. Individuals respond to such pressures because their 'tribal instincts' (Richerson and Boyd 2005) make them susceptible to identifying with the group. People have a need to 'belong', and in wanting to belong they will have to adapt their behavior to what is expected from members of the group.

While group membership is a widespread phenomenon in social organization, so are dominance hierarchies within groups. Individuals can derive status from their position in the hierarchy. Note that the source of such status is inherently scarce: the number of high-ranked individuals is limited by definition. Note also that such status is strongly correlated with access to other scarce resources (be it food, money, or mating opportunities). In fact, the status of dominant individuals is directly related to their power to control scarce resources. But the existence of dominance hierarchies within groups is also a source of selection pressures on the behavior of individuals. Given the existence of a dominance hierarchy, certain behaviors will be more successful than others. Higher placed individuals can literally enforce certain behaviors among lower placed individuals. Individuals respond to such pressure because of an evolved instinct to submit to power they cannot overcome (Buss 2004).

Although the previous two social selection mechanisms may have taken on particularly sophisticated forms in human societies, they are in fact widespread in nature. The third mechanism is not. Deriving status from authority requires language and symbolic culture. Whereas status as a result of hierarchical power rests on the ability to enforce control of resources, status as a result of authority rests on knowledge claims. These knowledge claims may take the form of metaphysical claims on the truth (epistemological claims), functional claims on what works (pragmatic claims), appreciative claims on what is worthwhile (esthetic claims), and moral claims on what is good (ethical claims). Such claims are what experts derive their status from. But to the degree that expert opinions are accepted, they also become a source of selection pressure on individual behaviors. Expert opinions establish rules, and specific individual behaviors will be more or less successful given the nature of these rules. Individuals respond to the selection pressures established by expert rules because of an evolved instinct that Simon (1990) has called docility: the tendency to learn vicariously by accepting the opinion of others.

THE FIRM AS A SOCIO-ECONOMIC SELECTION ENVIRONMENT

This chapter has argued for the need to build theories of socio-economic organization by applying Generalized Darwinism from the bottom up. Individual behavior should be the starting point of evolutionary theories in economics for both historical and ontological reasons. The chapter has furthermore argued that the evolution of individual behavior can be understood in Darwinian terms. Despite its ontogenetic nature, the population logic of Darwinism can be preserved by modeling individual learning as the selective retention of genetically transmitted and culturally learned behavioral dispositions in contexts of scarce economic and social resources. But what are the implications of such an approach for theories of socio-economic organization? Let us consider the contours of a Darwinian theory of the firm that reasons from the bottom up.

Such a theory of the firm would take the behaviors of individuals as its starting point. It would distinguish 'ultimate' and 'proximate' explanations of individual behavior. Ultimate explanations of behavior are given in phylogenetic (evolutionary) terms and take the form of statements about the evolved genetic dispositions (instincts) that drive human behavior. This is the domain of evolutionary psychology, which is rich in findings about universal drivers of human behavior that would allow us to build theories on behavioral assumptions that go beyond bounded rationality and opportunism. Possible examples of such behavioral assumptions are status consciousness, tribal instincts, submission, and docility. Proximate explanations are given in ontogenetic (learning) terms and take the form of statements about the evolved behavioral repertoires that drive the behavior of specific individuals. The evolution of behavioral repertoires can be understood as the result of the interplay between genetic dispositions, mental schemes grounded in evolving neural connections, and the specific socio-economic selection pressures that an individual faces.

A firm can then first and foremost be understood as a source of such socio-economic selection pressures. Individuals become members of a firm to meet their socio-economic needs, but in doing so need to adapt their behavior to the specific socio-economic context of the firm. From the point of view of the individual employee, behavior is successful if it helps secure scarce economic (money) and social (status) resources. Both the scarcity of economic resources and social status can be seen to exert selection pressure on the behavior of employees. This is, for instance, clear from how membership of a firm needs to be secured: employment opportunities are scarce, and employment at certain firms confers more status than employment at others. Moreover, once individuals have become members of a firm, their productive tasks are governed by market mechanisms, reciprocal relationships with peers, authoritative relationships within the context of the hierarchy, and rules established by experts. From the point of view of individuals, these aspects of socio-economic organization represent the selection environment to which they have to adapt. Given the nature of pressures from the market, from peers, from higher placed individuals, and from organizational rules (for example promotion criteria) certain individual behaviors will be more successful in securing money and status than others.

In other words, a Darwinian view of the firm from the bottom up would first consider the firm as a selection environment within which individuals compete for economic and social resources. But the existence of firms also introduces an additional level of analysis with its own emergent properties. Just as there is competition for resources between individuals within firms, so there is competition for resources between firms. In this competition, the success of firms depends in large part on their selection of employees and on how well they are able to coordinate the behaviors of these employees towards the goal of securing scarce resources from the environment. The success of such coordination, in turn, depends on the same four mechanisms discussed above. Firms coordinate the behaviors of their employees through the interplay of price mechanisms, peer pressure, hierarchical enforcement, and organizational rules. Together, these four mechanisms constitute the building blocks of the 'design' of the firm that enables its 'behavior' in interacting with the environment.

On this view of the firm, the question of the socio-economic selection of individual behaviors and the question of the internal organization of the firm collapse into one. From the point of view of the individual employees, the internal organization constitutes the socio-economic selection environment in which they compete for scarce economic and social resources. From the point of view of the firm, its internal organization constitutes a way to retain individual behaviors that contribute to the success of the system as a whole. From the point of view of the individual employee, behavior is successful if it helps secure scarce money and status. From the point of view of the firm, the behavior of individual employees should contribute to its ability to secure scarce resources from its environment in the competition with other firms. The internal organization, or 'design', of a firm can thus be seen as the essential linking pin in a multi-level view of socio-economic organization. In essence, the firm as a unit of socio-economic organization links within-group competition between individuals to between-group competition between firms (see Campbell 1994).

Applying Darwinism from the bottom up can help answer the two questions of a theory of the firm that Nelson and Winter did not address: why do firms exist and how are they organized? Generalized Darwinism shows that questions about the existence of the firm and its internal organization need to be framed in a multi-level selection framework that allows us to understand how the interaction between within-group competition and between-group competition plays out. In answering the question 'why do firms exist?', rather than looking for an answer in a comparison of the firm with the market, a Darwinian approach would take a historical perspective and look at how firms first originated and subsequently evolved as a form of economic organization (Stoelhorst 2005b). As argued in this chapter, firms can be seen as a social solution to the economic problem of securing the resources necessary for survival that makes use of cultural transmission mechanisms. The modern firm is, of course, a relatively recent solution to the economic problem, and has been preceded by a host of other social solutions that also made use of cultural transmission. This shows that the firm can only be understood as an accumulation of social design principles that work in relation to the broader socio-economic selection environment in which modern humans deal with the economic problem. Moreover, this broader environment has evolved a number of 'cultural cranes', such as property rights, that have made firms viable. Ultimately, the question 'why do firms exist?' can only be answered by taking into account the historical process by which the design principles of modern societies have evolved.

This brings us to the second question: how are firms organized? Firms are one of the ways in which humans are able to achieve large-scale coordination among individuals that are not genetically related. This ability is unique in the animal kingdom and represents a major transition in the accumulation of adaptive complexity. All major transitions require an explanation of how the new level of selection overcomes competition at the lower level of selection. From a Darwinian perspective, then, questions about the internal organization of the firm have to be answered in terms of an explanation of how firms channel within-group competition for resources in a way that allows the group as a whole to be successful in the competition for resources with other groups. This perspective opens up possibilities to unravel the internal organization of the firm in terms of the design principles that create a social selection environment that results in the successful coordination of individual behavior towards a common economic goal. The firm's internal organization is a way to preserve behaviors that work in light of this goal. In other words, in Darwinian terms, the ultimate causes of the firm's behavior can be found in the accumulation of design principles to channel within-group competition in order to coordinate human behavior to deal with the economic problem. The proximate causes for a firm's behavior need to be found in a more detailed understanding of the relationship between the specific design principles found in firms and the specific selection pressures to which they are subjected in their local environments. Such a perspective would combine an interest in universal design principles to achieve large-scale cooperation that play on genetically transmitted behavioral dispositions, on one hand, and an interest in design principles that are specific to the cultural and legal idiosyncrasies of different institutional environments, on the other.

CONCLUSION

This chapter has explored how Generalized Darwinism can be used to further evolutionary theories of socio-economic organization. Generalized Darwinism holds that the evolution of all open complex systems can be understood in terms of the Darwinian variation-selection-retention algorithm. This algorithm explains how open complex systems become adapted to their local environment, how the variety between them can be traced back to common origins, and how adaptive complexity, or design, accumulates. These explananda also point to the historical and ontological continuity of all evolutionary processes as an essential premise of Generalized Darwinism. The ontological continuity of all evolutionary processes means that Generalized Darwinism should be applied 'from the bottom up'. The evolution of individual behavior is both the historical and ontological linking pin between biological and cultural evolution and an essential component of understanding why and how such forms of social organization as the modern firm work.

The chapter has argued that the theory of socio-economic organization in Nelson and Winter (1982) represents an advance over earlier evolutionary theories in economics in its use of Darwinism, but that it does not yet offer a fully developed theory of the firm. Our current understanding of Darwinism makes it possible to take up the legacy of Nelson and Winter's view of the firm and further develop it in ways that are consistent with their original research agenda. Applications of Generalized Darwinism hold the promise of a third wave of theory development that will strengthen the ontological foundations of evolutionary theory in economics, add to the behavioral realism of our theories of socio-economic organization, and put within reach an evolutionary theory of the firm that can explain why firms exist, why and how they are different, and how they are organized.

In contrast to extant theory, an evolutionary theory of the firm that applies Generalized Darwinism from the bottom up would link up with theories of biological and cultural evolution and give individual behavior a central place in modeling competition between firms. The chapter has shown that, despite its ontogenetic character, the evolution of individual behavior can be understood in Darwinian terms. Such an understanding would preserve the population logic of Darwinism by seeing learning during an individual's lifetime in terms of the evolution of a behavioral repertoire. This evolution takes place as the result of feeding back the results of environmental interactions in a socio-economic context in which an individual faces selection pressures from markets, social groups, hierarchical relations, and expert opinions.

On such a view of the socio-economic selection of individual behavior the firm can be seen as a social solution to the economic problem of securing scarce resources that makes use of socio-economic selection pressures to retain behaviors that work. From a Darwinian perspective, the existence of such a solution needs first and foremost to be understood in terms of how firms channel competition for scarce resources within them in ways that make them successful in the competition for scarce resources with other firms. On this view, the internal organization of a firm can be seen as both a source of socio-economic selection pressures on individual behavior, and as an enabler of its success in securing scarce resources in the competition with other firms. Both the existence of firms and the nature of their internal organization need an explanation in terms of a multi-level selection perspective that links within-group competition to between-group competition. Applying Generalized Darwinism from the bottom up allows us to develop such a perspective in terms of the interplay between universal genetic dispositions, the specific mental maps of individuals, and culturally evolved socio-economic selection mechanisms.

NOTES

[1] While discussions of the possibility to develop ontological foundations for evolutionary economics on the basis of Darwinism originally referred to 'Universal Darwinism' (Hodgson 2002; Stoelhorst 2005a), it has now become customary to use the term 'Generalized Darwinism' (Hodgson and Knudsen 2006; Stoelhorst in press; Stoelhorst and Hensgens 2006). This term has the advantage of steering clear of Dawkins' (1983) original use of the term Universal Darwinism for the claim that all life anywhere in the universe would have evolved by way of Darwinian principles. This is a claim within the context of biological theory, whereas the claim here is that core Darwinian principles apply outside biology.

[2] This fear is exacerbated by a long tradition of influential critiques of the use of evolutionary theory in the social sciences. An influential critique within economics is Penrose (1952), while Gould (for example 1997) is among the natural scientists that would rather confine evolutionary theory to biology. The central argument against the use of an evolutionary view in the social sciences in Penrose and elsewhere is that social evolution is 'Lamarckian'. However, this does not in any way invalidate the usefulness of the Darwinian framework for developing theory in the social sciences (Hodgson 2001; Knudsen 2001).

[3] There is an ongoing discussion of the value of this premise: see for instance the special issues of *Journal of Economic Methodology* (Klaes 2004) and *Journal of Evolutionary Economics* (Witt 2006), as well as Stoelhorst (in press), Stoelhorst and Hensgens (2006), Vromen (2007).

[4] For a critical evaluation of the notion of routines and the analogy of 'routines as genes' see Becker and Lazaric (2002), Hodgson (2003) and Stoelhorst (2005a).

[5] The reference is to theories of evolution such as sociobiology, evolutionary psychology, gene-culture co-evolution and memetics. For a balanced overview see Laland and Brown (2002).

[6] It should be noted that while Witt seems to be on par with this part of Generalized Darwinism, he is sceptical about the generality of the Darwinian algorithm of variation, selection and retention (Witt 1999, 2003).

[7] Maynard Smith and Szathmary (1997, p. 6) present a tentative list of the major transitions in the evolution of complexity, which includes the origin of chromosomes, the origin of the genetic code, the origin of eukaryotes, the origin of sex, the origin of multicellular organisms, the origin of social groups, and the origin of language.

[8] Note that what follows is *not* meant to endorse either methodological individualism or methodological collectivism. Both individuals and groups are here seen as units of selection with their own emergent properties that are not fully reducible to lower levels of analysis (viz. genes and individuals). For a discussion of these issues from a Darwinian perspective see Hodgson (2004, chapter 2). What is argued here is that only individuals are endowed with *agency* in any sense that is meaningful to the social sciences. However, the collective behavior of a group of individuals has its own emergent properties, and these properties will typically need to be understood to achieve satisfactory explanations at the level of groups of individuals such as firms. In other words, the claim for only one level of agency does not reduce to a claim for

methodological individualism.
[9] For the application of Darwinian principles to different types of learning see for instance Skinner (1981) on operant learning and Campbell (1974) on conscious learning. See also Plotkin (1994) for a more general discussion of learning in Darwinian terms.
[10] Although an additional point of interest is how intentional reasoning can play a role in directing behavioral variations. More generally, the human ability to build mental models of the environment is an important part of evolving successful behaviors: this both allows adaptability to a wider variety of environments, and a faster way of learning by feeding back the consequences of behaviors into changes to the internal models of the environment.

REFERENCES

Barnard, Chester I. (1938), *The Functions of the Executive*, Cambridge, MA: Harvard University Press.

Becker, Markus C. and Nathalie Lazaric (2003), 'The Influence of Knowledge on the Replication of Routines', *Economie appliquée*, 61 (3), 65-94.

Bowles, Samual and Herbert Gintis (2003), 'The Origins of Human Cooperation', in: Peter Hammerstein (ed.), *The Genetic and Cultural Origins of Cooperation*, Cambridge, MA: MIT Press, pp. 429-444.

Buss, David M. (2004), *Evolutionary Psychology: The New Science of the Mind*, Boston: Pearson Education, Inc.

Campbell, Donald T. (1965), 'Variation and Selective Retention in Socio-Cultural Evolution', in: H.R. Barringer, G.I. Blanksten and R.W. Mack (eds), *Social Change in Developing Areas: A Reinterpretation of Evolutionary Theory*, Cambridge, MA: Shenkman, pp. 29-49.

Campbell, Donald T. (1974), 'Evolutionary Epistemology', in: P.A. Schilpp (ed.), *The Philosophy of Karl Popper, Vol. 14, I & II, The Library of Living Philosophers*, LaSalle, Ill: Open Court Publishing, 14-I, pp. 413-463.

Campbell, Donald T. (1994), 'How Individual and Face-to-Face Group Selection Undermine Firm Selection in Organizational Evolution', in Joel A. Baum and Jitendra V. Singh (eds), *Evolutionary Dynamics of Organizations*, Oxford: Oxford University Press, pp. 23-38.

Cziko, Gary (1995), *Without Miracles: Universal Selection Theory and the Second Darwinian Revolution*, Cambridge, MA: MIT Press.

Dawkins, Richard (1983), 'Generalized Darwinism', in D.S. Bendall (ed.), *Evolution from Molecules to Man*, Cambridge: Cambridge University Press, pp. 403-425.

Dennett, Daniel C. (1995), *Darwin's Dangerous Idea: Evolution and the Meanings of Life*, London: Penguin Books.

Eldredge, Niles (1995), *Reinventing Darwin: The Great Evolutionary Debate*, New York: John Wiley & Sons.

Fehr, Ernst and Urs Fischbacher (2003), 'The Nature of Human Altruism', *Nature*, 425, 785-791

Foss, Nicolai J. (1996), 'Knowledge-based Approaches to the Theory of the Firm: Some Critical Comments', *Organization Science*, 7 (5), 470-476.

Gould, Stephen Jay (1997), 'Evolution the Pleasures of Pluralism', *The New York Review of Books*, June 26.

Hodgson, Geoffrey M. (1993), *Economics and Evolution: Bringing Life Back Into Economics*, Cambridge, UK and Ann Harbor, MI: Polity Press and University of

Michigan Press.

Hodgson, Geoffrey M. (2001), 'Is Social Evolution Lamarckian or Darwinian?', in John Laurent and John Nightingale (eds), *Darwinism and Evolutionary Economics*, Cheltenham, UK and Northampton, USA: Edward Elgar, pp. 87-118.

Hodgson, Geoffrey M. (2002), 'Darwinism in Economics: From Analogy to Ontology', *Journal of Evolutionary Economics*, 12 (3), 259-281.

Hodgson, Geoffrey M. (2003), 'The Mystery of the Routine: The Darwinian Destiny of An Evolutionary Theory of Economic Change', *Revue Economique*, 54 (2), 355-384.

Hodgson, Geoffrey M. (2004), *The Evolution of Institutional Economics: Agency, Structure and Darwinism*, London: Routledge.

Hodgson, Geoffrey M. and Thorbjørn Knudsen (2006), 'Why we Need a Generalized Darwinism And Why a Generalized Darwinism is Not Enough', *Journal of Economic Behavior and Organization*, 61 (1), 1-19.

Holmstrom, B.R. and J. Tirole (1989), 'The Theory of the Firm', in: R. Schmalensee and R.D. Smilig (eds), *Handbook of Industrial Organization*, Amsterdam: North Holland, pp. 61-133.

Klaes, M. (2004) 'Ontological Issues in Evolutionary Economics', *Journal of Economic Methodology*, 11 (2): 121-124.

Knudsen, Thorbjoern (2001), 'Nesting Lamarckism within Darwinian Explanations: Necessity in Economics and Possibility in Biology?', in John Laurent and John Nightingale (eds), *Darwinism and Evolutionary Economics*, Cheltenham UK and Northampton, USA: Edward Elgar, pp. 121-159.

Knudsen, Thorbjoern (2002), 'Economic Selection Theory', *Journal of Evolutionary Economics*, 12, 443-470.

Laland, Kevin N. and Gillian R. Brown (2002), *Sense and Nonsense: Evolutionary Perspectives on Human Behaviour*, Oxford: Oxford University Press.

Maynard Smith, John and Eors Szathmary (1997), *The Major Transitions in Evolution*, Oxford: Oxford University Press.

Nelson, Richard R. (1991), 'Why do Firms Differ, and How does it Matter?', *Strategic Management Journal*, 12, 61-74.

Nelson, Richard R. (1995), 'Recent Evolutionary Theorizing About Economic Change', *Journal of Economic Literature*, 33, 48-90.

Nelson, Richard R. (2006), 'Evolutionary Social Science and Universal Darwinism', *Journal of Evolutionary Economics*, 16 (5), 491-510.

Nelson, Richard R. and Sidney G. Winter (1982), *An Evolutionary Theory of Economic Change*, Cambridge, MA: Harvard University Press.

Penrose, Edith (1952), 'Biological Analogies in the Theory of the Firm', *American Economic Review*, 42 (5), 804-819.

Plotkin, Henry C. (1994), *Darwin Machines and the Nature of Knowledge*, Harmondsworth: Penguin.

Richerson, Peter J. and Robert Boyd (2005), *Not By Genes Alone: How Culture Transformed Human Evolution*, Chicago: The University of Chicago Press.

Simon, Herbert A. (1990), 'A Mechanism for Social Selection and Successful Altruism', *Science*, 250, 1665-1668.

Skinner, B.F. (1981), 'Selection By Consequences', *Science*, 213, 501-504.

Sober, Elliot and David Sloan Wilson (1998), *Unto Others: The Evolution and Psychology of Unselfish Behavior*, Cambridge, MA: Harvard University Press.

Stoelhorst, J.W. (2005a), 'The Naturalist View of Universal Darwinism: An Application to the Evolutionary Theory of the Firm', in J. Finch and M. Orillard (eds), *Complexity and the Economy*, Cheltenham, UK and Northampton, USA: Edward Elgar, pp. 127-147. Reprinted in Hodgson, G.M. (2007), *The Evolution of Economic Institutions: A Critical Reader*, Cheltenham, UK and Northampton, USA: Edward Elgar, pp. 233-251.

Stoelhorst, J.W. (2005b), *Why Do Firms Exist? Towards an Evolutionary Theory of the Firm*, Working paper, University of Amsterdam.

Stoelhorst, J.W. (In press), The Explanatory Logic and Ontological Commitments of Generalized Darwinism, *Journal of Economic Methodology*.

Stoelhorst, J.W. and Robert Hensgens (2006), *On the Application of Darwinism to Economics: From Generalization to Middle-range Theories*, Working paper, University of Amsterdam.

Vromen, J.J. (2007), *Generalized Darwinism in Evolutionary Economics: The Devil Is in the Details*, Working paper, Erasmus University Rotterdam.

Winter, Sidney G. (2003), 'Understanding Dynamic Capabilities', *Strategic Management Journal*, 24, 991-995.

Witt, Ulrich (1999), 'Bioeconomics as Economics from a Darwinian Perspective, *Journal of Bioeconomics*, 1, 19-34.

Witt, Ulirch (2003), *The Evolving Economy: Essays on the Evolutionary Approach to Economics*, Cheltenham UK and Northampton, USA: Edward Elgar.

Witt, Ulrich (2004), 'On the Proper Interpretation of "Evolution" in Economics and its Implications for Production Theory', *Journal of Economic Methodology*, 11 (2), 125-146

Witt, Ulrich (2006), 'Evolutionary Concepts in Economics and Biology', *Journal of Evolutionary Economics*, 16 (5), 473-476.

3. Comparative Industrial Evolution and the Quest for an Evolutionary Theory of Market Dynamics

Guido Buenstorf

INTRODUCTION

The suitability of biology as a role model for evolutionary economics has been controversial ever since the times of Veblen and Schumpeter. In the present-day evolutionary community, the debate centers on whether and how concepts from Darwinian evolutionary biology can be fruitfully transferred to the study of economic processes. Positions in this debate range from squarely rejecting the relevance of biological concepts (which essentially replicates Schumpeter's view) to seeing them as the *conditio sine qua non* for any form of evolutionary theorizing. No convergence of positions seems to be on the horizon. Rather, the recent debate on 'Universal' or 'generalized' Darwinism (kicked off by Hodgson, 2002; see also the contributions to the *Journal of Evolutionary Economics* special issue edited by Witt, 2006) has served to renew the controversy.

Based on an earlier contribution to the debate (Buenstorf, 2006), this chapter suggests that, in understanding the dynamics of markets and industries, biological concepts are only of heuristic use. Moreover, since even biologically inspired heuristics entail framing effects and the discounting of some aspects of the processes under investigation, a pluralism of heuristics rather than the prescription of a specific 'evolutionary' heuristic seems warranted in applied research. To develop theories of industry evolution that go beyond a mere collection of empirical findings, the chapter then makes the case for an empirically grounded, 'bottom-up' approach to evolutionary industrial economics. This approach to theory building, which might be called 'comparative industrial evolution', is based on empirical studies of systematically selected industries that are comparable in key dimensions. It opens up opportunities for testing the relevance, preconditions, and generality of explanatory factors in industry evolution. An illustration of the approach is subsequently given by presenting some findings on the evolution of the historical US farm tractor industry.

The remainder of the chapter is organized as follows: The next section summarizes core controversies in the debate on Darwinian concepts in economics. The third section then develops a conceptual framework for comparative empirical work on the evolution of industries and discusses how evolutionary theorizing can be based on the empirical findings. The fourth section presents new results on the evolution of the US farm tractor industry. When juxtaposed to the well-analyzed automobile industry, the tractor industry offers interesting insights into industry evolution. The fifth section concludes.

CONTROVERSIES ON DARWINISM AND INDUSTRY EVOLUTION

The Heuristic Use of Biological Concepts

When, in 1898, Veblen posed his famous question why economics was no evolutionary science, he referred to the example of Darwinian biology providing a 'genetic account of an unfolding process' (Veblen, 1898, p. 388). In his article, Veblen conceives of evolutionary economics as a process theory of cultural and institutional development, which ultimately would have to take human psychology as its point of departure.[1] Beyond this basic commitment to causal explanations of developmental change, Veblen does not invoke any concepts from biology. His basic position is thus not too different from that of Schumpeter (1911, ch. 2) except for the terminology. Schumpeter not only rejected the analogical use of Darwinian concepts in the social sciences, but also the notion of evolution itself, which he considered discredited by dilettantism. Similar to Veblen, however, Schumpeter championed causal explanations of economic development based on qualitative change originating within the economy.

Concepts from Darwinian biology play a larger role in modern evolutionary economics, which took off with the seminal book by Nelson and Winter (1982). Their approach ingeniously combines behavioral organization theory with the metaphorical use of biological concepts. It culminates in the notion of organizational routines being the 'genes' of organizations (most notably business firms), which are subject to internal selection as well as external selection by the market process. The routine concept has been extremely influential in both evolutionary economics and management science, and the selection metaphor is a fundamental building block of Nelson and Winter's modeling approach. However, these authors openly confess to their eclectic 'borrowing' (Nelson and Winter, 1982, p. 9) of biological concepts. They dismiss biological accuracy as an objective in itself for evolutionary theorizing in economics, and likewise refrain from attempts at generalizing the Darwinian framework to an abstract, domain-unspecific theory.

In addition to selection, inheritance of organizational routines has also been used as a heuristic to make sense of evolutionary patterns in the development of industries, in particular the origination of capable new entrants (Klepper, 2001; Klepper and Sleeper, 2005). According to this interpretation of the empirical record, founders of intra-industry spin-offs are able to replicate organizational routines by transplanting them from the incumbent firm to the spin-off. Given that they have previously been tested in the industry, the routines taken over by spin-offs are on average expected to be superior to those accessible to startups whose founders have no background in the industry. Again, this heuristic has proved powerful. For example, it is commonplace terminology to talk about a spin-off's 'parent' firm. Likewise, the spin-offs of Fairchild Semiconductors (most notably Intel), which played a decisive role in the evolution of the semiconductor industry in Silicon Valley, have famously been referred to as the 'Fairchildren'.

Beyond these examples, the Darwinian metaphor of evolution operating through the selection and inheritance of organizational routines has been adopted in numerous evolutionary contributions. At the same time, prominent evolutionary economists have found it wanting. Foster (1997) argues that it is not doing justice to the historical character of economic evolution, where discontinuous structural change is highly relevant. According to Witt (1999, p. 24), the emphasis on selection 'may distract attention from a crucial source of economic evolution: human learning, cognition, and creativity'. Witt furthermore suggests that it may restrict the applicability of evolutionary analysis, thus limiting the potential of the evolutionary approach to economics (Witt, 2003, ch. 1).

From the applied evolutionary economist's perspective, framing the market process in terms of the variation, selection, and inheritance scheme is problematic insofar as it de-emphasizes those dimensions of competition that have no counterpart in the biological realm. Perhaps the most important aspect is a supply-side bias. Markets are loci of *voluntary* exchange where resources cannot simply be appropriated by force. Firms offer goods and services, and their performance depends on finding sufficiently many customers who are willing to pay enough for these goods and services for the firms to recover their costs. Thus, demand factors are crucial for understanding competition and the evolution of industries (Windrum, 2005). There are of course many ways for firms to actively influence the demand for their products, and superior skills in these activities are an important dimension of market competition. These marketing capabilities might be seen as part of a firm's routines, but in evolutionary models that have adopted the routine concept, little consideration seems to be given to them.

More generally, a dynamic view of market competition is not easily squared with the tendency inherent in the selection perspective to see firms as passive objects of selection. In spite of the notion of 'interactors' developed as part of a generalized Darwinist framework (Hull, 1988), there is typically little actual interaction between competing and cooperating firms in evolutionary characterizations of market processes. But this interaction is of course at the core of industrial economics, and numerous ways exist for firms to affect the competitive process and/or preempt its effects. A particularly important dimension of interaction is innovation. To trigger innovative efforts is an important effect of market competition. Successful innovation provides temporary profitability, which subsequently tends to be eroded by the competitive process.

There are likewise limits to the usefulness of the inheritance heuristic. For example, it is by no means obvious on what kinds of knowledge and experiences gained during their tenure at the parent firm spin-off founders actually draw to make their spin-offs successful; and the heuristic fails to offer guidance for finding out. Moreover, the spin-off process involves more than an attempt to copy the parent firm. There is ample evidence suggesting that, while important similarities exist between spin-offs and their parent firms, spin-offs are often based on business models that deliberately depart from the parent firm's strategy. Adverse developments at the parent firm and open disagreements between its management and the future spin-off founder (Klepper and Thompson, 2006) are frequent triggers of spin-off formation.

From Darwinian Heuristic to Darwinian Ontology?

In recent years, the debate on Darwinian concepts has been refreshed by the proposal to turn the approach of 'Universal Darwinism', which was originally developed in evolutionary biology (Dawkins, 1983), into a unifying foundation of evolutionary economics (Hodgson, 2002; Hodgson and Knudsen, 2006). The qualitative change this entails lies in that 'Universal' or 'generalized' Darwinism is an ontological position. Its proponents argue that, at a sufficiently high level of abstraction, all evolutionary processes share an identical basic structure, which can be described in terms of the Darwinian principles of variation, inheritance, and selection. 'It is not that social evolution is *analogous* to evolution in the natural world [...]. In this sense, social evolution *is* Darwinian' (Hodgson and Knudsen, 2006, p. 14, italics in original).

This position is less restrictive than it may seem at first glance. Consistent with the objective of generalization, no claim is made that the Darwinian principles are sufficient to explain the detailed workings of concrete evolutionary processes. Rather, the need for auxiliary, domain-specific explanations is emphasized (Hodgson, 2002). Also, the Lamarckian principle of inheritance of acquired traits is considered admissible as part of the generalized Darwinian scheme. In the most recent exposition, the applicability of the generalized Darwinian scheme is moreover limited to 'complex population systems', which are defined as systems that 'involve a variety of entities that interact with one another' (Hodgson and Knudsen, 2006, pp. 3-4).

These qualifications notwithstanding, because of the ontological claim underlying generalized Darwinism, the limitations of the Darwinian heuristic become even more critical. If the basic premises of generalized Darwinism are accepted, then it is but a small step to the position that all evolutionary theorizing must proceed in terms of its variation-selection-inheritance scheme. Framing market processes as selection and inheritance would then no longer be *a* possible heuristic to be evaluated on the basis of its usefulness, but become *the* perspective to be adopted on *a priori* grounds.

As such, the generalized Darwinian framework is too unspecific to offer much guidance for actual theory building in evolutionary economics. Accordingly, its proponents have attempted to make it more operational by specifying evolutionary economic processes in more detail. In particular, the Darwinian framework has been applied to the analysis of market competition and industry evolution (see, for example, Knudsen, 2002; Hodgson and Knudsen, 2004). At this level of application, firms are construed as interactors (generalized phenotypes), and organizational routines as replicators (generalized genotypes). As has been noted elsewhere (see Buenstorf, 2006, for a more detailed discussion), this approach raises some additional questions.

Organizational routines have attributes that render them less than ideal as units of inheritance or replication. First, routines as 'organizational memory' (Nelson and Winter, 1982) are located above the level of the individual employee; and they are at least partially tacit. Both characteristics complicate their replication through individual efforts. Routines may moreover be found at various levels of the organization. Simple routines relate to the firm's short-term behavior, while more involved, higher-order routines govern activities such as investment and innovation. These differences are not reflected in the generalized Darwinian scheme, as it is based on a homogeneous notion of routine replication.

There is also a variety of potential transmission channels, giving rise to different conditions for the replication of routines. They are argued to be replicated both in-house, for example in the set-up of new branch plants, as well as across organizations, where replication involves diverse channels such as imitation, consultancies, labor mobility, and spin-off activities. Finally, it is far from clear that routines are the only kind of knowledge that is replicated between firms. The imitation of product designs through reverse engineering is an obvious candidate for an additional replicator at the level of competing firms. However, the assumption of a single, homogeneous replication mechanism at the level of firm interaction implicitly underlies the application of the generalized Darwinian scheme in industrial economics.[2] This indicates how the biological template, in spite of the attempt to generalize it and minimize its domain-specificity, still structures the generalized Darwinists' thinking about economic processes.

It may well be that the above issues can be incorporated into future, even more general versions of generalized Darwinism. But that still leaves open the question what would be gained in the process. The abstract framework does not provide information as to how the various transmission channels function, how important they are in actual competitive processes, and how their relevance varies with changing industrial and environmental characteristics. In the final analysis, then, the payoffs from adopting this research strategy seem severely restricted. As a consequence, a rather different approach to theory building in evolutionary industrial economics will be advocated in the remainder of this chapter.

A COMPARATIVE APPROACH TO INDUSTRY EVOLUTION

The basic philosophy underlying the generalized Darwinian approach may be characterized as a 'top-down' strategy. It starts from an abstract framework and endeavors to identify the respective elements of the framework in empirical contexts. In this section, an alternative approach for building theories of economic evolution will be discussed. This approach follows a 'bottom-up' strategy, building on the strong empirical tradition in industrial dynamics, in particular the findings suggesting robust patterns in the long-term evolution of industries.

The basic idea is simple. It is to study systematically selected industries that share key characteristics while differing in others. In this way, the role of individual factors shaping the competitive process in different industries can be isolated. However, what seems simple in principle is considerably complicated in practice by the limits to available data. To have a full and comparable account of how industries develop, data are required that cover the complete populations of firms active in these industries over the entire time span of their development. A comparative approach to the study of industry evolution is therefore not easily accomplished. Nonetheless, existing studies have already yielded important results, providing an empirical foundation for theory building.

From its beginnings, the empirical work on industry evolution has been comparative in that developmental patterns have been studied for a variety of industries. The pioneering study by Gort and Klepper (1982) used trade register and patent data to trace the development of active producers and the extent and nature of innovations in a large set of US industries. A key finding of this study, as well as its subsequent refinement by Klepper and Graddy (1990), was to identify regularities of industry evolution (which subsequently became known as the 'industry life cycle', see Klepper, 1997). In particular, entry peaks early in most industries, and the industries then undergo a 'shakeout' phase during which the number of active producers is rapidly reduced. Also, the importance of product innovations, relative to process innovations, tends to decline as industries mature. Based on a study of four shakeout industries, Klepper (2002a) furthermore concludes that early entrants had a significantly higher likelihood of survival than later ones.

These regularities of industry evolution fall short of being universal laws, however. Not all industries develop in the same way. For example, in 19 out of the 46 industries studied by Klepper and Graddy (1990) no shakeout in the number of firms was observed. It is therefore a crucial task for research in industrial evolution to identify alternative developmental patterns as well as their drivers. One alternative pattern that has found much scholarly attention is observed in industries such as the laser industry, where products are heterogeneous and most producers specialize on a small number of submarkets (defined by product type). The US laser industry has been characterized by positive net entry and increasing numbers of producers over several decades. Also, early entrants did not survive longer than later ones in this industry (Sleeper, 1998; Klepper and Thompson, 2007).

Empirical regularities such as the shakeout phenomenon and advantages of early entry indicate that the competitive process undergoes significant changes as an industry matures. The Darwinian scheme of variation, selection, and inheritance of routines is of little use in trying to account for these changes. Why does the number of producers change, and why exactly is early entry beneficial? Answers to such questions are provided by theoretical models of industry evolution, for example by focusing on the larger size of earlier entrants, giving them more incentives to process R&D,

which in turn enhances future performance and raises the barriers to new entry (Klepper, 1996). Thus, an explanation is sought in terms of internal change in incumbent firms rather than changes at the population level focused upon by the Darwinian model. Indeed, declining entry rates in maturing industries suggest that population changes become less important over time for industry evolution. Likewise, the differences between alternative patterns of industry evolution are more amenable to an explanation in terms of product market characteristics (ultimately reflecting differences in demand patterns) than in terms of routines and their selection. For example, the specialization along submarkets found in the laser industry can be explained by pronounced product heterogeneity with low degrees of substitutability on the demand side, combined with lacking economies of scope on the supply side.

Numerous empirical studies have also found that the odds of success vary between entrants with different pre-entry backgrounds (Helfat and Lieberman, 2002). A pervasive finding is that diversifying producers from related industries on average outperform entrepreneurial *de novo* entrants (Klepper, 2002a). Substantial differences in performance are also observed within the latter group, with much effort being devoted to studies of intra-industry spin-offs, that is, firms started by former employees of incumbent firms in the industry. As a group, spin-offs are generally superior to other *de novo* entrants. In several industries they performed as well as diversifying entrants (Dunne et al., 1988; Sleeper, 1998; Agarwal et al., 2004). Spin-offs are more likely to originate in more successful firms (Buenstorf and Klepper, 2005), and the performance of parent and spin-off firm is positively related (Klepper, 2002b). Moreover, both the time of tenure and the position of spin-off founders at the parent firm predict spin-off performance (Dahl and Reichstein, 2006). At the same time, the importance of the alternative types of experienced entrants strongly varies across industries. For example, while the US automobile industry was dominated by spin-offs, spin-offs were inconsequential among producers of television receivers, and all major TV producers had originally been started as radio manufacturers (Klepper and Simons, 2000; Klepper, 2002b).

Many of these findings are consistent with the interpretation that inherited organizational capabilities are transferred to new markets (in the case of diversifiers) or new firms (spin-offs). This leaves open a number of crucial questions, however. Is it specific capabilities or general experience gained in previous activities that matter most for the performance in the new industry? Are there differences in the relevance of capabilities related to different activities, for example R&D, production, and marketing? How exactly are these capabilities transferred, and what role does the transfer of routines play? Also, what industry characteristics determine their effect on performance? And why are spin-offs and diversifiers not equally prevalent in all industries?

Comparing industries with different product characteristics helps to answer some of the questions regarding differences in evolutionary patterns and the effects of pre-entry experience. Further insight can be gained by comparative work along other dimensions, in particular by international comparisons. All initial studies of industry evolution were based on US data. In recent years, however, researchers have begun to analyze the same industry in different countries, or at least study whether patterns found in the US also characterize analogous industries in other countries. This kind of comparison is particularly important because it allows for a direct test of the assumption that technological factors (rather than, for example, institutional ones) are the critical determinants of the observed regularities, which implicitly underlies the theoretical work on industry evolution (Buenstorf, 2007).

Simons (2001) compares trends in the number of producers in the US and the UK for 18 of the industries featured in Gort and Klepper (1982). He finds remarkable similarities between both countries in both the timing and the severity of shakeouts in the various industries. A detailed analysis of two shakeout industries, tires and TV receivers, indicates that early-mover advantages were present in both countries. Cantner et al. (2006) study the German automobile industry. They find that the evolutionary patterns in this industry, most notably the effects of early entry and pre-entry experience on firm survival, mirrored those of the US automobile industry. In a similar vein, Boschma and Wenting (2007) compare the geographic structure of the British and the US automobile industries. Buenstorf (2007) studies lasers, a prominent non-shakeout industry, using data on German laser producers. Again consistent with the US patterns for the analogous industry, he finds an increasing number of producers over a 40-year period of industry evolution, no advantages of early entry, and no positive effects of accumulated industry experience on firm performance.

A complementary strategy exploits idiosyncratic historical events affecting the evolution of a national industry. For example, Buenstorf and Guenther (2007) study the effect of regional industry agglomerations on the location choice of German machine tool producers. To control for effects of regional 'birth potential' (Carlton, 1979; see also Buenstorf and Klepper, 2006), they specifically concentrate on analyzing firms that moved from East Germany to West German locations after World War II.

Finally, comparative work to identify key determinants of industry evolution can also be based on data for industries that manufacture closely related products and operate under similar institutional conditions. An example of this approach is provided in the next section, where some findings on the evolution of the US farm tractor industry are presented. This industry was selected because in its formative years its product was very similar to that of the automobile industry, which is one of the best studied industries in the literature on industry evolution. Indeed, in extreme cases, the boundary between the two products became blurred. For example, in the 1910s several producers marketed conversion kits allowing customers to use their automobiles as makeshift tractors. (In the long run, these conversion kits were unsuccessful because critical components such as radiators and bearings were overburdened in prolonged operation at low speeds.)

AUTOMOBILES AND FARM TRACTORS: LESSONS FROM COMPARING TWO (SEEMINGLY) SIMILAR HISTORICAL INDUSTRIES

To study the evolution of the US farm tractor industry, a new dataset was constructed with the objective to maximize comparability to prior work on the US automobile industry. The most important primary source of information on tractor producers is *Thomas' Register*, which was already used in Gort and Klepper's (1982) discovery of the shakeout phenomenon, and likewise in many later studies of industry evolution. However, in the case of tractors this source has two major shortcomings. First, in the industry's early years listings of tractors are lumped into the listings of (traction) engines, and the distinction between steam-powered traction engines (which are not included in the present analysis) and tractors with an internal combustion engine is not clear. Second, *Thomas' Register* does not list farm tractors separately from road tractors. Accordingly, among the more than 1,200 tractor firms listed many did not actually make farm tractors. To account for this, the dataset is restricted to firms that are listed as tractor producers both in *Thomas' Register* and in the *Encyclopedia of American Farm Tractors* (Wendel, 1979) and/or the *Standard Catalog of Farm Tractors, 1890-1960* (Wendel, 2000). The same sources were used to identify the backgrounds of firms.

In total, there were 319 confirmed entrants into the tractor industry until 1940. This number includes 56 prior engine producers (including producers of steam-driven traction engines), 40 prior producers of agricultural implements, 21 diversifying automobile and truck producers, and 22 preexisting firms with other backgrounds, including, for example, general manufacturing firms, makers of construction equipment, as well as a foundry. Some firms had experience in several of these industries, which is reflected in the coding of backgrounds. In addition, 13 spin-offs founded by employees leaving incumbent tractor firms could be identified.

The information on firm backgrounds already indicates substantial differences between the tractor and automobile industries. First, in tractors the share of spin-offs from incumbent firms in the industry was substantially smaller than it was in autos. Second, diversifiers came from a different set of industries, with prior implement producers being the second-largest group after engine producers. In contrast, makers of carriages and wagons, and bicycle producers, were (along with engine makers) the most prominent groups of diversifiers in the automobile industry (Klepper, 2002b). This prominence of implement makers suggests that relatedness in terms of markets and·customers may have been more important for the decision to diversify than technological relatedness. For example, it is not obvious what kind of technological capabilities should have enabled a plow manufacturer such as John Deere to become a successful tractor maker.

To study the role of background as a determinant of performance in the tractor industry, longevity is adopted as a performance measure, and an econometric survival analysis is conducted. Again, this approach follows the earlier work on the automobile industry, as well as the bulk of empirical studies on industry evolution. Using survival in the market as a performance criterion is in part dictated by the (non)availability of financial data on all but the largest firms in the population. There are, however, numerous reasons why longevity is a suitable proxy for performance. The underlying assumption is basically an opportunity cost argument. If firms leave a market, they do so either because they are forced to (that is, they are bankrupt) or because the firms' owners think there are better uses for their capital. Given irreversibility of at least some earlier investments, one can (at least for manufacturing industries like the one considered here) be quite certain that the decision to voluntarily leave the market indicates a substandard performance of the respective firms.[3]

Generally speaking, survival analysis models the risk ('hazard') of succumbing to some event conditional on vectors of explanatory variables. A variety of specifications are available for survival models. Below, the fully parametric Gompertz specification is adopted. This model setup has two characteristics that are helpful in the present context. First, in contrast to other specifications, notably the popular semi-parametric Cox regression, proportionality of hazards among different groups of entrants need not be assumed. Second, the influence of firm age (time after entry) on the exit hazard is explicitly modeled.

Results of the survival analysis are reported in Table 3.1. Model 1 is the proportional benchmark model in which the age-dependent part of the exit hazard is not separately estimated for the various types of entrants. The model includes dummy variables denoting the various types of diversifiers (prior makers of implements, engines, autos and trucks, and other diversifiers) as well as spin-offs; other *de novo* entrants are the non-reported control group (they are referred to as startups below). The model also includes a set of dummies that sort entrants into age cohorts, where each cohort corresponds to a decade of entry. Estimation results suggest that among the diversifiers, only firms with a background in agricultural implements and prior engine producers performed systematically better than the startups. In contrast, the diversifying auto and truck producers and the residual group of diversifiers with diverse backgrounds have lower exit hazards than the startups, but these effects are smaller and statistically insignificant. The same holds for the group of spin-offs, even though their coefficient estimate suggests that their performance was comparable to that of the diversifying engine producers. The cohort dummies indicate that once the background of entrants is accounted for, there were at best weak advantages of early entry in the tractor industry. The oldest cohort has a slightly lower hazard than the control (cohort 4), whereas both intermediate cohorts have substantially larger hazards. Only the coefficient estimate for cohort 2 is marginally significant (at the 0.10 level), however.

Table 3.1: Survival and Firm Characteristics in the US Farm Tractor Industry (entrants through 1940; hazard models in Gompertz specification)

	Model 1	*Model 2*	*Model 3*	*Model 4*
Agric. Impl.	−0.967***	−0.996***	−0.995***	−1.021***
Diversifiers	(0.229)	(0.232)	(0.314)	(0.315)
Engine	−0.417**	−0.333	−0.345	−0.395
Diversifiers	(0.206)	(0.207)	(0.274)	(0.274)
Auto/ Truck	−0.230	−0.139	−0.069	−0.124
Diversifiers	(0.239)	(0.240)	(0.295)	(0.298)
Other	−0.055	−0.079	−0.761**	−0.814**
Diversifiers	(0.227)	(0.227)	(0.364)	(0.367)
Spin-offs	−0.391	−0.402	−0.253	−0.299
	(0.328)	(0.220)	(0.423)	(0.432)
Own Engine				0.176
				(0.223)
Purchased				−0.172
Engine				(0.147))
Cohort 1	−0.040	−0.466	−0.453	−0.457
	(0.436)	(0.642)	(0.655)	(0.654)
Cohort 2	0.675*	0.792	0.809	0.848
	(0.390)	(0.583)	(0.583)	(0.584)
Cohort 3	0.627	0.860	0.883	0.919
	(0.405)	(0.601)	(0.602)	(0.604)

Constant	−2.393***	−2.457***	−2.463***	−2.443***
	(0.389)	(0.577)	(0.576)	(0.581)
Agric. Impl.			0.001	0.001
Diversifiers * t			(0.015)	(0.015)
Engine			0.003	0.004
Diversifiers * t			(0.014)	(0.014)
Auto/ Truck			−0.008	−0.009
Diversifiers * t			(0.024)	(0.024)
Other			0.131***	0.129***
Diversifiers * t			(0.044)	(0.044)
Spin-offs * t			−0.027	−0.024
			(0.056)	(0.057)
Cohort 1 * t		0.026	0.024	0.023
		(0.033)	(0.034)	(0.034)
Cohort 2 * t		−0.014	−0.018	−0.017
		(0.033)	(0.033)	(0.033)
Cohort 3 * t		−0.031	−0.030	−0.028
		(0.037)	(0.037)	(0.037)
t	−0.023***	−0.019	−0.019	−0.019
	(0.006)	(0.031)	(0.031)	(0.031)
No. firms	319	319	319	319
(uncens. exits)	(271)	(271)	(271)	(271)
Log-likelihood	−444.403	−438.906	−434.813	−433.607
$P > chi^2$	0.000	0.000	0.000	0.000

Notes: Standard errors in parentheses; ***P≤0.01; **P≤0.05; *P≤0.10.

In Model 2 (Table 3.1) the hazard of the entry cohorts is allowed to vary over time. For each cohort, there are now two coefficient estimates. The estimates reported in the upper part of Table 3.1 denote the hazard that firms of the respective type had at age 1, whereas the second set of estimates denote the age-dependent hazards. Including these terms wipes out the significance of the performance effect of prior engine production, while the effect of prior production of agricultural implements is robust to this modification. Both sets of coefficient estimates for the cohort variables are statistically indistinguishable from zero, but the log-likelihood of the model increases significantly relative to Model 1, suggesting that the age-dependent hazard terms are jointly significant and the proportionality assumption underlying Model 1 cannot be upheld.[4]

Model 3 adds another set of age-dependent hazard terms for the alternative kinds of pre-entry experience. In comparison to the earlier models, there is one substantial change in the results: the aggregate group of diversifiers with diverse backgrounds has a significantly lower initial hazard than the control group. In fact, their early performance almost matches that of the best performing group, the prior implement makers. At the same time, they are the only group whose exit hazard significantly increases with firm age. In contrast, the initial performance of diversifiers from the automobile industry as well as spin-offs is even less distinctive than suggested by the earlier models, indicating that these entrants benefited little from the capabilities they brought to the tractor industry. Finally, another piece of information on tractor producers is included in Model 4. It is well known that many early tractor firms did not produce their own engines but purchased engines as components from other producers. For a number of firms, the *Standard Catalog* (Wendel, 2000) reports whether they installed own or purchased engines in their earliest tractor model. This information can be interpreted as a proxy for the technological capabilities that an entrant possessed. Surprisingly, Model 4 finds that, if anything, those entrants of which we know they entered using own engines performed below average, whereas entrants using purchased engines may have fared better than average. Both coefficient estimates are not significantly different from zero, however.

How can we explain the substantial performance differences among tractor producers as indicated by the survival analysis? Perhaps the most striking result is that in the tractor industry, prior producers of agricultural implements benefited more from their pre-entry experience than either engine producers or automobile firms did. This is puzzling since, first, the engine is the most complex component of a tractor and, second, tractors and automobiles (and trucks) were closely related technologically in the early 20th century, which would suggest some kind of scope economies between both markets. Apparently, performance differentials were not primarily driven by technological capabilities. This interpretation is consistent with the finding that tractor firms constructing their own engines (which presumably were among the more technologically versed entrants) did not outperform other producers.[5]

Automobile producers were in the technological vanguard of manufacturing in the early 20th century, adhering to stricter engineering standards than most other firms, including implement makers. Production volumes for autos also picked up speed much quicker than those for tractors, turning automobile firms into large-scale organizations accustomed to standardization and mass manufacturing (Williams, 1987). Presumably, therefore, automobile producers possessed both technological capabilities and more general organizational capabilities allowing them to dominate the tractor industry. Indeed, major US automobile producers, most notably Ford but also others such as General Motors, Maxwell, and Chandler, tried to gain control of the tractor market. Ford was the most aggressive. Similar to their prior strategy in the auto industry, they introduced a low-cost, mass-produced tractor in 1917. Ford's entry boosted production volumes and helped to raise engineering standards in the tractor industry. The firm also started a price war by drastically cutting its prices, but eventually lost out to International Harvester and temporarily withdrew from production in the US in 1928 (ibid.).

In addition to severe design flaws of its 'Fordson' tractor, Ford's defeat has been attributed to the firm's failure to set up a distinct distribution network for tractors and to sell tractors as part of a larger system of farm equipment.[6] In contrast, agricultural implement producers had extensive networks of marketing outlets in the rural US. Their decisive competitive advantage thus appears to have been their superior access to customers, which made them better informed about customer needs, enabled them to introduce commercially successful product innovations, and may also have made them more credible in the eyes of their customers. Based on their familiarity with the farm equipment market, implement makers like International Harvester were able to introduce design innovations such as the general-purpose tractor, which was attractive to the average US farmer, including growers of row crops, and decisively widened the tractor market (Williams, 1987, chs. 4 and 5).

The second major difference between the tractor and the automobile industries is that, while spin-offs played a crucial role in the evolution of the automobile industry, they were relatively rare and their performance was unspectacular in the tractor industry. This may have had to do with the strong showing of implement makers leaving little room for innovative spin-offs. Klepper (2006) conjectures that the degree of technological novelty in a new industry conditions the success of diversifiers from related industries, and the extent to which opportunities open up for innovative spin-offs. The present analysis indicates that diversifiers' ability to transfer capabilities depends on the relatedness of markets in terms of demand factors as well as technological proximity. This is in line with Klepper's basic conjecture, however, that the spin-off process may only be prominent in industries where diversifiers leave enough room for it.

The finding regarding spin-offs is moreover interesting with regard to the evolution of the tractor industry's geographic structure. Whereas the automobile industry became heavily concentrated in and around Detroit, the tractor industry was characterized by much less geographic concentration. These patterns are entirely consistent with a spin-off-based account of industrial clustering (Klepper, 2006, 2007; Buenstorf and Klepper, 2005). In the automobile industry, the Detroit cluster mainly emerged due to high-performance spin-offs that originated in the region and located close to their geographic roots. In contrast, the diversifiers that became dominant in the tractor industry were much more widely spread out (mostly throughout the Midwest), while the spin-off process was too weak to drive a process of regional agglomeration.

CONCLUSION

This chapter discussed alternative approaches to evolutionary research on industrial dynamics. It juxtaposed two basic research strategies. One strategy is based on the adoption of the abstract framework of Darwinian evolutionary biology, which is then used as a template for economic analysis. In its heuristic form, this strategy has been popular in evolutionary economics for the past 25 years, going back to Nelson and Winter (1982). It has evidently been very successful, despite some potential pitfalls of the heuristic that have been pointed out above. More recently, a 'generalized' Darwinist framework has been advocated as the shared ontological foundation of processes in, among other fields, biology and economics. As has been argued in this chapter, the ensuing endeavor to use generalized Darwinism as the foundation of an operational framework for studying industrial dynamics – interpreted as being driven by the selection and inheritance of organizational routines – has left many issues unresolved.

Comparative empirical work has been suggested as an alternative research strategy. There is a wealth of empirical studies on industry evolution, and, implicitly, this strand of literature has been comparative in nature from the beginning. In addition to the study of different industries in the same country, studies of the same industry in different countries have recently been taken up. Moreover, models of industry evolution have been developed that are evolutionary in character, but have at most cursory and heuristic recourse to the Darwinian framework.

The chapter's principal conceptual objective was to make more explicit the comparative character of the empirical work, and to propose the strategic selection of industries as a deliberate 'bottom-up' research strategy enabling the development and refinement of theories of industry evolution. In addition to cross-national comparative work, studies of industries that are or have been subject to nation- or industry-specific exogenous shocks, as well as an analysis of closely related industries have been advocated as research designs allowing new insights to be gained into the processes and determinants of evolutionary dynamics in industries. With this emphasis on the comparability of industry studies, the chapter was also intended to help shape an agenda for empirical research in industry evolution that is conducive to theory building. This resonates with the recent proposal to focus empirical attention on irregularities rather than regularities of industry evolution (Klepper and Thompson, 2007).

The chapter then illustrated this approach with an empirical example. Results for the historical US farm tractor industry were presented and discussed against the backdrop of findings on the automobile industry, which was very similar in terms of product technology and has been thoroughly studied before. The example indicated substantial differences between the two industries in the prevalence and performance effects of pre-entry experience. Most importantly, diversifiers from agricultural implement-making dominated the tractor industry, and there were few spin-offs, which mostly had little impact on the industry's further development.

The patterns in the tractor industry suggest that knowledge about customer needs and marketing capabilities are important success factors in innovative industries. This conclusion from studying the tractor industry is consistent with earlier findings in a study of German laser producers (Buenstorf, 2007). While spin-offs were numerous and on average quite successful in lasers, another group of entrants performed just as well: prior laser distributors that integrated into laser manufacturing. These firms could neither bring in detailed knowledge about organizational routines from successful laser producers, as their founders had not been insiders to these firms before, nor were they distinctive in their technological capabilities. (University spin-offs, on the other hand, that presumably did have superior technological capabilities, tended to be among the least impressive performers in the laser industry.) Furthermore, the small number and unimpressive performance of spin-offs in the tractor industry coincided with the absence of a pronounced geographic concentration. This lends support to the theories of spin-off-induced clustering that have been derived from earlier industry studies. Apparently, spin-offs are not only conducive to the emergence and evolution of geographic concentrations, but a lack of spin-offs may also prevent clusters from forming.

Findings like these indicate the potential of the comparative approach to lead to new, detailed insights into the kinds of individual knowledge and organizational capabilities that can be transferred between firms and industries, shaping the competitiveness of new entrants and the way that industries develop. The concrete findings, albeit still preliminary and sketchy in nature, are much more specific than the notion of inherited routines derived from the framework of generalized Darwinism, and they are open to subsequent testing and refinement.

There are, of course, limitations also to the 'bottom-up', comparative research strategy proposed here. Some are inherent in that as an essentially inductive approach, it requires complementary sources of research questions and testable hypotheses. This is where heuristics from biology may play a role, then being a complement to the detailed empirical work. However, there is no obvious reason why biological concepts should necessarily play a special role in this context. Other sources of inspiration may be just as fruitful, for example concepts borrowed from disciplines other than biology, historical and contemporary case study evidence, and more applied theoretical models. Other limitations to the approach derive from data availability. To date, no industry study has had access to full information on the complete firm population, including dimensions such as output and profitability statistics, product prices, detailed information on customers and market segments, etc. However, more and more empirical work on industry evolution is being done, and new datasets are increasingly becoming available to the applied researcher. Thus, the frontier of knowledge about industry evolution is gradually shifting.

NOTES

[1] The spirit of this position is remarkably close to the 'naturalistic' version of evolutionary economics proposed by Witt (2003) (see also Cordes, 2007).

[2] Consistent with some approaches to evolutionary biology, Hodgson (2002, p. 273) stresses the multi-layered nature of economic evolution. He does not discuss, however, the possibility of multiple replication mechanisms at the same level, for example, competing firms, which has no counterpart in biology.

[3] Some firms disappear from the dataset because they are acquired by other tractor firms. In these cases, exit does not provide systematic information on performance. Accordingly, the fact of being acquired is not taken into account in the survival analysis, but only the information that the firm survived up to the time of its acquisition (that is, acquisitions are treated as censored exits).

[4] This finding also rules out the use of alternative survival techniques such as the Cox regression.

[5] The development over time in the hazards of diversifiers with various backgrounds suggests that many of them entered the tractor industry opportunistically, expecting quick profits, and not without initial success.

[6] When Ford was able to make a comeback in 1939, this was due to the duplex hitch invented by Harry Ferguson, a self-taught British mechanic (Williams, 1987, ch. 6). Ford is treated as a continuing producer in the survival analysis.

REFERENCES

Agarwal, R., R. Echambadi, A.M. Franco and M.B. Sarkar (2004), 'Knowledge transfer through inheritance: spin-out generation, development and survival', *Academy of Management Journal*, Vol. 47: 501-522.

Boschma, R. and R. Wenting (2007), 'The Spatial Evolution of the British Automobile industry. Does location matter?' *Industrial and Corporate Change*, Vol. 16: 213-238.

Buenstorf, G. (2006), 'How useful is generalized Darwinism as a framework to study competition and industrial evolution?', *Journal of Evolutionary Economics*, Vol.

16: 511-527.

Buenstorf, G. (2007), 'Evolution on the shoulders of giants: entrepreneurship and firm survival in the German laser industry', *Review of Industrial Organization*, Vol. 30: 179-202.

Buenstorf, G. and C. Guenther (2007), 'No Place Like Home? Location Choice and Firm Survival after Forced Relocation in the German Machine Tool Industry', *Jena Economic Research Papers* # 2007-53.

Buenstorf, G. and S. Klepper (2005), 'Heritage and Agglomeration: The Akron Tire Cluster Revisited', Max Planck Institute of Economics: *Papers on Economics and Evolution # 0508*.

Buenstorf, G. and S. Klepper (2006), 'Why Does Entry Cluster Geographically? Evidence from the U.S. Tire Industry', Mimeo.

Cantner, U., K. Dressler and J.J. Krueger (2006), 'Firm survival in the German automobile industry', *Empirica*, Vol. 33: 49-60.

Carlton, D.W. (1979), 'Why New Firms Locate Where They Do: An Economic Model', in: W.C. Wheaton (ed.): *Interregional Movements and Regional Growth*, Washington DC: The Urban Institute.

Cordes, C. (2007), 'Turning economics into an evolutionary science: Veblen, the selection metaphor, and analogical thinking', *Journal of Economic Issues*, Vol. 41: 135-154.

Dahl, M.S. and T. Reichstein (2006), 'Heritage and Spin-offs: Quality of Parents and Parent-tenure of Founders', Mimeo.

Dawkins, R. (1983), 'Universal Darwinism', in: D.S. Bendall (ed.): *Evolution from Molecules to Men,* Cambridge: Cambridge University Press, pp. 403-425.

Dunne, T., M.J. Roberts and L. Samuelson (1988), 'Patterns of firm entry and exit in U.S. manufacturing industries', *RAND Journal of Economics*, Vol. 19: 495-515.

Foster, J. (1997), 'The analytical foundations of evolutionary economics: from biological analogy to economic self-organization', *Structural Change and Economic Dynamics*, Vol. 8: 427-451

Gort, M. and S. Klepper (1982), 'Time paths in the diffusion of product innovations', *Economic Journal*, Vol. 92: 630-653.

Helfat, C. and M. Lieberman (2002), 'The birth of capabilities: market entry and the importance of pre-history', *Industrial and Corporate Change*, Vol. 11: 725-760.

Hodgson, G.M. (2002), 'Darwinism in economics: from analogy to ontology', *Journal of Evolutionary Economics*, Vol. 12: 259-281.

Hodgson, G.M. and T. Knudsen (2004), 'The firm as an interactor: firms as vehicles for habits and routines', *Journal of Evolutionary Economics*, Vol. 14: 281-307.

Hodgson, G.M. and T. Knudsen (2006), 'Why we need a generalized Darwinism, and why generalized Darwinism is not enough', *Journal of Economic Behavior and Organization*, Vol. 61: 1-19.

Hull, D.L. (1988), *Science as a Process*, Chicago: University of Chicago Press.

Knudsen, T. (2002), 'Economic selection theory', *Journal of Evolutionary Economics*, Vol. 12: 443-470.

Klepper, S. (1996), 'Entry, exit and growth, and innovation over the product life cycle', *American Economic Review*, Vol. 86: 562-583.

Klepper, S. (1997), 'Industry life cycles', *Industrial and Corporate Change*, Vol. 6: 145-181.

Klepper, S. (2001), 'Employee startups in high-tech industries', *Industrial and Corporate Change*, Vol. 10: 639-674.

Klepper, S. (2002a), 'Firm survival and the evolution of oligopoly', *RAND Journal of*

Economics, Vol. 33: 37-61.

Klepper, S. (2002b), 'The capabilities of new firms and the evolution of the US automobile industry', *Industrial and Corporate Change*, Vol. 11: 645-666.

Klepper, S. (2006), 'The evolution of geographic structure in new industries', *Revue de l'OFCE*, June: 135-158.

Klepper, S. (2007), 'Disagreements, spinoffs, and the evolution of Detroit as the capital of the U.S. automobile industry', *Management Science*, Vol. 53: 616-631.

Klepper, S. and E. Graddy (1990), 'The evolution of new industries and the determinants of market structure', *RAND Journal of Economics*, Vol. 21: 27-44.

Klepper, S. and K.L. Simons (2000), 'Dominance by birthright: entry of prior radio producers and competitive ramifications in the U.S. television receiver industry', *Strategic Management Journal*, Vol. 21: 997-1016.

Klepper, S. and S.D. Sleeper (2005), 'Entry by spinoffs', *Management Science*, Vol. 51: 1291-1306.

Klepper, S. and P. Thompson (2006), 'Intra-industry spinoffs', Mimeo.

Klepper, S. and P. Thompson (2007), 'Submarkets and the Evolution of Market Structure', *RAND Journal of Economics*, Vol. 37: 862-888.

Nelson, R.R. and S.G. Winter (1982), *An Evolutionary Theory of Economic Change*, Cambridge MA and London: Belknap Press of Harvard University Press.

Schumpeter, J.A. (1911), *Die Theorie der wirtschaftlichen Entwicklung*, München: Duncker & Humblot.

Simons, K.L. (2001), 'Product Market Characteristics and the Industry Life Cycle', mimeo.

Sleeper, S.D. (1998), *The Role of Firm Capabilities in the Evolution of the Laser Industry: The Making of a High-Tech Market*, PhD Dissertation, Pittsburgh: Carnegie Mellon University.

Veblen, T. (1898), 'Why is economics not an evolutionary science?', *Quarterly Journal of Economics*, Vol. 12: 373-397.

Wendel, C.H. (1979), *The Encyclopedia of American Farm Tractors*, Sarasota FL: Crestline.

Wendel, C.H. (2000), *Standard Catalog of Farm Tractors, 1890 to 1960*, Iola WI: Krause.

Williams, R.C. (1987), *Fordson, Farmall and Poppin' Johnny. A History of the Farm Tractor and Its Impact on America*, Urbana IL and Chicago: University of Illinois Press.

Windrum, P. (2005), 'Heterogeneous preferences and new innovation cycles in mature industries: the amateur camera industry 1955-1974', *Industrial and Corporate Change*, Vol. 14: 1043-1074.

Witt, U. (1999), 'Bioeconomics as economics from a Darwinian perspective', *Journal of Bioeconomics*, Vol. 1: 19-34.

Witt, U. (2003), 'Evolutionary economics and the extension of evolution to the economy', in: U. Witt (ed.): *The Evolving Economy. Essays on the Evolutionary Approach to Economics*, Cheltenham, UK and Northampton, MA, USA: Edward Elgar, pp. 3-34.

Witt, U. (ed.) (2006), 'Special Issue on Universal Darwinism', *Journal of Evolutionary Economics*, Vol. 16 (5).

4. European Contributions to Evolutionary Institutional Economics: The Cases 'Open-Systems Approach' (OSA) and 'Cumulative Circular Causation' (CCC)

Sebastian Berger and Wolfram Elsner

INTRODUCTION

This chapter is about pioneering contributions to evolutionary economics, namely the Open-Systems Approach (OSA) and the conception of Circular Cumulative Causation (CCC). These were developed by the European institutionalists Nicholas Georgescu-Roegen, Karl William Kapp and Gunnar Myrdal (Berger 2007).

OSA and CCC ideas or formal modules are frequently used in modern evolutionary institutional economics but there appears to exist some kind of 'intra-paradigmatic loss', due to the fact that the original contributions, for whatever reason, have not been fully made use of yet. This chapter argues that a reconstruction of the original approaches, including the 'lost' dimensions of the original OSA and CCC, may contribute to better inform and perhaps to improve modern evolutionary institutional economics. Systematic recourse to 'lost' dimensions of earlier contributions in the development of economic theory may in fact help in improving current economic theorising (Elsner 1986).

The first part of the chapter discusses the origins and intended contexts and meanings of OSA and CCC, thus paving the way for better information on modern evolutionary institutional economics. Examples of current uses of OSA and CCC will be considered vis-à-vis their originally intended meanings.

The second part will consider OSA's and CCC's potential contributions to modern evolutionary institutional economics in the context of some recent theoretical developments. We will tentatively compare the two conceptions' broad scopes and methodological stances with conceptions, such as self-organisation, Universal Darwinism and path-dependence.

This chapter contends that OSA and CCC may contribute to the development of modern evolutionary institutional economics mainly in two ways. First, because they were designed to deal with socio-ecological degradation resulting from the economic process, they have the potential to integrate, and put high on the agenda, critical themes in modern evolutionary institutional economics. Second, the conceptions include methodological lessons regarding the integration of trans-disciplinary knowledge and the role of values in the process of theory formation.

RECONSTRUCTING CCC AND OSA

One of the main branches of modern evolutionary institutional economics originates from Veblen's work. In this tradition, the understanding of 'evolution' rests on Veblen's conception of 'cumulative causation'. The two potential core modules of evolutionary institutional economics that we deal with in this chapter, CCC and OSA, can in fact be related to the Veblenian tradition although they originated independent of American Institutionalism. OSA and CCC were developed by Georgescu-Roegen, Kapp and Myrdal to deal with environmental disruption and the 'vicious circle' of poverty. They have triggered much fruitful applied research in the fields of developmental economics and ecological economics (see, for example, Steppacher 1976; 2006).

However, given the celebrity of and frequent references to these ideas it is surprising that OSA and CCC do not play a major role in modern evolutionary institutional economics. The latter addresses issues such as growth, innovation, technological diffusion, organisational change, etc. by means of conceptions like self-organisation, Darwinism and path-dependence. Recourse to the original meaning of OSA and CCC will help to use their full potential for evolutionary economics.

CCC

Approaches that dealt with 'cumulative' effects were common in Europe in the 1920s, especially in England, Germany and Sweden. Suffice to mention the cost controversy between Young and Marshall, the work of Lowe and the 'Kiel School' on the causes of the trade cycle (for example, Krohn 1987, p.

65; Forstater 2003, pp. 309ff.), as well as Wicksell's work on inflation and Myrdal's work on the dynamics of savings and investment rates (for example, Sandelin 1991, pp. 186ff.). Therefore, it is questionable whether CCC can be said to emerge from Veblen's conception of 'cumulative change' (CC) (for example, Argyrous and Sethi 1996, p. 485; O'Hara 2000, pp. 25, 29) and whether the two are more or less identical (for example Mayhew 2001, p. 243). Likewise, the full implications of important differences with Kaldor's 'cumulative causation' seem to be underestimated (for example, Skott 1994, p. 119; Toner 1999, p. 25).

Myrdal fully developed CCC in Appendix 3 of his 'American Dilemma' (Myrdal 1944) and used it as a hypothesis to explain the circular (i.e. self-reinforcing) causation between general prejudices, that is institutionalised patterns of thought and valuation, and poverty which constitutes a vicious circle, leading to increasing inequalities, instabilities and finally crises of the whole socio-economic system. Myrdal derived the conception from his earlier models on 'Monetary Equilibrium' (1939) (see Myrdal 1944, p. 1065, fn. b; Lundberg 1994, pp. 426, 430; see also Wahid 2002, p. 85).

The two distinct elements of CCC are the circular (self-reinforcing) causation and its cumulative effect. Myrdal (1968) defined the first element, circularity, in 'Asian Drama – An inquiry into the poverty of nations':

> circular causation will give rise to a cumulative movement only when [...] a change in one of the conditions will ultimately be followed by a feed-back of secondary impulses [...] big enough not only to sustain the primary change, but to push it further. Mere mutual causation is not enough to create this process [...] (p. 1875).

The second element, cumulativity, has been formulated in the following way:

> Because of such circular causation a social process tends to become cumulative and often to gather speed at an accelerating rate. (Myrdal 1957, p. 13).

Thus, CCC has become one of the early abstract definitions, and in Myrdal's work also exact empirical applications, of the ancient idea of the vicious circle to socio-economic problems (Richardson 1991, pp. 77ff.). It already contained the conception of a 'positive feedback loop' as used in systems or complexity approaches such as Forrester's later 'system dynamics' approach.

Without delving into the details of Veblen's much-cited conception of CC (see, for example, Jennings and Waller 1998, pp. 196ff.), the differences between CC and CCC become evident from Veblen's very own definition:

> For the purpose of economic science the process of cumulative change that is to be accounted for is the sequence of change in the methods of doing things – the methods of dealing with the material means of life. (Veblen 1898, p. 387)

and:

> Evolutionary economics must be a theory of cultural growth as determined by the economic interest, a theory of a cumulative sequence of economic institutions stated in terms of the process itself. (p. 393)

Veblen thus used his conception to underline just the sequential character of the socio-economic process as well as the importance of causal inquiry that does not abstract from historical and empirical facts. Again:

> The economic life history of the individual is a cumulative process of adaptation of means to ends that cumulatively change as the process goes on [...]. (p. 391)
> Accordingly, the main characteristic of an evolutionary economist is that he insists on an answer in terms of cause and effect [...] the notion of cumulative causation. (p. 377)

Of course, similarities do exist between CC and CCC because Myrdal pursued 'causal' analysis and Veblen, on the other hand, was aware of the self-reinforcing nature of institutions. The remaining difference, however, is that Veblen's conception, per se, did not contain the full idea of a circular causation (a self-reinforcing 'positive' feedback) that leads to cumulative effects (see also, Myrdal 1976, p. 215; Angresano 1997, p. 85; Bellets and Sosthe 2006).

CCC also needs to be distinguished from Kaldor's conception of 'cumulative causation'. As Kaldor stated:

> what Myrdal called the principle of 'circular and cumulative causation' [...] is nothing else but the existence of increasing returns to scale [...]. (Kaldor 1978, p. 143)

and:

> This [...] is the principle of cumulative causation whereby some regions gain at the expense of others, leading to increasing inequalities between relatively prosperous and relatively poor areas. (Kaldor 1985, p. 74).

Also, some similarities do exist between Myrdal and Kaldor. In fact, Myrdal dealt with increasing returns as a special case of CCC. The latter is more comprehensive because it includes circular causations between many variables of the socio-economic system, comprising institutional factors and 'backwash effects' that can offset development policy efforts and lead to 'vicious circles'. Because he does not explicitly deal with institutional factors, Kaldor seems to be closer to traditional growth theories that was criticised by Myrdal and Kapp (for example, Kapp 1965, pp. 51ff.; Myrdal

1968, pp. 1866ff.). Reducing the complex character of CCC to 'increasing returns' would imply a loss of explanatory potential. The larger potential of CCC seems to lie in the fact that CCC is a research hypothesis and a 'real type' (see below for a methodological discussion) which can be actualised in many different cases and on different levels to address critical issues. Therefore, it seems to be important for evolutionary institutional economics to distinguish between CCC and other versions of CC.

CCC has been applied to understand the dynamics of societal systems in a wide array of fruitful research in developmental and ecological economics (for example, Kapp 1965, 1973; Steppacher 1976), for instance, the 'centre-periphery' approach (for example, Galtung 1975) or the 'domination effect' (Perroux 1950, 1964, pp. 32ff.). Myrdal analysed, for instance, the role of institutions in traditional societies and showed that the 'economic factor', e.g. foreign investment, does not necessarily gain dominance over the 'institutional factor' and does not necessarily lead to better development. Thus, as a real type and applicable research hypothesis, CCC captures central characteristics of socio-economic processes.

However, Myrdal explicitly refers to the possibility of reversing the vicious into a virtuous circle by state intervention and planning (Myrdal 1960, 1968, pp. 1878-1903). A comprehensively designed and long-run policy and reform orientation is what CCC shares with OSA (see also Myrdal 1976, p. 215).

OSA

It is also important to differentiate carefully between OSA and the concept of an open system as used, for instance, in Critical Realism (see, for example, Bhaskar 1979, 1989; Lawson 1994), Bertalanffy's general systems theory (see, for example, Hodgson 1995, p. 476; 1999, p. 145; Mearman 2002, p. 573), and not to reduce OSA to a metaphorical approach only (for example Hodgson 2005, p. 133).

OSA analyses the economic system in interaction with the natural and the social systems and focuses both on physical and biological, and institutional interactions between the economic system and its environment. Its specific pioneering contribution seems to be that it reconsiders and elaborates on the ('direct') significance of the physical-biological theories of open systems for economics. It thereby seems to have pioneered a truly interdisciplinary 'direct' integration of one of the important scientific advances of the 20th century. The term 'open system' then gains specific meanings on different dimensions, or 'levels' of organisation. The latter are: the inanimate matter, living organisms and human society.

The biological and thermodynamic dimensions of organisation
The biological theory of open systems is directly applicable only to the level of living organisms. Since the 1930s, Schroedinger and Bertalanffy developed elements for a theory which tries to bring together the seemingly contradicting implications of classical thermodynamics and biology (Schroedinger 1944; Bertalanffy 1950). According to the second law of thermodynamics, entropy will continually and irreversibly increase in an isolated system (that is the universe), which in turn tends towards a thermodynamic equilibrium in which entropy is at its maximum. High entropy means disorder and reduction of complexity. The obvious increase of complexity in biological systems, however, points to the opposite direction. Schroedinger's and Bertalanffy's approaches tried to solve the 'puzzle' by investigating how living organisms are thermodynamic open systems that import low entropy to build up structure and export high entropy. Referring to Bertalanffy, Kapp put it this way:

> [Living organisms] are open systems which maintain themselves in a steady state due to an influx and efflux of nutrients and waste materials. [...] [they] use materials from their environment for the maintenance of orderly processes [...] [and show] the most complex and often instantaneous coordination of processes [...] It is these superimposed self-regulating mechanisms which tend to restore balance [...] and give the appearance of purpose and direction not found in the inanimate closed systems [...]. (Kapp 1961, p. 93)

Thus, complexity-building of the life process (that is of an open system) appears compatible with the implications of the entropy law (that is of an isolated system) (which is to be comprehended, though, in a stochastic world). Referring to Schroedinger, Georgescu-Roegen states:

> life does not feed on mere matter and mere energy but – as Schroedinger aptly explained – on low entropy. [...] There is then nothing wrong in saying that life is characterized by the struggle against the entropic degradation of mere matter. It would be a gross mistake to interpret this statement in the sense that life can prevent the degradation of the entire system, including the environment.[...] life speeds up the entropic degradation of the whole system. (Georgescu-Roegen 1966, p. 82)

Consequently, the economic process, from a physical point of view, basically is an entropic transformation since it transforms low into high entropy, which is irrevocable waste (see also op. cit., p. 97).

In this way, OSA's 'direct' and non-metaphorical integration of interdisciplinary knowledge into economics facilitated a reformulation of the 'evolutionary' interaction of the economic system with its natural environment and led to important implications dealt with, for instance, in modern ecological economics.

The bio-cultural conception of the human being

Another key to understanding the foundations of the openness of the economic system is the individual human being. Kapp's 'bio-cultural concept of man' allows for understanding human conduct via the enculturation process that consists of the interactions of a biological structure with a man-made cultural environment:

> if we consider the physical proportions and the highly specialized equipment with which all other mammals are born, the human infant is born in a quasi-embryonic state. [...] A relative short period of gestation produces a relatively immature infant which, unlike animals, does not enjoy the relative safety and protection of a fixed instinctual organization. The fundamental importance of this concept of 'premature birth' and subsequent 'extra-uterine existence' for understanding man's unique position [...] cannot be overestimated. (Kapp 1961, pp. 142f.)

The quasi-embryonic state results in an extreme dependence of the infant, and the completion of the biological process of maturation has to take place in interaction with a highly variable environment. Man is born with a non-differentiated system of drives and with a high degree of plasticity. Human basic needs of cooperation and communication are the outcome of the human experience of helplessness and isolation. These experiences call for assurance which can only be established in interpersonal relationships in which man is able to affirm his self-esteem, to adapt, to coordinate, etc. This interaction is a precondition for the development of man's potentialities and he depends on a process of enculturation to become a human being. Hence individuals become culturally conditioned and view reality through their acquired linguistic and symbolic system (op. cit., pp. 155ff.). This bio-cultural foundation of human conduct has been defined as openness on the individual level (Steppacher 1994, p. 438) which is another reason to contribute to the openness of the 'aggregate' level of the whole economic system. Of course, given this framework, the approach also can fruitfully integrate interdisciplinary knowledge from psychology and anthropology.

The institutional dimension of societal organisation

Finally, OSA focuses on the organising principles of the socio-economic system that determine the speed of that entropic transformation process and of socio-ecological degradation (Kapp 1977, pp. 532ff.; Georgescu-Roegen 1966, pp. 96, 126). In order to understand these organising principles, as well as their interaction with the socio-ecological systems, and their effect on socio-ecological degradation, we have to proceed from the level of thermodynamics to an institutional analysis of the more complex dimension of organisation, that is human society. Kapp and Georgescu-Roegen have developed the understanding that this dimension cannot be understood with the knowledge of the natural sciences alone, nor simply through analogies or metaphors taken from the natural sciences. Both Kapp and Georgescu-Roegen emphasised the distinction to be made between the two organisational dimensions, physico-biological and societal. The conception of an 'open system' in thermodynamics needs to be differentiated from its actualisation on the 'higher' and more complex level of societal organisation, with the enculturation of the immature individual as a bridging process.

To understand the economic system at the complex level of human society means to understand its prevalent economic institutions. Both dimensions ('levels'), and their interaction, basically imply discontinuous and nonlinear feedbacks that characterise the dynamic interdependencies between the subsystems as well as of each subsystem with the composite whole. The comprehension and analysis of both dimensions, or 'levels' of organisation, is necessary to fully understand the dynamics of the economic system.

Implications

OSA was elaborated to address socio-ecological disruption that results from the organising principles of an open economic system, especially the capitalist 'market' mechanism which seems to be specifically designed to make maximum use of the unavoidable openness in order to exploit the other two subsystems at a maximum rate if, and as long as, they are not properly embedded, directed and restricted. This constitutes the tradition of Kapp's lifelong work on social control and environmental policy to reduce environmental degradation and social disparities.

In his article 'The Open System Character of the Economy and its Implications' (1976a, b) and in 'Umweltkrise und Nationaloekonomie' (1972a), Kapp considered the advantages of a 'new' systems thinking along those lines, but also cautions that this is but a first step to (1) view reality anew, (2) order empirical findings in a new way, (3) develop terminologies that are adequate to the problems, and (4) establish a basis for an adequate causal analysis which takes physical/biological and institutional causal chains into account (Kapp 1972a, p. 236; 1976a, p. 97). Kapp further clarifies that the open system character of the economy requires a new approach since the effects of the economy on the natural (and social) environment(s) can threaten the reproduction of the whole society through negative feedbacks:

> as soon as the open character of economic systems is fully realized the formulation of social goals and objectives and the problem of collective choices can no longer be avoided. Such objectives and choices with respect to the maintenance of dynamic states of ecological and economic balance for the maintenance and improvement of the conditions of social and individual existence (quality of life) must become the point of departure of a normative science of economics. [...] In short, a normative science of economics taking account of the open system

character of the economy would imply a complete reversal of the analytical procedures of the discipline as heretofore practiced and applied. [...] the new task of economics would be to elucidate the manner in which collectively determined social goals and objectives could be attained in the most effective and socially least costly manner. (Kapp 1976b, p. 101-102)

Kapp's lifelong search for remedies against socio-ecological degradation resulting from the capitalist 'market' mechanism dated back to his dissertation 'Planwirtschaft und Aussenhandel' (1936) which was a contribution to the planning debate of the 1920s and 1930s, and the starting point of what was to become one of the most powerful attacks on orthodox economics in his most famous work 'The Social Costs of Private Enterprise' (1950). Here, he identified the cause of socio-ecological degradation in what Weber had called the formal rationality of an accounting system based on 'market' values and what Veblen had called the ceremonial and emulative 'business' principle of investment for profits. In this framework, firms systematically shift maximum portions of the costs of production to third parties, to the commons, and to future generations, that is 'social costs'. This is in accordance with the institutional framework and culture of a capitalist society which defines 'costs' in specific (and deliberately reduced) ways, thus reducing the socio-ecological responsibility of the economic agents, particularly of the most powerful ones who can shift the greatest amounts of costs. Costs are what we seek responsibility for:

Although the evidence was all around us, few [...] economists, have warned us against the dangers inherent in the fact that production and economic growth, particularly under the influence of modern technology, tend to give rise to social costs which are not accounted for in entrepreneurial outlays. (Kapp 1977, p. 528)

It is questionable whether there would be any 'growth' at all, as defined by the 'market', if all social costs had to be borne by those who generate them. In turn, this implies that economic growth measured in terms of market values is only possible because those who pay the social costs are too weak to defend themselves against this redistribution. Kapp, like Georgescu-Roegen, developed an interdisciplinarily informed production theory where industrial growth depends on non-renewable stocks of low entropy. Renewable biotic resources, over all, cannot generate such growth.

The open-system character of the economy is the reason why socio-ecological degradation cannot be understood through an economic approach that remains within the confines of 'markets'. Mainstream approaches that deal with 'social costs' (as clearly definable and allocable externalities, such as Pigou or Coase), fail to reflect the nature of the problem (see also Kapp 1972b). They simply lack knowledge about the complex causations and dynamics. Recent complexity research seems to suggest that formal approaches to complexity are infeasible in the last instance (see, for example, Delorme 2005).

According to Kapp, socio-ecological indicators should replace, or at least be added to, the GDP index to account for the heterogeneous and complex processes at the material level of the economic process. He proposed alternative instruments of planning and control like, for instance, environmental and social quality standards that force economic units to take adequate account of the negative socio-ecological effects of their activities (including the choice of technologies and inputs, and the location of production). According to Kapp, technology is just a dependent variable which must be chosen in accordance with societal and environmental objectives (Kapp 1977, pp. 534-539).

Kapp's approach to decision-making, thus, is not artificially closed like the formal individualistic rationality of the 'market' but open like substantive rationality. Based on Weber's conception of substantive rationality ([1925] 2005, pp. 77ff.), Kapp linked economics to societal goals and basic human needs. He developed a conception of social minimum standards, or thresholds, as an operational basis for human needs and coined this 'rational humanism' to humanise economics:

> the criteria of rationality in a new humanism have to be of a substantive nature, that is, they have to be sought and found in the degree to which they guarantee concrete conditions of life or satisfy basic existential needs. Concrete and relatively constant measures of basic needs or minimal limits of tolerance have to take the place of value functions with undetermined content. (Kapp 1985, p. 108)

Goal definition, conflict mediation, impact studies and implementation are all societal processes involved. Here, Kapp refers to J. Dewey's pragmatist 'means-ends' psychology (for example Kapp 1971, pp. 111-142; Berger and Forstater 2007). This involves normative economics, although basic human needs, for instance, can also largely be made objective by empirical evidence. In his unfinished manuscript 'The Foundations of Institutional Economics', Kapp said that

> any substantive treatment of human needs and the resulting notion of substantive rationality is based in part on the normative axiom that human life and human development and survival are values which need no further proof or demonstration. (Kapp, undated, p. 11)

and:

> This distinction [between basic and higher needs] is necessary for the formulation of a substantive principle of rationality in face of the dangers to humanity in a technical age. (p. 110)

In the final instance, Kapp held that the secular environmental crisis could not be solved without addressing the role of private property, the core institution of capitalist 'markets' (for example Kapp 1972a, p. 247), a conclusion that he shared with Veblen and the late classical political economy. Private property therefore becomes a prime research subject in socio-ecological degradation (Steppacher 2006).

Our reconstruction of OSA suggests that neither Kapp nor Georgescu-Roegen attempted to develop a biological-analogy approach to evolutionary institutional economics. Finally, it should also have become clear that OSA is more than a philosophical concern, as in Critical Realism, and that its purpose is different from Bertalanffy's general systems theory.

CCC'S AND OSA'S POTENTIALS FOR MODERN EVOLUTIONARY INSTITUTIONAL ECONOMICS

A Broader Institutional and 'Political-Economic' Perspective?

Our contention here is that OSA and CCC could help evolutionary economics strengthen its institutional, ecological and 'political-economic' dimensions because they were designed and elaborated to capture increasing ecological degradation, economic inequalities, and crises in the 'market' economy.

To illustrate this potential significance for the scope and method of evolutionary institutional economics, we may just mention some of the developments of its subject fields and theory. Many approaches focus on phenomena only *within* the logic of the 'market' economy, such as the evolution of markets and market structures, the evolution of firms and their strategies, or the diffusion and adaptation of technology. Phenomena like systemic social costs, asymmetric power distribution, vested interests, and socio-ecological degradation fall outside the attention of many approaches.

The conception of path-dependence tends to divert interest in causal relations towards focussing just on short-cut random events. The research interests of OSA applications would basically not be random modelling. For instance, OSA and CCC consider that it is an institutionalised practice to hold prices low mainly by shifting costs on the socio-ecological subsystems in conjunction with manipulative advertising, generating systemic wasteful consumption patterns that make for pathdependent sales and 'growth.' Any neglect of these underlying causes is equivalent to treating the economic system as a closed system. Even if the economy is considered an open system, pathdependence theory tends to overlook this open character vis-à-vis the socio-ecological systems. The self-reinforcing mechanism of CCC can elucidate the interactions of the full range of potential variables of the socio-economic system. OSA and CCC had been designed to be open for the consideration of new variables and relations. One of the reasons for this openness towards a broader empirical perspective certainly is that they were intended for analysing non-equilibrium processes.

Considering the reasons why economic science tends to restrict itself to 'economic' variables, Kapp referred to Veblen:

> In an age of business enterprise, Veblen wrote, new facts and ideas will impose themselves upon the imagination of a wider audience of economists [...] only if they are expressed in terms of business finance and the market-test. Veblen felt that ingrained habits of thought reflecting the predominant climate of opinion characteristic of a system of business enterprise have a tendency of being • transmitted from one generation of economists to the next as they did in the past: via 'institutions of higher learning'. (Kapp, 1976b, p. 104)

According to Veblen, evolutionary economics should be a theory of cause and effect so that economic growth and technological change can be explained in causal terms by virtue of their cumulative character. In addition, evolutionary institutional economics in the traditions of Kapp, Myrdal and Georgescu-Roegen will have to contribute to analyses of socio-ecological degradation and distributive problems. This, as should have become clear, would have to be pursued in the framework of a normative political economy that deals with policy processes, social control and democratic decision making.

The Methodological Issue

Biological, thermodynamic and other metaphors as well as ontologies play a major role in the analysis of evolutionary processes. Prominent examples are conceptions of 'self-organisation' (see, for example, Witt 1997; Foster 2005), path-dependence (for example, Arthur 1994; David 2002), and Universal Darwinism (Hodgson 1999). Without delving deeper into these approaches it seems that OSA and CCC have pursued a different approach. Kapp, Myrdal and Georgescu-Roegen were aware of the specific difficulties of theory formation in economics. Here, more than in natural sciences, theories depend on the pre-analytical values of the observer because they are man-made actualisations of aspects of reality (see, for example, Myrdal [1929] (1976); Kapp [1963] (1987); 1972b). Approaches which do not question the status quo are clearly influenced by the observer's value premises. These have to be made explicit to avoid implicit and hidden manipulation. For example, the value premises behind the conception of social costs were clearly spelled out by Kapp and are very critical of core institutions of the modern market economy.

This is why analogies imported from the natural sciences also have to be explained in terms of the value premises of the researcher because they often lend themselves to all kinds of hidden normative elements. A prominent example seems to be the conception of 'natural selection' used in neoclassical and Austrian market theories to keep and strengthen the optimisation and equilibrium approach (see, for example, Rosenberg 1994). Another example is the analogy of 'self-organisation' derived from Prigogine's non-equilibrium thermodynamics. Especially Austrian economics and also some Neo-Schumpeterian economists (see, for example, Foster 2001, 2005) use this analogy to lend support to the idea of 'spontaneous order' in the 'market' system. They do not consider the role of vested interests, asymmetric power relations, deliberate coercion and manipulation, systemic information and coordination problems, and social costs. Sometimes the issue of theory formation tends to be shifted over to ontology formation that is, of course, also dependent on value premises (Vromen 2004, p. 213). For instance, it is claimed that parts of Darwin's evolutionary theory can be integrated in economics to describe all kinds of evolutionary processes (that is, Universal Darwinism – see Hodgson 1999, 2002).

Both Kapp (1961) and Georgescu-Roegen (1966) have emphasised the problems of using theories of the natural sciences to understand processes at the much more complex level of human society. Reasoning by analogies would facilitate evading the need to clearly develop notions of the subject matter (for example Kapp 1961, pp. 56-60). While they are useful for creative and heuristic associations, analogies tend to oversimplify and misrepresent reality by imputing similarities to very distinct phenomena that belong to distinct levels of organisation with different levels of complexity. By imposing an analogy upon the material, the collection of data, testing etc. tends to lose its specificity by considering as similar and identical what actually is diverse. It might even be facilitated to neglect, and withdraw from investigating, those events which do not fit the analogy:

> Once the intellectual operation based upon the analogy is in full swing, it is usually too late to remind oneself of the imperfect character of the original analogy upon which the whole enterprise rests. (Kapp 1961, p. 58)

On the other hand, directly integrating interdisciplinary knowledge at the adequate level of complexity is less problematic. An example is the biological theory of open systems which is applied to gain fundamental knowledge about the entropic transformation process on the material level of the economy as discussed above. Other examples are the bio-cultural understanding of individual human development as discussed, but also psychology and anthropology which may be integrated to attain a better understanding of human conduct and existential needs.

OSA and CCC thus use 'real types' and research hypotheses to capture processes of socio-ecological degradation and increasing inequalities in 'market' systems. This is different from developing elaborate analogies and ontologies. Kapp proposes 'real types' for the study of complex social structure in the tradition of Spiethoff and Weber (Kapp 1961, pp. 194ff.; Georgescu-Roegen 1966, p. 114). 'Real types' refer to specified problem situations:

> Their 'real' character stems from what is empirically given. They are derived from the observed regularities of the social process, which are however, isolated from their historically unique and accidental context. What is retained for purpose of analysis are regularities as they are observed within the socio-cultural context. (Kapp 1961, pp. 198-199)

The advantage of the 'direct' integration method is that it does prevent economics from working with preconceived causal mechanisms and conceptions taken from natural sciences which may prematurely filter information and may divert attention from the very nature of the problem situation.

CONCLUSION

By reconsidering the outlines of OSA and CCC from their original sources, we have tried to suggest core areas and ways of a potential compensation for 'intra-paradigmatic' losses in evolutionary institutional economics through 'direct' integration of specific bio-physical knowledge. We have tried to show how the two core modules could be used to increase the fund of research interests and research questions, and the 'knowledge fund' of modern evolutionary institutional economics. This may be performed first through making use of their potential of institutional, ecological and systemic 'political-economic' themes and approaches. These stand in, reiterate, resume and further develop, the radical classical-economic and Veblenian traditions. Second, this could be pursued through the specific non-metaphorical and non-ontological ways of ('direct') integration of interdisciplinary knowledge and theory formation.

Formal dynamic modelling (agent-based modelling, system dynamics, network analysis, dynamic graphs etc.) might profit from the core modules OSA and CCC as perceived in their original intentions and designs. Impulses might be provided in quite diverse analytical areas, such as the generation of new variables and relations, reconfigurations of 'endogenous' and exogenous' etc. This has to be left, though, to future research in a perhaps revived OSA-CCC-Kappian-Myrdalian research tradition.

Finally, an intra-paradigmatic loss compensation seems possible which might in turn provide considerable knowledge net gains to modern evolutionary institutional economics in a broad array of topical questions, fields and theories.

REFERENCES

Angresano, James (1997), *The Political Economy of Gunnar Myrdal: An Institutional Basis for the Transformation Problem*, Cheltenham, UK and Lyme, USA: Edward Elgar.

Argyrous, G. and Sethi, R. (1996), 'The Theory of Evolution and the Evolution of Theory: Veblen's Methodology in Contemporary Perspective', *Cambridge Journal of Economics*, 20, 475-495.

Arthur, Brian W. (1994), *Increasing Returns and Path Dependence in the Economy*, University of Michigan Press.

Bellets, Michel and Sosthe, Frank (2006) 'Anticipations, Institutions, and Market Process Theories: A Re-interpretation of Myrdals Institutionalism' (internet version),
http://dossier.univ-stetienne.fr/creuset/www/pubwp/WP_CREUSET99_2.pdf. [visited 14.4.2006].

Berger, Sebastian (2007), *Europäischer Institutionalismus*, Frankfurt am Main: Peter Lang Verlag.

Berger, Sebastian and Forstater, Mathew (2007), 'Towards a Political Institutional Economics: Kapp's Social Costs, Lowe's Instrumental Analysis, and the European Institutionalist Approach to Environmental Policy', *Journal of Economic Issues*, 41, 2, 539-546.

Bertalanffy, Ludwig von (1932), *Theoretische Biologie*, Bd. 1: *Allgemeine Theorie, Physikochemie, Aufbau und Entwicklung des Organismus*, Berlin.

—— (1950), 'The Theory of Open Systems in Physics and Biology', *Science*, 111, 23-29.

Bhaskar, Roy (1979), *The Possibility of Naturalism*, The Harvester Press.

—— (1989), *Reclaiming Reality – A Critical Introduction to Contemporary Philosophy*, Verso.

Cohen, I. Bernard (1994), *Interactions: Some Contacts between the Natural Sciences and the Social Sciences*, Cambridge, MA.

David, Paul A. (2002), 'Path Dependence, its Critics, and the Quest for Historical Economics', in T. Cowen and E. Crampton (eds), *Market Failure or Success*, Cheltenham, UK and Northampton, MA, USA: Edward Elgar, 79-104.

Delorme, Robert (2005), *Notes on Effective Complexity: A Post-Simonian Modelling of Very Ill-Structured Problem Situations*, International Workshop on Evolutionary Macroeconomics, The University of Queensland, Brisbane 14-17 July 2005.

Elsner, Wolfram (1986), *Economic Institutions Analysis – The Paradigmatic Development of Economics and the Significance of a Recourse to the Economic Classics: The Example of Institutional Analysis* (German: Ökonomische Institutionenanalyse), Berlin: Duncker & Humblot, Volkswirtschaftliche Schriften,

No. 367.

Forstater, Mathew (2004), 'Cumulative Causation à la Lowe: Radical Endogeneity, Methodology, and Human Intervention', in G. Argyrous, M. Forstater and G. Mongiovi (eds), *Growth, Distribution, and Effective Demand – Alternatives to Economic Orthodoxy. Essays in Honor of Edward J. Nell*, London: M.E. Sharpe, 309-16.

Foster, John (1997), 'The Analytical Foundations of Evolutionary Economics: From Biological Analogy to Economic Self-Organization', *Structural Change and Economic Dynamics*, 8, 427-51.

—— (2005), 'The Self-Organizational Perspective', in Kurt Dopfer (ed.), *The Evolutionary Foundations of Economics*, Cambridge, UK: Cambridge University Press, 367-90.

Galtung, Johan (1975), *Development From Above and The Blue Revolution: The Indo-Norwegian Project in Kerala*, International Peace Research Institute, Oslo, PRIO Publication No. 2-12.

Georgescu-Roegen, Nicholas (1966), *Analytical Economics – Issues and Problems*, London: Oxford University Press.

—— (1971), *The Entropy Law and the Economic Process*, Cambridge, MA: Harvard University Press.

—— (1976), *Energy and the Economic Myths – Institutional and Analytical Economic Essays*, New York: Pergamon Press.

Hodgson, Geoffrey M. (1995), 'The Evolution of Evolutionary Economics', *Scottish Journal of Political Economy*, 42, 469-88.

—— (1999), *Evolution and Institutions: on evolutionary economics and the evolution of economics*, Cheltenham, UK and Northampton, MA, USA: Edward Elgar.

—— (2002), 'Darwinism in Economics: from Analogy to Ontology', *Journal of Evolutionary Economics*, 12, 259-81.

—— (2005), 'Decomposition and Growth: biological metaphors in economics from the 1880s to the 1980s', in Kurt Dopfer (ed.), *The Evolutionary Foundations of Economics*, Cambridge, UK: Cambridge University Press, 105-50.

Jennings, Ann and Waller, William (1998), 'The Place of Biological Science in Veblen's Economics', *History of Political Economy*, 30, 189-217.

Kaldor, Nicholas (1978), *Further Essays in Economics*, London.

—— (1985), *Economics without Equilibrium*, New York, Cardiff.

Kapp, Karl W. (1936), *Planwirtschaft und Aussenhandel*, Genf.

—— (1950), *The Social Costs of Private Enterprise*, Cambridge, MA: Harvard University Press.

—— (1961), *Toward a Science of Man in Society – A Positive Approach to the Integration of Social Knowledge*, The Hague: Martinus Nijhoff.

—— [1963] (1987), 'Social Costs and Social Benefits – A Contribution to Normative Economics' (translated into German), in Rolf Steppacher and Christian Leipert (eds), *Für eine ökosoziale Ökonomie – Entwürfe und Ideen. Ausgewählte Aufsätze*, Frankfurt: Fischer, 71-102.

—— (1965), 'Economic Development in a New Perspective: Existential Minima and Substantive Rationality', *Kyklos*, 18, 49-79.

—— (1971), 'Implementation of Environmental Policies. United Nations Conference on the Human Environment 1971', in John E. Ullmann (ed.), *Social Costs, Economic Development and Environmental Disruption*, New York, 111-42.

—— (1972a), 'Umweltkrise und Nationalökonomie', *Schweizerische Zeitschrift für Volkswirtschaft und Statistik*, 108, 231-48.

—— (1972b), 'Social Costs, Neoclassical Economics, Environmental Planning: A Reply', *Social Science Information*, 11.1, 17-28.

—— (1973), Entwicklungspolitik in neuer Perspektive – Bemerkungen zu Gunnar Myrdal's "Politisches Manifest über die Armut in der Welt"', Institut für Sozialwissenschaften, Universität Basel, Nr. 110.

—— (1976), 'The Open-System Character of the Economy and its Implications', in Kurt Dopfer (ed.), *Economics in the Future*, London: Macmillan Press.

—— (1977), 'Environment and Technology: New Frontiers for the Social and Natural Sciences', *Journal of Economic Issues*, 11, 527-40.

—— (undated), 'The Foundations of Institutional Economics' (unfinished Ms.), Kapp Archive, University of Basle.

Krohn, Claus-D. (1987), *Wissenschaft im Exil – Deutsche Sozial- und Wirtschaftswissenschaftler in den USA und die New School for Social Research*, Frankfurt am Main, New York: Campus Verlag.

Lawson, Tony (1994), 'Philosophical Realism', in G.M. Hodgson, W.J. Samuels and M.R. Tool (eds), *The Elgar Companion to Institutional and Evolutionary Economics*, Vol. 2, Aldershot, UK and Brookfield, US: Edward Elgar, 219-25.

Lundberg, Erik (1994), 'Studies in Economic Instability and Change', in Rolf Henriksson (ed.), *Eric Lundberg Studies in Economic Instability and Change: selected writings through five decades together with an obituary by William J. Baumol*, SNS Förlag.

Mayhew, Ann (2001), 'Human Agency, Cumulative Causation, and the State', *Journal of Economic Issues*, 35, 239-250.

Mearman, Andrew (2002), 'To What Extent is Veblen an Open-System Theorist?', *Journal of Economic Issues*, 36, 573-580.

Myrdal, Gunnar [1929] (1976), *Das politische Element in der national-ökonomischen Doktrinbildung*, Bonn-Bad Godesberg.

——(1944), *American Dilemma*, New York, London: Harper and Row.

——(1957), *Economic Theory and Under-Developed Regions*, London: Gerald Duckworth.

——(1960), *Beyond the Welfare State – Economic Planning in the Welfare States and its International Implications*, London.

——(1968), *Asian Drama – An inquiry into the poverty of nations*, New York: Pantheon.

——(1976), 'Remarks upon Receipt of the Veblen-Commons Award', *Journal of Economic Issues*, 10, 215-216.

O'Hara, Phillip (2000), 'How can Economics be an Institutional-Evolutionary Science?', in Francisco Louca and Mark Perlman (eds), *Is Economics an Evolutionary Science? The legacy of Thorstein Veblen*, Cheltenham, UK and Northampton, MA, USA: Edward Elgar, 25-40.

Perroux, François (1950), 'The Domination Effect and Modern Economic Theory', *Social Research*, 17, 188-206.

—— (1964), *L'économie du XXème siècle*, 2nd edition, Paris.

Richardson, George P. (1991), *Feedback Thought in Social Science and Systems Theory*, Philadelphia.

Rosenberg, Alexander (1994), 'Does Evolutionary Theory give Comfort or Inspiration to Economics', in Philip Mirowski (ed.), *Natural Images in Economic Thought: 'Markets read in tooth and claw'*, Cambridge, UK: Cambridge University Press, 384-408.

Sandelin, Bo (1991), *The History of Swedish Economic Thought*, London, New York:

Routledge.

Skott, Peter (1994), 'Cumulative Causation', in G.M. Hodgson, W.J. Samuels and M.R. Tool (eds), *The Elgar Companion to Institutional and Evolutionary Economics*, Vol. 1, Aldershot, UK and Brookfield, US: Edward Elgar, 119-124.

Schroedinger, Erwin (1944), *What Is Life?*, Cambridge, UK.

Steppacher, Rolf (1976), *Surplus, Kapitalbildung und wirtschaftliche Entwicklung*, Liebefeld, Bern: Lang Druck AG.

—— (1994), 'K. William Kapp', in G.M. Hodgson, W.J. Samuels and M.R. Tool (eds), *The Elgar Companion to Institutional and Evolutionary Economics*, Vol. 1, Aldershot, UK and Brookfield, US: Edward Elgar, 435-41.

—— (2006), 'Property, Mineral Resources and "Sustainable Development"', in Otto Steiger (ed.), *Property Rights, Creditor's Money and the Foundation of the Economy*, Marburg: Metropolis.

Toner, Philip (1999), *Main Currents in Cumulative Causation – The Dynamics of Growth and Development*, London: Macmillan Press.

Ullmann, John E. and Preiswerk, Roy (eds) (1985), *K. William Kapp, The Humanization of the Social Sciences*, London.

Veblen, Thorstein B. (1898), 'Why is Economics not an Evolutionary Science', *The Quarterly Journal of Economics*, 12.4, 373-97.

—— (1907), 'The Socialist Economics of Karl Marx and His Followers', *The Quarterly Journal of Economics*, 21.2, 299-322.

Vromen, Jack (2004), 'Conjectural Revisionary Economic Ontology: Outline of an Ambitious Research Agenda for Evolutionary Economics', *Journal of Economic Methodology*, 11, 213-47.

Wahid, Abu N.M. (2002), *Frontiers of Economics – Nobel Laureates of the Twentieth Century*, Greenwood Press.

Weber, Max [1925] (2005), *Wirtschaft und Gesellschaft*, repr. Verlag Zweitausendeins.

Witt, Ulrich (1997), 'Self-organization and Economics – What is New?', *Structural Change and Economic Dynamics*, 8, 489-507.

—— (2005), 'The Evolutionary Perspective and the Firm', in Kurt Dopfer (ed.), *The Evolutionary Foundations of Economics*, Cambridge, UK: Cambridge University Press.

5. Institutions as Determinants of Preference Change: A One Way Relation?

Martin Binder and Uta-Maria Niederle

INTRODUCTION

During the recent decades, there has been a growing interest by economists in relaxing some of the assumptions of neoclassical economic reasoning. One assumption, which has been discussed prominently, is that of static, exogenously given preferences. In the case of institutional economics, endogenizing preferences has been most prominently worked out by Bowles (1998, 2004). To our understanding, these attempts reflect economists' growing explanatory reservations concerning the standard assumptions on preferences (non-satiability, convexity, transitivity, etc.), economic decision making (assumption of perfect rationality, perfect information), and the optimization/maximization calculus.[1]

In this chapter, we follow a naturalistic approach and analyze changing preferences in a more 'consilient' way (see Wilson 1998), that is, concepts and explanations in the social sciences – economics being one of them – should in any case be compatible with findings in the natural sciences on more fundamental levels. Following Witt (1987, 1991, 1999), who has introduced this 'naturalistic perspective', we feel that economists can learn a lot from other social sciences. Having more material conjectures and hypotheses about the content of preferences and the way they are formed and change *systematically* over time will improve economic reasoning on dynamic, long-term phenomena, such as new consumer markets or emerging institutions. Socio-biology and especially social psychology seem to be promising fields to gain insights from whence to try to establish a more substantive view of preferences. In particular, we want to focus on how an account of preference change could benefit our understanding of institutional change. Drawing on Bowles (1998) on how institutions affect preferences (see also Frey 2005) we want to present a conceptual framework in which this relationship is bi-directional.

The chapter is organized as follows: The next section gives an account of the 'substantive' physiological and psychological underpinnings of preferences generally observed in situations of choice. In the third section we turn to examine how learning affects these preference bases over time. The insights gained from this conceptual framework are then related to the dynamics of institutional change in the fourth section. The fifth section concludes.

SUBSTANTIVE PREFERENCES

Standard economic theorizing focuses on a very narrow picture of an individual's preferences. To fruitfully apply the mathematical calculus of constrained maximization in utility theory, several formal requirements for preferences are necessary (see Warke 2000; Witt 2005). Standard subjective preference orderings thus rely on several formal axioms (such as completeness, transitivity, etc.) which are *ad hoc* and do not conform to real-world situations. According to Witt (2001, p. 24), a theory of substantive preferences, on the contrary, wants to address several issues which are *expressis verbis* excluded from orthodox preference theory (in the clause of 'given tastes and preferences'), namely such questions as: what is the content of our preferences (do we universally share some preferences across individuals), how do we come to our preferences (are they innate, or learnt) and if preferences change, is there a systematic way to describe their change.

The present chapter distinguishes between the well-known 'revealed' preferences in a given situation, dealt with in economic decision theory, and a more 'substantive' version of preferences that is more long-term oriented. Substantive preferences are grounded on physiological and psychological wants of the individual (see Witt 2001, pp. 25-27), on 'social instincts' in the case of social interaction, as well as on attitudes (see Niederle 2006, pp. 81-83).

We argue that these three elements, namely wants and social instincts (as motives for behaviour), and attitudes (as beliefs and evaluation of outcomes), comprise the most important influencing factors of an individual's preferences. While wants and social instincts belong to the more stable part of our preference basis, attitudes are more easily changeable but less persistent in their effect on our preferences. The three concepts will now be discussed in turn.

Wants

There have been already different attempts in economics at elaborating a theory of wants[2] (for example Menger 1950 or Georgescu-Roegen 1954). However, those attempts often suffer from the *ad hoc* fashion in which wants (or hierarchies thereof) are introduced. We will rely therefore on Witt's (2001) theory of wants, which draws on Menger's theory but provides it with a behavioural foundation.

Witt (2001) defines a want as a behavioural disposition that arises out of a state of deprivation of the organism (for example hunger, thirst, the need for air, sociability, etc.). Our urge to satisfy a want motivates our actions, hence the use of the term 'motive' in psychological literature (Reiss 2000, Ch. 1). The satisfaction of a want gives an individual a pleasant sensory experience while deprivation is a (more or less) painful experience.

A key feature of all wants is that consumption of certain goods leads to their satiation for a certain period of time, during which excessive consumption would even lead to unpleasant sensory experiences. A prominent example is food, where after having eaten a certain amount, hunger is satiated, and 'overconsumption' makes the individual feel worse off. But also in the case of cognitive and social needs, e.g. socializing with others, satiation takes place. Satiation in all these cases is, however, temporary so that after a period of time, deprivation occurs again.

Witt (2001) classifies wants on the one hand as *innate* and on the other hand as *acquired* or *learnt*. He claims that there exists a finite (and possibly very small) set of innate wants, which are physiologically determined (such as those mentioned above;[3] see also, for example, Millenson 1967, p. 368; Maslow 1987 and Reiss 2000). These innate wants can be seen as synonymous to 'needs' as used in psychology. Innate wants are a stable component of substantive preferences and are not subject to change.

The category of learnt or acquired wants is possibly the more important one for economic and behavioural analysis. Witt's conjecture is that acquired wants are neither few nor finite in number. The argument in this case is based on innate learning dispositions which are common to all humans and which allow for the growth of very refined wants. Acquired wants can change over time. We will discuss the related learning mechanisms in the third section. In any case, learnt wants also have their beginning in innate basic wants.

Now, what do wants have to do with institutions? Nothing directly, one should say, because there is no such thing as an individual want for a specific social institution. But technical progress and organizational developments to better satisfy wants (and combinations thereof) create conditions that necessitate new arrangements of coordination, hence new rules and institutions. Here, wants influence institutions latently via social needs like status contributing to the formation and diffusion or disapproval of rules. This connection, however, remains indirect and is more mediating in character.

The concrete means to satisfy wants are subject to attitude formation, but before elaborating this relation let us turn to social instincts as the invariant source of preference formation in social interaction.

Social Instincts

A second important influence on our preferences is social instincts.[4] There seem to be clear biological underpinnings of behavioural expectations in social interaction, like a sense of reciprocity and fairness in cooperation (see Jones 2001, p. 1182).[5] Such biological underpinnings of behaviour are adaptive in the sense that they have responded to and have enhanced survival and reproductive chances in a selective environment – for the individual herself and in the social group. In this way 'evolutionary processes inevitably and importantly contribute to the *common origins* and ordering of some preferences' (Jones 2001, p. 1166, emphasis added). In this sense, people are no *tabula rasa*.

In the social context one might speak of social instincts as innate impulses to act. These social instincts, in the end, support the satisfaction of individual (basic) wants. For example, cooperating and reciprocating for gaining food ultimately serves satisfying not only bodily needs but also, by acting and being treated cooperatively, even serves social-psychological wants like social integrity.

A list of such instincts in social (or strategic) interaction should at least comprise the following five elements: reciprocity (in cooperation and retaliation),[6] conformity,[7] commitment and loyalty,[8] readiness to help others[9] like giving and sharing, and possessiveness.[10] Since it is a tentative compilation, this list does not claim completeness. Single elements given in the list, however, are discussed in diverse contexts of social interaction in socio-biology and evolutionary psychology (for an exhaustive discussion of those social instincts, see Niederle 2006).

In the present context of tracing the influence of preferences on institutions (and *vice versa*) we will draw on social instincts as direct influencing factors. Instinctive behavioural impulses have to be controlled and channelled as well as supported by institutional arrangements for a small group as well as a great society to function. Otherwise no complex organization as has been observed all along human history would be possible. Nevertheless, concrete institutional rules are supported or refused on the basis of attitudes, which are examined in the next section.

Attitudes

In contrast to social instincts and basic wants, as rather unchanging substance of preferences, the more variable bases of preferences relate to changeable attitudes. Attitudes are 'learned predispositions to respond in a consistently favorable or unfavorable manner with respect to a given object' (Fishbein and Ajzen 1975, p. 6, emphasis omitted). In other words, attitudes represent a person's general feeling of favourableness or unfavourableness toward some stimulus object,[11] which can also consist of a means-end-relationship. As a person forms beliefs about such an object, she automatically and simultaneously acquires an attitude toward that object. The relation is such that each belief links the object to some attribute, and the person's attitude toward the object is a function of her evaluations of these attributes (Fishbein and Ajzen 1975, p. 216). Since attitudes are learnt, they are mouldable. They change with experience of the stimulus objects, i.e. they change with the experience of goods and services and with social rules or institutions. The evaluative part of attitudes can easily be likened to a psychological interpretation of preferences as 'expressions of an affective response' rather than the reflectively reasoned orderings in economics (see Kahneman 2003, p. 1463). In the same manner, attitudes are defined by the affective value of (the mental representation of) objects and not by choices (Kahneman et al. 1999, p. 206).

Attitude formation is also a function of the beliefs, that is subjective probability judgements about an object's or event's attributes or relation to other objects or events (see Fishbein and Ajzen 1975, p. 131, and Albarracín et al. 2005, p. 3). Briefly, the scheme is as follows:

> [F]rom direct observation, other sources of information, and inference, a person forms beliefs about the attributes of an object. Beliefs are thus statements about whether or not, or in what ways, the object possesses certain attributes. Attributes are evaluated independently in terms of their 'favourableness' or 'unfavourableness'. Both beliefs and evaluations are taken to be exogeneously [sic!] and independently determined. The person's attitude toward an object then depends on his beliefs about the attributes of that object together with his evaluations of those attributes. Attitudes, in turn, generate intentions, and intentions determine behaviour. (Katzner 1989, p. 136)

In the course of a person's life, her experiences lead to the formation of many different beliefs about various objects, actions and events. These beliefs may result from direct observation or from inference processes as forms of social cognitive learning. Some beliefs may persist over time, others are less stable, and new beliefs may be formed. This is due to a growing body of experiences and knowledge accumulation.

Change of both positive and evaluative components of attitudes, namely beliefs and evaluations, depends upon (expected) experience of pleasure and pain from the stimulus objects. This experience is connected to primary reinforcers. As such, attitudes are underlying the same learning mechanisms as learnt wants (see below).

To sum up, social instincts and basic wants can account for invariants in institutional arrangements, whereas mechanisms of attitude change and the changing acquired wants may help to predict the variants. However, the mechanisms described above make it more ambiguous to predict social behaviour from attitudes than from social instincts, since the latter are more immediate, and even behavioural responses (to stimuli), whereas attitudes are valuations of mental representations with no immediate impulse to act. How social instincts, wants and attitudes are moulded is discussed in the next section.

LEARNING WHAT WE LIKE

After having elaborated the three pillars of substantive preferences, namely individual wants, social instincts and attitudes, we will now examine the mechanisms affecting the formation and change of them. We argue that innate behavioural learning mechanisms can be identified as the necessary 'transition laws' (Witt 1996, p. 712) to account for the systematic change of preferences. Learning mechanisms are part of the human genetic inheritance, and while the objects of learning may vary, the processes of learning are quite stable.[12]

'Learning' characterizes the procedures and mechanisms via which animals and human beings acquire, retain and modify modes of behaviour. These mechanisms mostly elude direct observation and thus are hypothetical entities to explain observed phenomena. We can broadly distinguish between two kinds of learning, namely cognitive (social) learning and non- (or sub-) cognitive reinforcement learning. We will see, however, that this distinction is only a conceptual aid, as for humans, reinforcement learning is partly also cognitively mediated (Bandura 1977, p. 38). While, on the one hand, primary reinforcers (for example pleasant experiences, pain, aggression) are genetically programmed and species-specific, and thus serve as a 'guide to learning' (Pulliam and Dunford 1980, p. 25),[13] learning mechanisms, on the other hand, allow for a wide variety of behaviours to emerge and to get associated with primary reinforcers. Especially in humans, our cognitive abilities seem to allow for wide ranges of learnt behaviours (which can, in the case of social learning, be even transmitted across generations). Both forms of learning will be discussed in more detail in the next subsections.

Classical and Operant Conditioning

Classical and operant conditioning both are classic and well-researched forms of sub-cognitive learning. Both forms have been intensively studied with animals and (to a certain degree) humans as well. Classical conditioning was discovered and studied by Ivan Pavlov in his famous experiments with dogs (Hilgard and Bower 1966, p. 48). Generally speaking, classical conditioning refers to involuntary behaviour that occurs whenever a certain stimulus induces a predetermined unconditioned response or reflex (UR). When such an unconditioned stimulus (US) if sufficiently often coupled with another stimulus (i.e. another stimulus precedes or coincides with the US), the new stimulus becomes a conditioned stimulus (CS), which elicits the same response as the US. This response is then called a conditioned reflex (CR). This form of conditioning works largely sub-cognitively and allows for previously neutral stimuli to become either conditioned as appetitive (positive relation, for example when a certain stimulus is associated with a rewarding experience) or aversive (negative relation, for example when a certain stimulus is associated with punishment). It only works when US and CS are temporally related (principle of contiguity, see Anderson 1995, pp. 56-58). The association of the CS with an US depends on the intensity of the stimuli and the number of repetitions in which CS and US are paired. If CS and US are decoupled after a while, 'extinction' (or 'unlearning') begins and the CR does not occur anymore.[14]

It has to be noted that in the case of classical conditioning, there are some characteristics which severely limit its scope: unconditioned responses are part of our innate behaviour and not subject to change. Consider for example the increase of our pulse in the case of pain or the reflex that closes the eyelids when something comes near our eyes. Such reactions are usually not subject to our control and such responses occur automatically (Franke and Kühlmann 1990, p. 122). Furthermore, in classical conditioning, no new modes of behaviour are learnt since innate responses are (merely) associated with different stimuli. Classical conditioning can thus not explain how humans acquire complex forms of behaviour. Although it is quite possible to associate chains of conditioned stimuli with an unconditioned stimulus, this does only partially work with very intensive unconditioned responses such as avoidance of pain. Classical conditioning has nonetheless been shown to be useful in advertising, where stimuli from such areas as eroticism or recreation (etc.) are associated with the products to be advertised (a classical example would be a girl in a bikini praising a brand of beer at the beach, see, for example, Gorn 1982; Stuart et al. 1987; Shimp et al. 1991; Kroeber-Riel 1992, pp. 124-135).

Similar to classical conditioning is operant conditioning (operant reinforcement), which is closely related to the work of B.F. Skinner (1953).[15] Contrary to classical conditioning, which requires stimulus-linked behaviour in the first place, operant conditioning starts with a behavioural response. If such behaviour is followed by a rewarding experience (a stimulus), an individual learns to adjust her behaviour such that the shown response is more likely to occur in the future (this reversal was called the 'law of effect' by Thorndike, see Anderson 1995, p. 15). The valuation of a sensory experience thus determines the probability of repetition of that response. The difference between classical conditioning (which is called respondent behaviour in Skinner's terminology) and operant conditioning is that the former is a form of passive reaction while the latter is behaviour for which no conditioned or unconditioned stimulus is observable beforehand. Operant conditioning allows human beings to learn behaviour leading to certain behavioural consequences. This is the reason why it is also called 'instrumental conditioning'. As for classical conditioning, operant learning requires a temporal vicinity of behaviour and its consequences ('contingency'). Events that follow operant behaviour and increase the probability of its future repetition are called reinforcers (see Skinner 1953, pp. 72-75). There is a difference between 'positive reinforcers', such as food, whose presence increases future operant behaviour and 'negative reinforcers' (punishments such as electric shocks), which increase future operant behaviour when removed. It is also important to distinguish two classes of reinforcers, namely primary and secondary reinforcers. Primary reinforcers are generally reinforcing (this is often species-specific), such as food. Their reinforcing character wants not be learnt (or is genetically programmed in species). Secondary (conditioned) reinforcers acquire their reinforcing power via their association with another primary or some strong other secondary reinforcer (for example money, grades). Note, that in classical and operant conditioning, no assumptions about inner human processes are made ('black box models').

While Skinner does not do so, reinforcers can be related to human wants: It can be argued that only these things are (positively) reinforcing that tend to satisfy human wants (see, for example, Hull 1943; Witt 2001). Since there is sufficient genetic variance in the weights individuals attach to the satisfaction of different wants (this is not so for the more physiological wants such as the need for air, warmth etc.), this accounts for the differences that are experienced in experiments about what is reinforcing for the individual (for example for some people, grades or status are more reinforcing than money, for others not).

Reinforcement learning has been shown to be effective in companies, for example for improving punctuality and other aspects of work (see Hamner and Hamner 1976 for a survey). However, due to the complexity of the business environment, it clearly has its limits. Another instance of operant conditioning would be the business practice of trial subscriptions where customers ideally learn to like the product due to its reinforcing characteristics (see Franke and Kühlmann 1990, p. 140). Another – institutional – example would clearly be ostracism and other sanctions for deviation from social rules, or some governmental campaigns to reward and reinforce courageous behaviour.

Some reinforcing processes clearly are not in the individual's consciousness, but often operant conditioning does depend on cognitive processes as well, e.g. concerning the attention processes: what we tend to notice can be experienced as reinforcing. The same is the true when learning depends on the individual's knowledge of means-ends relationships. Thus, classifying operant conditioning as a form of sub-(non-)cognitive learning is somewhat problematic and should be seen as a conceptual aid inasmuch as it highlights the relative unimportance of (highly) cognitive activities in this form of learning compared to social learning. This will be discussed in the next subsection.

Cognitive (Social) Learning

It has become clear that new and complex ways of behaviour cannot be explained with the forms of learning discussed so far. For example, children do not learn language via continuous reinforcement by their parents. The same holds true for learning to behave correctly while driving a car. Trial-and-error reinforcement processes would soon reach their limits in such cases (see Franke and Kühlmann 1990, p. 141; Zimbardo and Gerrig 1996, p. 337). Psychologists have thus identified another important learning process. This process has been called social learning (synonymous: imitational learning, vicarious learning, observational learning) and is closely associated with Bandura (1977, 1986) who has made important contributions to it. He conjectures that most learning (especially in humans) is achieved in the form of imitational learning. Social learning means that a person learns behaviour by observing (and later on by imitating) someone else performing that behaviour and being (more or less obviously) reinforced by its consequences. To understand the processes of observational learning, however, some assumptions about the underlying cognitive processes have to be made. This highlights an important difference to classical and operant conditioning, where the learner is seen as a black box and learning is solely interpreted in terms of his or her overt behaviour. Inner processes do not count in such black box models. With imitational learning, (cognitive) psychology opens this black box.

In social learning models, two broad phases of learning have to be distinguished, namely the acquisition phase, where behaviour is observed and learnt, and the performance phase, where such behaviour is exhibited after learning. Imitational learning thus can take place without the learner actually performing the behaviour she has learnt, since the learning takes place in the acquisition phase. This has been shown in empirical experiments (see Bandura 1965). While learning in the first place does not depend on actual reinforcement, performing learnt behaviour then does.[16] The consequences of behaviour thus only play a role in the second phase of learning. 'Vicarious reinforcement/punishment' (that is the reinforcement/punishment of the observed role model) influences the probability of displaying imitative behaviour later (see Bandura 1986, pp. 301-303[17]). The more similar the observer is to the role model, the more readily such vicarious learning takes place (see also Paulus and Seta 1975).

Observational learning can be criticized for some of its assumptions: though it has been proven fruitful in experimental research, the focus on internal (unobservable) processes is problematic.[18] The same holds true for a sharp distinction of what processes are exactly engaged in a certain learning situation, since so many different characteristics of the modelled events and the observer can potentially play a role. And, finally, the sequential character of Bandura's model is very contestable and could not be shown to work linearly in experiments (Franke and Kühlmann 1990, p. 146). Nonetheless, imitational learning has been shown to be a very important form of human learning and has been fruitfully employed in 'mental training', in business life or in marketing (think of the typical role models shown in commercials, see Franke and Kühlmann 1990, p. 148; Kroeber-Riel 1992, pp. 645-660).

We will argue in the following sections that imitational learning plays a crucial role in the formation and change of preferences and attitudes and their relationship to institutions. Before we link the psychological findings to institutions, we will discuss shortly how learning affects the triangle of substantive preferences.

How Learning Affects Preferences

From the previous sections we can conclude that preferences are shaped in a twofold way: 'We acquire preferences through genetic inheritance and cultural learning' (Bowles 2004, p. 372, see also Bowles 1998, pp. 77-79).

Differentiating the three components of substantive preferences also allows for differentiating between observed behaviour, the underlying motives to act (wants and social instincts) and evaluation of potential alternatives (attitudes). As has been discussed in the second section, (basic) wants and social instincts are two innate bases of substantive preferences.

Because of their genetic basis, they are more resistant to change than acquired wants and attitudes, which are generally (socially) learnt. Attitudes and acquired wants both are subject to the same processes of change, namely reinforcement and the more cognitive forms of learning.

Before we deal with how they change specifically, a few more words on the attitude-want relation are in order. At the same time that we acquire new wants we form a corresponding attitude toward the stimuli serving as means of satisfaction. Here, attitudes can be interpreted as an evaluative shortcut to learnt schemes of pleasure and pain-generating events. In this way they connect some motive to act (a want or a behavioural impulse) to a positive aim, i.e. a means or situation giving pleasure, or to an aversion to avoid pain. These aims or aversions are mostly learnt and can be very specific and diverse across individuals depending on their history of learning, that is the presence of certain means of satisfaction when a motive is actually activated. People learn what to like and what to avoid through reinforcement on the described primary and secondary level. But this reflexive way is only valid to a certain extent. People are also capable of reflecting their wishes and expectations, and hence do change their likings or attitudes via more reflective cognitive mechanisms as will be seen. For example, people can refrain from impulse purchases,[19] and they ponder on whom to vote for in elections, representing the course that institutions are going to take.

In the case of acquired wants, human beings are motivated to satisfy them because satisfaction produces pleasant sensory experiences. In essence, all goods, services and interactions, serving to satisfy wants, can be primarily reinforcing. Also former neutral or unknown stimuli can become (secondary) reinforcers, when they are experienced with primary ones.[20] If certain behaviour is thus reinforced, new wants can emerge or existing wants can change. In other words: reinforcement processes are at work as a basic learning mechanism. During an individual's lifetime, she acquires a plethora of associations between formerly neutral stimuli and primary reinforcers. In this way, multiple wants may emerge which give learned pleasurable sensory experiences to an individual. Consider for example how we may learn to associate pleasure with good grades, an accepted publication or other awards that increase one's status. The same holds true when we learn to enjoy rule conformity via the positive encouragement (reinforcement) of our relevant peer group. This can work the other way round as well, when we experience negative sanctioning during socialization for the deviation from norms and social rules. The same is true for change of both positive and evaluative components of attitudes, namely beliefs and evaluations. They, too, depend upon (expected) experience of pleasure and pain from the stimulus objects. This experience is also connected to primary reinforcers:

> Primary reinforcers imply genetically programmed neural pathways that classify some sensations as pleasant and others as unpleasant. In this sense the primary reinforcers correspond to [...] 'innate, built-in values'. Specific primary reinforcers arouse sensations that humans call feelings or emotions. [...] Emotions and the reinforcers that evoke them are indicators of comfort and, as such, are bases for evaluating experiences. (Pulliam and Dunford 1980, pp. 25-26)

Hence, because of reinforcement 'attitudes may unwittingly be coloured by the context in which an object has been experienced' (Stroebe and Jonas 1996, p. 244). Furthermore,

> the plasticity of people's memories may turn unexpected consequences into conscious aims, and the malleability of their preferences may make formations they once feared or opposed desirable after the fact. (Kuran 1991, p. 269)

This mechanism helps to reduce cognitive dissonance, or regret. Mere exposure to the same – novel – stimuli effects a (positive) change in attitudes, whereas exposure to familiar stimuli does not have such an effect (Fishbein and Ajzen 1975, pp. 281-283).[21] Thus, the same object may evoke different valuations depending on its description or framing and on the context in which it is evaluated (Kahneman et al. 1999, p. 206).

It becomes clear that such learned associations as discussed above do have some interesting features. First, they are based on a few innate motives that seem to be common to all humankind. But, as learning histories differ from culture to culture and even from individual to individual, their concrete specification can take many different forms. This means that the objects of encouragement are a matter of the social group we belong to. Secondly, acquired wants themselves shape the attention processes guiding our learning so that we may expect path-dependence in learning histories. Once one has acquired a want for award-specific status, the person will be more open and susceptible to information pertaining to such status enhancement thus refining ever more this acquired want. But also in the opposite direction, our (often random) shifts in attention may well lead to the acquisition of new wants that are then reinforced.

As for social learning, for example, when we see that behaving in a certain way is associated with status and success, we imitate that behaviour if we consider the modelling person a role model. This can happen very consciously but also unbeknownst to the imitator. Such observational learning does play a vital role in the acquisition of new wants. The formation and change of attitudes in the sense discussed above is also something inherently social. To stress the social components in attitude change, the role of social interaction in learning mechanisms has to be re-emphasized. The process of attitude formation starts early in childhood with the acquisition of language and the identification of meaning and continues during a lifetime with communication and socializing with others. The more frequent and intense the interactions between agents are, the more likely it is that tacit, socially shared commonalities emerge in their subjective interpretations and valuations (Bandura 1986, Chs. 2 and 4).

What we want to show now is how this triangle of substantive preferences changes in relation to social institutions.

A MODEL OF CO-EVOLUTIONARY PREFERENTIAL AND INSTITUTIONAL CHANGE

In the preceding sections we have introduced the necessary elements allowing us to show how institutional change depends systematically on a change in preferences. We now would like to exemplify how the different elements of substantive preferences influence the dynamics of institutional evolution.

In his seminal paper, Bowles (1998) has examined how several effects of institutions determine preferences. He has identified five effects of how institutions influence values and motivations (ibid., pp. 76-77), namely via framing (the framing of institutions influences preferences), extrinsic and intrinsic motivation (the nature of market rewards can induce preference changes), evolution of norms (institutions shape social interaction and thus influence preferences), task performance effects (institutions structure the task of everyday life and thus influence individuals' values) and effects on the process of cultural transmission (cultural learning processes are influenced by institutions and thus transmitted values are affected). It is evident that this one-way relationship is incomplete and can be complemented with a causal relationship in the other direction, once the black box of human preferences is opened.[22] For example, Bowles (2004, part III) introduced a simulated agent-based model of multi-level selection for the early co-evolution of pro-social predispositions and institutions of resource sharing and segmentation. To begin with, in our understanding of the issue we fully agree with his view on institutions:

> Institutions [...] are the laws, informal rules, and conventions that give a durable structure to social interactions among the members of a population. Conformity to the behaviors prescribed by institutions may be secured by a combination of centrally deployed coercion (laws), social sanction (informal rules), and mutual expectations (conventions) that make conformity a best response for virtually all members of the relevant group. Institutions influence who meets whom, to do what tasks, with what possible courses of action, and with what consequences of actions jointly taken. (Bowles 2004, pp. 47-48, emphasis in original removed)

We want to follow this lead and focus on how the learning mechanisms for preferences affect the change of institutions. The difference to Bowles's approach is that, for one thing, we interpret 'co-evolution' more loosely as the interrelation between preferential and institutional change in our times, and, for the other, we focus on Witt's (2001) naturalistic learning approach and not on a formal *a priori* account of this evolution.[23] In the following we would like to shed light on the interplay of motives (wants and social instincts) and attitudes (1, 2), attitudes and institutions (3) and the possibly direct connection between motives and institutions (4). This is a complicated interplay that is not yet well understood, but in our model we show how these relationships may change the elements interdependently and what role learning plays therein. We would like to give special attention to status and conformity as well as possessive behaviour in the example of changing institutions of the welfare state (especially unemployment and retirement).[24]

How Motives Shape Attitudes

We have seen in the second section that motives are a strong pillar of substantive preferences. Whether they be divided into (basic) wants or social instincts in the isolated case is of no importance here, since the striving for status, the need for conformity, or security can equally be termed status defence, conformism, or possessive behaviour to use the more behavioural terms of instinctive impulse. In the present context it seems better to speak of a motive to act for both social instincts and wants than to try and analyse them separately, notwithstanding the differences mentioned in the second section.

Humans possess more or less innate motives. We argue that they form the most basal and most stable influencing pillar of substantive preferences concerning institutions. Humans' social instincts and basic needs are genetically coded and those parts, which can be learnt, are acquired during infancy, where at early developmental stages the specifications of rule-related preferences such as reciprocity, fairness, or helping ('altruism') are learnt. At later ages, we possess quite stable ideas about what we consider to be fair or not (the same is true for the other social instincts mentioned above). The same holds for basic inborn wants that might combine but do not change dramatically over time as has been argued above.

These motives mostly unconsciously influence our attitudes towards our environment and towards institutions in particular. As such, their influence on attitudes is much stronger than vice versa. Consider, for example, how the motive to gain or keep social status and possessions can influence an individual's attitudes toward institutional rules concerning retirement regulation and pension payments. Assume a rule to freeze pensions for the next few years and to prolong working times within a lifetime. Although there are, of course, the usual economic reservations against such financial losses, resentment might be greater than rationally justifiable. This may be due to basic motives of status and possessiveness. On a basic level, when an individual with a relatively strong quest for social status perceives that it is a sign thereof to see one's income rise with those of others, his or her attitude toward freezing pensions will be negative. Note that this effect differs from the perception of commutative fairness of earning what one deserves in that rising pensions do not compensate work performance and hence achievement in this respect is not touched. There is also a strong drive to try and keep and value more what one possesses. This effect of an innate motive of security is expressed in prospect theory. This has implications for how one assesses welfare reforms that seemingly cut back one's standard of living. It becomes clear that an individual's (genetically programmed) endowment is reflected in her attitudes towards rules (and other issues) that affect the satisfaction of her personal structure of motives.

How Attitudes Influence Motives

Following from the argument above, attitudes cannot really change motives but they may help to qualify and put into perspective their importance. They might do so in the following way. Attitudes as learnt (un-)favourable predispositions towards objects play a role in guiding human attention processes. Those objects in the environment towards which an individual has a strong attitude (be it positive or negative) tend to be noticed much more easily. Thus, when one has a strong, accessible attitude towards an object that tends to reinforce a motive, it is quite possible to alter the motive via having acquired the attitude. This process, however, is not entirely independent of the strength of the basic motive initiating the attitude formation in the first place: objects that are not related to the satisfaction of relatively intense parts of our motives usually escape our attention.

Generally, it can be possible that through the shaping of attitudes, individuals can exert influence over some of their motives. This, again, is conditional upon the strength of the motive and the weight an individual attaches to it. For example, if someone has an innate tendency to strive fervently for social status, then it will not be easy for that person to acquire attitudes that contain propositions contrary to that motive, for example, give up increases in income or pension as an expression of status. If, however, status is not too important a motive, one can consciously adopt attitudes towards status and the means to satisfy this motive that demean the importance of the motive still further and thus exert some influence in decreasing the weight of the status motive, or at least decrease the importance of certain means of satisfaction, like monetary income. This process can be supported by role models strengthening certain motives as opposed to others via imitation of their attitudes. This relation shows how the media could shift attitudes toward support of institutional rules that otherwise seem to attack basic motives of status and possessiveness. Also, a general positive attitude toward reform of the welfare state can make one think over security and status motives in this respect and reassess specific attitudes toward some cutback in pensions or prolonging working time.

The Co-Evolution of Attitudes and Institutions

Here we analyse the role of attitudes that translate into institutional change. What we want to answer is the question of how the attitudinal change influences the variation of old and the acceptance of novel institutional rules.

Attitudes help categorizing incoming information, such as new experiences, along established evaluative dimensions (Stahlberg and Frey 1996). In that way, attitudes help to simplify and categorize, for example, the complex institutions of the welfare state.

When analysing institutional change, two attitudinal effects are at work. The first is changing positive attitudes toward old rules into negative ones. Here, two effects work in opposite directions. Dissatisfaction with the status quo works into the negative direction of attitude change, while support of the existing status quo through habituation impedes this change of attitude. The second effect for institutional change is generating a positive attitude toward a new rule.

To show the role of the two effects in the process of attitudinal change towards institutional rules, let us consider the example of welfare reform and assume the status quo of the welfare state and some reform cutting back on pensions and prolonging work time. People not being advantaged by the old system, like people who had to privately ensure retirement payments via life insurance, probably hold a neutral to negative attitude toward the old expensive welfare system serving others but not themselves. Now, being dissatisfied with the old situation may trigger a positive attitude toward potential reform. Nevertheless, due to some habituation effect dissatisfied individuals might still value the old security system just for having experienced it in contrast to a reform whose outcome one cannot yet grasp. It is a simple fact that people often adapt their attitudes toward their situation rather than changing that situation to reduce cognitive dissonance springing from behaviour being incoherent with original attitudes (see Stroebe and Jonas 1996, passim). Hence, there exists some habituation effect of the status quo on attitudes towards the status quo. This connection impedes the change to negative attitudes towards the status quo of rules at the cost of formation of positive attitudes towards new rules. As for the actors being advantaged by the old welfare system, a change of attitudes in the negative direction is only to be expected, when they are outweighed by strong positive attitudes toward reform, which seems a foremost cognitively mediated process. Generally,

> attitudes that are changed as a result of considerable mental effort tend to be stronger than those changed with little thought and thus are more persistent, resistant to counterpersuasion, and predictive of behaviour than attitudes that are changed by processes invoking little mental effort in assessing the central merits of the object. (Petty and Wegener 1998, p. 370)

The process of attitudinal change might include an effect of 'mere exposure' to new stimuli (Zajonc 1968, 2001), for example frequent discussions on welfare reform, supporting the formation of a positive attitude towards the new system beside the obvious positive effect that positive expectations from a new welfare rule have. This is due to the role that reinforcement has to play in the process of attitude formation and change (see Stroebe and Jonas 1996). Being exposed to ever the same argument for a new rule (in the right situation) tends to be persuasive in character and may form a positive attitude toward it. In the same manner, discontent with the status quo of existing rules opens up the mind for new rules. Public agents or so-called 'political entrepreneurs' in the mass media play a role in this process of attitude change.

The other direction of the co-evolution of attitudes and institutions is quite clear. Once institutions have changed they exert the above-mentioned influence of mere exposure and habituation until forces of changing attitudes toward the existing institutions have become powerful enough again to support institutional change.

The Interrelation of Motives and Institutions

As we have identified social instincts and (basic) wants as the most enduring and mostly unchanging pillar of substantive preferences, we will start with their impact on institutional reform for the example of the welfare state (see also Niederle 2006, pp. 133-139, for a static examination of the unilateral influence of social instincts on institutions in general).

It is our motives that shape the institutional set-up of our societies. When we take again the motives for status and possession we can readily infer their powerful impact on welfare institutions. All rules supporting the personal standard of living and furthering social security serve these motives. Conversely, without these deeply ingrained motives no rules would have been created of such extremity like guaranteeing a payment after retirement almost equal to income during work times. Possessiveness and preserving status is also a strong motive for not agreeing to rule change in the direction of lesser payments in the future, even if they were economically necessary. In this way, basic motives shape institutional settings and make other institutions unfeasible in the long run, for example replacing familial support entirely for state subsidies or publicly organizing a minimum support for the disadvantaged. There is also no society where there is not a minimum support through family relationships. Neither is there a society where there is no voluntary help appreciated or propagated through religion (charity), suggesting being deeply ingrained in human nature.

The status motive is an important factor of propagating rules as well, which can also take the form of defecting from former, existing rules. Individuals with high status, for example political or religious leaders in stratified societies, have the power to bring new rules on the agenda and promote them.[25] In the process of welfare reform, political leaders with high reputation in the public can influence rule support among the voters. Whether new rules do actually disseminate is also determined by other motives, but promotion of rules by high status authorities serves to legitimize rules and furthers acceptance.

On the other hand there exist many social and legal rules as well as sanctions to exert an influence on human motives. There are, for example, specific rules limiting payment in the pension system and balancing the burden, contributing in a way to mitigating excessive possessiveness and income-orientated status-seeking along. So, our exposure to institutional rules and sanctions is likely to shape our motives (where they are not entirely invariant but mouldable in a limited fashion) since institutions define what motives (and the behaviour resulting from them) are positively reinforced and what motives and behaviours, respectively, are not.

CONCLUSION

In this chapter, we have provided a conceptual framework to understand the co-evolution of preferences and institutions. We have used the naturalized concept of substantive preference bases, consisting of three pillars, namely social instincts, (basic) wants and attitudes. These concepts were derived from socio-psychological, socio-biological and anthropological findings. To endogenize preferences, we have examined how innate learning mechanisms lead to a systematic change of the substantive preference bases. Here, it was argued that social instincts along with human wants, both being motives to act, account for the most resistant and difficult to change pillar of substantive preferences. Attitudes toward means of serving the motives were identified as the malleable part of human preference formation. An important contribution of a substantive theory of preference change is that it allows the identification of a meaningful mutual relationship between changing bases of preferences and changing institutions that cannot be given in standard theory where preferences are assumed to be given and where no conjectures regarding their content and change exist. A co-evolutionary framework of preferential and institutional change has been developed, sketching out the specific interrelations between institutional rules, motives and attitudes.

From our analysis, some tentative implications for the design of institutions may be derived in exemplary fashion. On the basis of our model, we can make the following five statements: Because of the importance of social learning (positive) role models can vicariously reinforce intended behaviour and thereby promote institutional arrangements. Attention processes must be ensured, for example by the media, so that role models could indeed set the agenda for pressing institutional topics (agenda-setting effect). It should be taken into account that the mere exposure effect can create support of institutional rules which otherwise would not be chosen. Since there is a negative learning bias for harmful effects (Fazio et al. 2004), reinforcement from negative sanctioning versus positive incentives should also be considered. Lastly, the powerful motives of possessiveness and status-seeking and the resulting 'rat race' problems should be taken seriously, especially when thinking of the struggle for downplaying worldly possessions and propagating donations in the many religions.

The next step in our research would be to formalize the relationship between changing attitudes and institutions and the repercussions on wants and social instincts in order to get to a more rigorous analysis. This would have to be complemented with a case study for empirical foundation.

NOTES

[1] Of course, there have been attempts to keep the neoclassical assumptions, the most prominent of which is 'De gustibus non est disputandum' (Stigler and Becker 1977), where the authors can take preferences as given because of an igenious new argument in the utility function, catalysing all the change that would otherwise be understood as a change in preferences (see also more extensively Becker 1996).

[2] The idea of wants can already be found in Plato's *Republic*.

[3] A more elaborate list of basic wants may contain air, water or other drinkable liquid, sleep, means of maintaining body temperature, nutrition, sexual activity, maternal care, shelter, cognitive arousal or entertainment, social recognition or status, and others (see Witt 2001, pp. 26-27).

[4] See for the following two subsections Niederle (2006).

[5] See also Henrich et al. (2001).

[6] The (genetic) evolution of strong reciprocity, as a component in the repertoire of human preferences, in the sense of adhering to a social norm and punishing violators is shown in Bowles and Gintis (2000). The inclination to punish deviators is also termed 'moralistic aggression'.

(See also Cialdini and Trost 1998, pp. 175-177, for a discussion of reciprocation as a universal norm.) The coming about of these basic social preferences or instincts via natural evolution is not the subject of this chapter, however.

[7] See Cialdini and Trost (1998), p. 167.

[8] See Richerson and Boyd (2001).

[9] See for this social instinct Darwin (1981, p. 72). Altruism, when interpreted as an instinct and not as a motive, could be subsumed here (see Niederle 2006 for a discussion).

[10] See Niederle (2004) for an analysis.

[11] Of course, a stimulus object can also be of an abstract form, such as a concept or idea.

[12] On the genetic basis of learning behaviour see also more extensively Lumsden and Wilson (1981), Chs. 2 and 3.

[13] The same can be conjectured for emotions as well.

[14] On classical conditioning in general see, for example, Hilgard and Bower (1966), Ch. 3, Anderson (1995), Ch. 2.

[15] On operant conditioning see, for example, Hilgard and Bower (1966), Ch. 5, Anderson (1995), Chs. 3 and 4.

[16] In experiments with children, it was shown that they learned aggressive behaviour by observing it but only performed this behaviour when being reinforced for doing so (see Dubanoski; Madsen 1968 and Parton 1971).

[17] This can encompass very long time spans until imitative behaviour is shown (see Hamilton 1970).

[18] Bandura has identified four subprocesses governing observational learning (1986, p. 52). In sequential order, these are *attentional processes*, *retention processes*, *production processes* and *motivational processes*. For this exposition, we will not go into detail on the relevance of these four subprocesses here.

[19] Nevertheless, although not buying anything, a person may have a special liking for the available good, and this even more so than for another good.

[20] See also Witt (2001) for accounts of change via conditioning processes such as operant learning.

[21] This seems to have something in common with an agenda-setting effect in that, for example, new behavioural rules may be eventually accepted simply because they are extensively propagated.

[22] While Bowles (1998, p. 79) argues that it is important to divide the effects of the incentives and constraints of institutional set-ups on behaviour on the one hand, and their effects on preferences *per se* on the other hand, we follow North (1994, pp. 4-5) that these two are closely related in the following way: while one could explain institutional change with changes in relative prices, our approach is more fundamental since a change in preferences leads to different mental models of an individual and thus to changed perceived relative prices.

[23] Thus, we agree with Sugden (2005) that the Bowlesian account neglects many of the findings of (European continental) evolutionary economics.

[24] See also the discussion of values and attitudes (solidarity) for the case of labour market institutions (for example, unemployment benefits) in Argandona (2002).

[25] For an example from anthropology see Ensminger and Knight (1997).

REFERENCES

Abravanel, E., Levan-Goldschmidt, E. and Stevenson, M.B. (1976), 'Action Imitation: The Early Phase of Infancy', in: *Child Development*, Vol. 47, 1976, 1032-1044.

Albarracín, D., Johnson, B.T., Zanna, M.P. and Kumkake, G.T. (2005), 'Attitudes: Introduction and Scope', in: Albarracín, D., Johnson, B.T. and Zanna, M.P. (eds), *The Handbook of Attitudes*, Lawrence Erlbaum Associates, Publishers:

Mahwah/New Jersey.

Anderson, J.R. (1995), *Learning and Memory: An Integrated Approach*, John Wiley & Sons: New York.

Argandona, A. (2002), 'The Social Dimension of Labour Market Institutions', in: Argandona, A. and Gual, J. (eds), *The Social Dimensions of Employment: Institutional Reforms in Labour Markets*, Edward Elgar: Cheltenham, UK and Northampton, MA, USA, 49-75.

Bandura, A. (1965), 'Influence of Models' Reinforcement Contingencies on the Acquisition of Imitative Responses', in: *Journal of Personality and Social Psychology*, Vol. 1, 589-595.

―― (1977), *Social Learning Theory*, Prentice-Hall: Englewood Cliffs/New Jersey.

―― (1986), *Social Foundations of Thought and Action – A Social Cognitive Theory*, Prentice Hall: Upper Saddle River/New Jersey.

Barkow, J.H., Cosmides, L. and Tooby, J. (1992), *The Adapted Mind: Evolutionary Psychology and the Generation of Culture*, Oxford University Press: Oxford.

Becker, G. (1996), *Accounting for Tastes*, Harvard University Press: Cambridge/Mass.

Bowles, S. (1998), 'Endogenous Preferences: The Cultural Consequences of Markets and other Economic Institutions', in: *Journal of Economic Literature*, Vol. 36, 75-111.

―― (2004), *Microeconomics – Behavior, Institutions, and Evolution*, Princeton University Press: Princeton/New Jersey.

Bowles, S. and Gintis, H. (2000), *The Evolution of Strong Reciprocity*, University of Massachusetts, Amherst (mimeo).

Cialdini, R.B. and Trost, M.R. (1998), 'Social Influence: Social Norms, Conformity, and Compliance', in: Gilbert, D.T., Fiske, S.T. and Lindzey, G. (eds), *The Handbook of Social Psychology*, 4, McGraw-Hill: Boston.

Cordes, C. (2005), 'Long-term Tendencies in Technological Creativity – a Preference-based Approach', in: *Journal of Evolutionary Economics*, Vol. 15, 149-168.

Cosmides, L. and Tooby, J. (1994), 'Better than Rational: Evolutionary Psychology and the Invisible Hand', in: *American Economic Association Papers and Proceedings*, Vol. 84, 327-332.

Darwin, C. (1981), *The Descent of Man, and Selection in Relation to Sex*, Princeton University Press: Princeton.

De Houwer, J., Thomas, S. and Baeyens, F. (2001), 'Associative Learning of Likes and Dislikes: A Review of 25 Years of Research on Human Evaluative Conditioning', in: *Psychological Bulletin*, Vol. 127, 853-869.

Dubanoski, R.A. and Parton, D.A. (1971), 'Imitative Aggression in Children as a Function of Observing a Human Model', in: *Developmental Psychology*, Vol. 4, 489.

Ensminger, J. and Knight, J. (1997), 'Changing Social Norms: Common Property, Bridewealth, and Clan Exogamy', in: *Current Anthropology*, Vol. 38, 1-24.

Fazio, R.H., Eiser, J.R. and Shook, N.J. (2004), 'Attitude Formation Through Exploration: Valence Asymmetries', in: *Journal of Personality and Social Psychology*, Vol. 87, 293-211.

Fishbein, M. and Ajzen, I. (1975), *Belief, Attitude, Intention and Behavior: An Introduction to Theory and Research*, Addison-Wesley Publishing Company: Reading, Menlo Park, London etc.

Franke, J. and Kühlmann, T.M. (1990), *Psychologie für Wirtschaftswissenschaftler*, Verlag Moderne Industrie: Landsberg/Lech.

Frey, B.S. (2005), 'Institutions Shape Preferences: The Approach of "Psychology & Economics"', in: Schubert, C. and v.Wangenheim, G. (eds), *Evolution and Design of Institutions*, Routledge: London.

Frey, B.S. and Stutzer, A. (2002), *Happiness and Economics*, Princeton University Press: Princeton/New Jersey.

Georgescu-Roegen, N. (1954), 'Choice, Expectations and Measurability', in: *The Quarterly Journal of Economics*, Vol. 68, 503-534.

Gorn, G.J. (1982), 'The Effects of Music in Advertising on Choice Behavior: A Classical Conditioning Approach', in: *The Journal of Marketing*, Vol. 46, 94-101.

Hamilton, M.L. (1970), 'Vicarious Reinforcement Effects on Extinction', in: *Journal of Experimental Child Psychology*, Vol. 9, 108-114.

Hamner, W.C. and Hamner, E.P. (1976), 'Behavior Modification on the Bottom Line', in: *Organizational Dynamics*, Vol. 4, 3-21.

Henrich, J., Boyd, R., Bowles, S., Camerer, C., Fehr, E., Gintis, H. and McElreath, R. (2001), 'In Search of Homo Economicus: Behavioral Experiments in 15 Small-Scale Societies', in: *American Economic Review (Papers and Proceedings)*, Vol. 91, 73-78.

Hilgard, E.R. and Bower, G.H. (1966), *Theories of Learning*, 3rd edn, Appleton-Century-Crofts: New York.

Hull, C.L. (1943), *Principles of Behavior – An Introduction to Behavior Theory*, Appleton-Century-Crofts: New York.

Jones, O.D. (2001), 'Time-shifted Rationality and the Law of Law's Revenge: Behavioral Economics meets Behavioral Biology', in: *Northwestern University Law Review*, Vol. 95, 1141-1205.

Kahneman, D. (2003), 'Maps of Bounded Rationality: Psychology for Behavioral Economics', in: *The American Economic Review*, Vol. 93, 1449-1475.

Kahneman, D., Ritov, I. and Schkade, D. (1999), 'Economic Preferences or Attitude Expression?: An Analysis of Dollar Responses to Public Issues', in: *Journal of Risk and Uncertainty*, Vol. 19, 203-235.

Katzner, D.W. (1989), 'Attitudes, Rationality and Consumer Demand', in: Kregel, J.A. (ed.), *Inflation and Income Distribution in Capitalist Crisis. Essays in Memory of Sidney Weintraub*, New York University Press: New York.

Kroeber-Riel, W. (1992), *Konsumentenverhalten*, 5th rev. edn, Verlag Franz Vahlen: München.

Kuran, T. (1991), 'Cognitive Limitations and Preference Evolution', in: *Journal of Institutional and Theoretical Economics*, Vol. 147, 241-273.

Lumsden, C.J. and Wilson, E.O. (1981), *Genes, Mind and Culture: The Coevolutionary Process*, Harvard University Press: Cambridge/Mass.

Madsen, C., Jr. (1968), 'Nurturance and Modeling in Preschoolers', in: *Child Development*, Vol. 39, 221-236.

Maslow, A.H. (1987), *Motivation and Personality*, 3rd edn, Harper Collins: New York.

Menger, C. (1950), *Principles of Economics*, The Free Press: Glenco/Illinois.

Millenson, J.R. (1967), *Principles of Behavioral Analysis*, MacMillan: New York.

Nicholson, N. (1997), 'Evolutionary Psychology: Toward a New View of Human Nature and Organizational Society', in: *Human Relations*, Vol. 50, 1053-1077.

Niederle, U.-M. (2005), 'From Possession to Property: Preferences and the Role of Culture', in: Finch, J. and Orillard, M. (eds), *Complexity and the Economy: Implications for Economic Policy*, Edward Elgar: Cheltenham, UK and Northampton, MA, USA, 77-104.

—— (2006), 'Preferences in Social Interaction and Their Influence on Formal Institutions', in: Schubert, C. and v. Wangenheim, G. (eds), *Evolution and Design of Institutions*, Routledge: London, 79-99.

North, D.C. (1994), *Institutional Change: A Framework of Analysis*.

Paulus, P.B. and Seta, J.J. (1975), 'The Vicarious Partial Reinforcement Effect: An Empirical and Theoretical Analysis', in: *Journal of Personality and Social Psychology*, Vol. 31, 1975, 930-936

Petty, R.E. and Wegener, D.T. (1998), 'Attitude Change: Multiple Roles for Persuasion Variables', in: Gilbert, D.T., Fiske, S.T. and Lindzey, G. (eds), *The Handbook of Social Psychology*, 4, McGraw-Hill: Boston.

Pulliam, H.R. and Dunford, C. (1980), *Programmed to Learn: An Essay on the Evolution of Culture*, Columbia University Press: New York.

Reiss, S. (2000), *Who Am I? The 16 Basic Desires That Motivate Our Actions and Define Our Personalities*, Berkeley Books: New York.

Richerson, P.J. and Boyd, R. (2001), 'The Evolution of Subjective Commitment to Groups: A Tribal Instincts Hypothesis', in: Nesse, R.M. (ed.), *Evolution and the Capacity for Commitment*, Russell Sage Foundation: New York.

Rozin, P. (1986), 'One-Trial Acquired Likes and Dislikes in Humans: Disgust as a US, Food Predominance, and Negative Learning Predominance', in: *Learning and Motivation*, Vol. 17, 180-189.

Shimp, T.A., Stuart, E.W. and Engle, R.W. (1991), 'A Program of Classical Conditioning Experiments Testing Variations in the Conditioned Stimulus and Context', in: *Journal of Consumer Research*, Vol. 18, 1-12.

Skinner, B.F. (1953), *Science and Human Behavior*, Macmillan: New York.

Stahlberg, D. and Frey, D. (1996), 'Attitudes: Structure, Measurement and Functions', in: Hewstone, M., Stroebe, W. and Stephenson, G.M. (eds), *Introduction to Social Psychology: A European Perspective*, Blackwell Publishers: Oxford and Cambridge.

Stigler, G.J. and Becker, G.S. (1977), 'De Gustibus Non Est Disputandum', in: *The American Economic Review*, Vol. 67, 76-90.

Stroebe, W. and Jonas, K. (1996), 'Principles of Attitude Formation and Strategies of Change', in: Hewstone, M., Stroebe, W. and Stephenson, G.M. (eds), *Introduction to Social Psychology: A European Perspective*, Blackwell Publishers: Oxford and Cambridge.

Stuart, E.W., Shimp, T.A. and Engle, R.W. (1987), 'Classical Conditioning of Consumer Attitudes: Four Experiments in an Advertising Context', in: *Journal of Consumer Research*, Vol. 14, 334-349.

Sugden, R. (2005), 'Samuel Bowles's Post Walrasian Economics', in: *Journal of Economic Methodology*, Vol. 12, 331-336.

Warke, T. (2000), 'Mathematical Fitness in the Evolution of the Utility Concept from Bentham to Jevons to Marshall', in: *Journal of the History of Economic Thought*, Vol. 22, 5-27.

Wilson, E.O. (1998), *Consilience – The Unity of Knowledge*, Alfred Knopf: New York.

Witt, U. (1987), *Individualistische Grundlagen der evolutorischen Ökonomik*, Tübingen.

—— (1991), 'Economics, Sociobiology, and Behavioral Psychology on Preferences', in: *Journal of Economic Psychology*, Vol. 1991, 557-573.

—— (1996), 'A "Darwinian Revolution" in Economics?', in: *Journal of Institutional and Theoretical Economics*, Vol. 152, 707-715.

—— (1999), 'Bioeconomics as Economics from a Darwinian Perspective', in: *Journal of Bioeconomics*, Vol. 1, 19-39.

—— (2001), 'Learning to Consume – A Theory of Wants and the Growth of Demand', in: *Journal of Evolutionary Economics*, Vol. 11, 23-36.

—— (2005), *From Sensory to Positivist Utilitarianism and Back – A Rehabilitation of Naturalistic Conjectures in the Theory of Demand*.

Zajonc, R.B. (1968), 'Attitudinal Effects of Mere Exposure', in: *Journal of Personality and Social Psychology Monograph Supplement*, Vol. 9, 1-27.

—— (2001), 'Mere Exposure: A Gateway to the Subliminal', in: *Current Directions in Psychological Science*, Vol. 10, 224-228

Zimbardo, P.G. and Gerrig, R.J. (1996), *Psychology and Life*, 14th edn, HarperCollins: New York.

PART TWO

COMPLEXITY, NON-KNOWLEDGE AND
STRATEGY

6. Complex Individuals: The Individual in Non-Euclidian Space

John B. Davis

INTRODUCTION – THE RECENT CHANGE IN ECONOMICS

Economics is widely seen as neoclassical economics, whose core is the idea of rational self-interested individuals interacting in markets. Yet when one conducts a census of kinds of research being published in 'leading' economics journals over the last three decades one find considerable *prima facie* evidence that a not insignificant share of this work employs non-neoclassical types of theorizing, tools and methods of empirical analysis, whereas in the first three postwar decades that share was far smaller. If one extends this empirical investigation to journal births in the last three decades, one finds evidence that non-neoclassical journal births significantly exceed neoclassical journal births, implying (with far fewer journal deaths over the same period) that non-neoclassical research appears to be a rising share of what is being published in economics journals as a whole. Further, conceptual evaluation of much of this recent non-neoclassical research indicates that it has origins outside of economics in other sciences, and thus it imports into economics assumptions from these other sciences about the nature of scientific explanation and about how to conceive the object of investigation in economics that depart from what underlies conventional neoclassical views (Davis, 2006b). While it is possible that this process might ultimately eliminate economics as a distinct domain of investigation in the future, the more likely possibility given economics' historical ability to absorb other science contents in the past (Mirowski, 1989; Blaug, 2003), is that economics' shape and objectives will be transformed, but that it will broadly remain a science of human interaction, production and exchange.

Yet under this very general description a wide range of frameworks can be imagined, and this invites us to ask how the new approaches now being pursued in economics target the fundamental assumptions of standard theory.

Indeed many of these assumptions, long taken for granted and thus rarely examined, are cast into stark relief in arguments that begin with different starting points in the new approaches. Arguably as fundamental as any of these assumptions in standard theory are those regarding the nature of economic agents, who are conventionally taken to be human individuals all of essentially the same kind of make-up, and who are thus all taken to behave in essentially the same way across their many different possible forms of interaction. This dual conception – like individuals and like forms of interaction – is challenged in many recent evolutionary-complexity-computational accounts of the economy that alternatively suppose that individual economic agents and their forms of interaction are inescapably heterogeneous. Indeed for some the stimulus for this different view of individuals lies in their perception that replacing the standard conception of the individual is key to developing new economic understanding. For example, Kirman (1997) traces the breakdown of axiomatic general equilibrium theory, particularly as associated with the Sonnenschein-Mantel-Debreu results, to the standard view of the individual, and argues for a new approach to individuals as central to new forms of economic theory. What then might be the basis of such an alternative dual conception of individuals?

One explanation of the heterogeneity of agents and interaction advanced in evolutionary-complexity-computational approaches derives from an alternative conception of space that rejects the classical view of space as a real field that operates in neoclassicism. The standard real field or Euclidian view treats space as undifferentiated except by arithmetic measure. Non-Euclidian views of space, particularly as developed for economics and social science (see Frenken, 2006), are often elaborated using alternative mathematical methods such as graph theory to investigate structures of network relationships between agents, thus further differentiating space by identifying positions specific to particular networks and according to specific structural relationships between networks. In contrast to the standard real field view of space in which you can always go from one point to another with the only issue being the arithmetic distance between those points, in non-real space one often cannot get from one point to another, because connections or pathways do not exist for doing so between different structural locations. This introduces 'irreversibilities' into the actions of agents, and more generally makes it possible to treat agents and their interactions as heterogeneous by virtue of their different locations and correspondingly different opportunities for interaction. One question it raises is whether this is enough to explain individuals as heterogeneous and non-atomistic. Another question it raises is whether an evolutionary-complexity-computational view of the world is possible without a non-atomistic account of individuals.

This chapter discusses the differences between neoclassical and evolutionary-complexity-computational views of individuals and their interaction in terms of their different underlying accounts of space. The two contrasting accounts of the individual are termed the atomistic view and the relational views. The second section of the chapter begins by further distinguishing the field and non-field concepts of space, comments on how they figure in recent debates in evolutionary biology in terms of competing interpretations of the idea of a fitness landscape, and then ties this to recent evolutionary-complexity-computational approaches' somewhat mixed rejection of the classical view of space as a field. The third section argues that this alternative understanding of space implies a relational conception of the individual, and that the standard atomistic individual conception employs a Euclidian understanding of space. I characterize the individual in the relational conception as a complex individual. The fourth section introduces the evolutionary-complexity-computational approach to individuals known as agent-based modelling, and then critically evaluates the interpretation of this approach, Potts (2000) provides attempts to combine non-Euclidian geometries of space with a conception of individuals as heterogeneous. I argue that, despite his non-Euclidian turn, he still treats individuals as homogeneous, thus showing that escaping the atomistic conception requires tying the heterogeneity of individuals directly to their relations to one another rather than to such things as path-dependence and their different locations in a differentiated space. The fifth section uses an identity analysis to further explain complex individuals, distinguishing between individual identity and personal identity, tying the former concept to how individuals are changed by social interaction and the latter concept to their being self-organizing, reflexive agents. This overall view of individuals is applied to Mirowski's (2007) 'markomata' computational view of markets, and it is argued that together they provide an understanding of markets and individuals as interlinked and everywhere complex and diverse. The sixth section closes with brief comments about social economic policy towards individuals on this understanding.

TWO GEOMETRIES OF SPACE

Complexity economics is the investigation of non-linear dynamics of economic systems made up of heterogeneous agents exhibiting co-evolving expectations. Mirowski (2007) traces the origins of complexity-computational approaches in economics to the gradual abandonment of physics as the chief model for scientific explanation in economics, and the emergence of the sciences of computation and evolutionary biology as alternative models for economic explanation. Early neoclassical utility theory was modelled on Euclidian field theory and the energy metaphor of late nineteenth century classical mechanics, and has largely sustained this image for a century (Mirowski, 1989). Fundamental to this conception is the idea of real space, R^n, understood as a well-defined given field or metric in which any one point can be related to any other, such as embodied in the standard neoclassical notion of the economy as a homogeneous, continuous commodity space in which individual agents have demands and supplies for all goods whatsoever, and no part of the economy is partitioned off, inaccessible, or can be said to be near or distant.[1] While the real field concept of space is intuitive and familiar in mathematics as the generalization of arithmetic, algebra, and as the foundation of the integral and differential calculus, it is hardly the only concept or geometry of space or understanding of economic space. Graph theory (see Ellerman, 1984; Kirman, 1987; Mirowski, 1994) offers an alternative geometry of space based on the idea that systems can be conceived of in terms of set of elements (or vertices) and different combinations of connections (or edges) between them that make it possible to speak of 'neighborhoods' of elements. Since all neighborhoods are not connected to one other, neither are all their elements. Varying degrees of inaccessibility from any given point to particular neighborhoods accordingly makes it possible to explain space in terms of the concepts of nearness and distance. Further, adding hierarchies of neighborhoods generates higher-level systems (hyperstructures or systems of systems) that extend this basic idea by representing systems themselves as the elements having different connections to one another, as illustrated in Simon's decomposable modular decision-making systems for organizations (Simon, 1962).

Arguably the analogue of real space in evolutionary biology is the idea of a fitness landscape defined independently of the evolutionary processes that occur within it, which thus lacks 'neighborhoods' or other asymmetries that reflect particular evolutionary processes ongoing in that given space, seen as if it were a neutral container. Similarly, in standard economics, that all goods are substitutable for one another in agent choice means that neighborhoods do not exist in real commodity space. In contrast, the idea of there being 'neighborhoods' in which mutation and selection occur effectively defines space in terms of these evolutionary processes. Thus a number of recent contributors to evolutionary biology begin from the idea that the concept of space is inseparable from the concept of behavior, is therefore structured according to the distribution of different types of behavioral agents, and then examines how the processes of mutation and selection operate along pathways which are irreversible and unique, reflecting the existence of 'neighborhoods' in which different kinds of agents happen to be located

(Fontana, 2003).

Many recent evolutionary-complexity-computational approaches draw in one way or another on evolutionary metaphors, but do so with differing degrees of sensitivity to the difference between Euclidian and non-Euclidian concepts of space. Even in accounts that emphasize that space is heterogeneous and differentiated, there is still often a tendency to think of this 'non-Euclidian' space as a given space in the form of a 'social-economic' fitness landscape. I suggest that one possible reason for this mixed understanding lies in a vestigial attachment to the atomistic conception of the individual. Most approaches replace the standard preference conception of the individual with a characterization of the individual in terms of search algorithms, in order to explain behavior as involving travel across a heterogeneous landscape. This appears to involve a non-subjectivist sort of characterization of individuals – thus a non-atomistic one – but the idea of search is easily associated with the idea of search across a given landscape, albeit a differentiated one. That is, the idea that the space and the behavior of agents is jointly constituting is missing also, implying that not only is space not a given (in whatever form), but that neither are the characteristics of the individual. I attempt to make this point clearer in the next section's comparison of the atomistic conception of the individual with what I take to be its genuine alternative, a relational conception.

TWO CONCEPTIONS OF THE INDIVIDUAL

The two geometries of space, the Euclidian and non-Euclidian, I argue, imply two different conceptions of individuals. The classic Euclidian field concept of real space supports an atomistic conception of the individual, whereas the various possible non-Euclidian concepts of space support a relational conception of the individual. In the case of the field concept, since space is homogeneous and continuous, no place within it can be distinguished from any other, except by being arithmetically distant from some arbitrarily given point. The character of space, then, does not itself distinguish entities of any kind from one another, so that they cannot but be defined both strictly in terms of themselves and also in the same way – or as indistinguishable atoms. Non-Euclidian space, in contrast, is differentiated by virtue of patterns of connections between sets of elements, so that these elements, or whatever types of entities they may be, must differ in kind according the different combinations of connections they have to other elements. Entities in non-Euclidian space, that is, are complex in virtue of having different kinds of relations to other entities, which are themselves similarly complex. Such entities cannot therefore be self-contained atoms, and are thus neither defined strictly in terms of themselves nor all in the same way.

In the atomistic conception, since atoms are essentially self-contained entities that are complete in themselves, individuals thus understood are analogously defined strictly in terms of their own characteristics and all in terms of the same kinds of characteristics. Accordingly the dominant interpretation of the individual in economics – the neoclassical atomistic conception – defines all individuals solely in terms of their own preferences (whether defined in psychological terms in the classical cardinal and ordinal utility tradition or more formally in Samuelsonian revealed preference terms as a binary relationship between ranking systems) and their own (Savage-based) subjective expectations, both of which constitute characteristics of the individual that require no reference to other individuals. As the familiar fable has it, Robinson Crusoe was a complete man on his desert island before Friday arrived, would have remained one had Friday never arrived, and indeed remained one after he did.

In contrast to this and other atomistic conceptions of the individual, relational conceptions of the individual define individuals in terms of their relationships to and communication with other individuals, or more accurately in terms of their different sets of relationships to and different forms of communication with other individuals. Indeed, on the relational conception individuals cannot be defined in isolation without undermining their characterization as individuals.[2] Intuitively, the simple idea underlying the relational conception is that something cannot be attributed the status of being an entity or individual unless it can be shown to be distinct from a like thing; that is, it is 'individuated' by comparison to a like thing. In non-Euclidian space, this simple point is compounded, as it were, since individuals are positioned in space by virtue of having connections to many individuals who they are like in different ways. Consequently their individuality is the result of their being individuated in different ways. But as their different connections to others are a function of individuals being differently positioned in space, their different connections to others are generally incommensurable. Individuals thus understood must be complex in that – despite being unitary entities – they are made up of incommensurable characteristics. Accordingly the relational conception of individuals must be an account of *complex individuals*.

One example of a relational conception of the individual is the collective intentionality account of individuals, which treats the individual's capacity for forming shared we-intentions as an individuating characteristic of individuals that can be exercised in multiple contexts (see Gilbert, 1989; Tuomela, 1995; Davis, 2003). The simple principle of individuation it employs is that individuals are individuated relative to others they are like in virtue of the belief they have that a possible we-intention is shared.[3] But the abundance of forms and occasions in which we-intentions are expressed differentiates individuals from other individuals in multiple ways. Though proponents of collective intentionality theory do not explicitly employ any particular conception of space, their conception of individuals cannot but be complex in light of the heterogeneous nature of we-intentions. What, then, of Robinson Crusoe? In this particular relational conception, since individuals are understood to have a capacity for forming we-intentions, Crusoe can only be an individual, because Friday is possible, whether Friday ever arrives on the island, since Crusoe needs the possibility of Friday, or rather many Fridays, to be able to form we-intentions. Crusoe, then, is a complex individual, not a simple, self-contained individual, because he is made up of relations to many different Fridays.

The contrast between the atomistic and relational conceptions of the individual can be made sharper by comparing their respective treatments of differences between individuals. In the atomistic conception, though individuals can be different in having different preferences and expectations, nothing in this conception requires it, so that they can in principle all have identical preferences and expectations. Are they still distinct individuals? Representative agent models effectively use this identity to treat many individuals as one individual, implying that the differences between individuals are irrelevant. But such models can be shown to be really one-agent models (Kirman, 1992). In the argument here, they are not even that. Since in the relational conception individuals must be different from sets of other like individuals to exist as individuals, the solitary representative individual by definition cannot even exist as an individual, but rather operates as a *faux* construct for the underlying neoclassical model (and close kin to another mythical agent, the Walrasian auctioneer). This all raises an interesting question: if individuals in the relational conception are seen as complex individuals who are all different from one another, is it possible to say *anything* about them in general other than that they are all different from one another? I will argue that there is indeed one important thing we can say, namely, that they are reflexive entities. But before doing so, and for purposes of contrast, in the next section I review Potts (2000) agent-based modeling account of individuals, and argue that, despite his intention to break with the atomistic individual conception, he still ends up treating individuals as homogeneous and undifferentiated.

NEO-EUCLIDIAN AGENT BASED MODELING

Agent-based modeling, as a part of agent-based computational economics, consists of a variety of computational methods used to simulate and investigate the properties of dynamic systems of different kinds of autonomous agents who interact according to different sets of decision rules (see Tesfatsion, 2006). Whereas in traditional general equilibrium models agent interaction is indirect, and is mediated by a price coordination process that operates through the artificial device of a Walrasian auctioneer, in agent-based models individuals interact directly with one another according to how, for example, their rules for acquiring and supplying goods match up. Agents are also seen to learn from their interactions with others, and then change their decision rules according to simple revision procedures, such as reinforcement learning. Because systems of such agents exhibit emergent properties that are not properties of the agents themselves, they are known as complex adaptive systems. Agent-based computational economics and agent-based modeling have accordingly often been characterized as a 'bottom-up' or 'culture dish' approach, since all aggregate patterns of behavior are explained in terms of individual interactions. At the same time, the emergent properties of complex adaptive systems also produce feedback effects on individual behavior, so that micro behavior and macro system or aggregate regularities operate as a two-way street.

Agent-based modeling is formulated in terms of non-Euclidian space in virtue of its representation of agents as directly interacting with one another. In standard equilibrium models, the existence of the Walrasian auctioneer creates a real space in which all agents' demands and supplies are related to one another through the medium of the equilibrium price vector. Minus the auctioneer, individuals and their demands and supplies are no longer all related to one another, so that which individuals they are modeled as directly interacting with effectively creates the space in which they act – a space which is accordingly differentiated and uneven. This non-Euclidian view of the space of agent interactions when understood dynamically requires that the paths individuals take across a sequence of interactions be seen as heterogeneous as well. Thus individuals, it follows, must also be heterogeneous. In effect, path-dependency, as an aspect of modeling agent behavior in non-Euclidian space, explains the nature of individuals.

Potts adopts this general framework, argues explicitly for abandoning Euclidian real space as necessary for progress in economics, and regards the agent-based computational conception of the individual as an advance on the atomistic conception. He formulates his view using graph theory, as developed by 'theoretical biologists and systems ecologists,' and considers it a method of analysis able to provide a 'universal framework for the study of complex systems' (Potts, 2000, 55ff), citing Kauffman, a theoretical biologist attached to the Santa Fe Institute, and author of the influential *The Origins of Order: Self-Organization and Selection in Evolution* (1993), as a key contributor. The main implication of this approach for our thinking about individuals, Potts argues, is that individuals need to be treated as heterogeneous, and indeed he recommends we adopt the label of *Hetero economicus* for his agent-based modeling conception of the individual. But is the sense in which Potts understands individuals to be heterogeneous sufficient to distinguish his view of the individual from the atomistic view? What we find, it turns out, is that despite the fact that graph theory allows us to look upon entities as related to other entities in neighborhoods and networks, Potts does not employ a relational conception of the individual, and indeed goes on to define individuals atomistically entirely in isolation from all other individuals, remarkably even employing the traditional image of Robinson Crusoe to motivate his 'new' type of understanding.

> We begin with just a single agent in an environment stocked with resources (a Robinson Crusoe formulation, as such). The model is then initially of two sets – an environment state V^* and an agent resource set V – where we shall initially define V^* as an infinite set of elements in the environment from which we draw a subset as the resource elements held by the agent (Potts, 2000, 114).

The set V^* represents all 'nature's endowments' from which the agent resource set V for our 'Robinson Crusoe … might represent clams, rocks, firewood, coconuts and suchlike' (114). Crusoe's problem, then, is to 'find the good combinations' of these resources by engaging in a process of 'experimentation by combination, searching through the space of possibilities for useful combinations' – or a 'search in state-space' (115). How are the different combinations evaluated as 'good' or not? 'We may … suppose that the agent's rankings of these technologies is an expression of the agent's preferences,' which we learn 'are engaged only after all technologies have been sampled' (116). Thus, Potts's argument is that since different Crusoes have different locations in space, and since non-Euclidian space is differentiated, agents are heterogeneous in having different locations. But this does not tell us that they are different in any important respect in themselves, and indeed Potts treats individuals – albeit in their different locations – as being all essentially the same type of agents. That is, they are homogeneous agents who appear to be different by being located in different places.

Potts makes this clear when he gives us the definition of *Hetero economicus* as an algorithmic man, meaning an agent that employs a sequential set of operations or rules as a decision algorithm, 'which we may suppose to be an innate property of an autonomous agent' that can be formally represented as (117):

$<Y>$ = <LIST: CONSTRUCT: RANK: SELECT> (Potts, 2000, 117).

More generally, the agent is defined as a set of resources, a set of behavioral algorithms, and a selected set of technologies. The agent is indeed a boundedly rational agent in the tradition of Simon (1959) and more recently Holland (1995), because abandoning Euclidianism implies that the reach of agent behavior no longer extends to resources at any point in space. Individuals are boundedly rational, because their cognitive abilities only operate on objects in their immediate neighborhoods. Bounded rationality, however, is not actually a property of individuals on this interpretation, but rather a property of the locations that individuals occupy – a bounded view or perspective – in a differentiated and asymmetric space. The same thing can be said about the ways in which individuals revise and adopt their different decision rules as they travel through differentiated space. Different rules are adopted as the result of traveling through specific sequences of locations in space, not because of inherent limitations of individuals, but because they only encounter specific locations. Thus any agent who travels a given path would adopt the same decision rules, and accordingly all individuals are the same type of homogeneous agents who each exhibit the same 'innate property of an autonomous agent.'

Note, then, that in Potts's account thus far Friday has yet to arrive on the scene. How will things be influenced by Friday's arrival? Nothing, we unfortunately learn, is really changed by the addition of other individuals, and in fact other individuals turn out to simply be opportunities for Crusoe to locate new sets of resources that were previously inaccessible to him. As Potts (2000) says,

> The problem that agents now face is the decision of which other agent to interact with. It seems reasonable to presume that interaction between agents will be engaged according to the same logic by which the agent interacts with the environment. (125)

More fully, now 'the agent's environment [also] consists of the resources and technology sets of other agents,' which when somehow displayed to our Crusoes on the occasions of their interaction, trigger them to record the locations of these other resources (following the analysis of Holland) with 'tags' given to each other. Should any Crusoe's tags match tags created by other Crusoes, then an exchange of resources becomes possible that increases the resources available to all (126). That is, all Crusoe's Fridays are but occasions for new combinations of 'clams, rocks, firewood, coconuts and suchlike,' as well as application of the new technologies different Fridays have for their combination. In such circumstances, Potts tells us, a 'multiagent' can be formed, such as is understood as a firm or a household in standard economics (129), which if stable, merges the preferences of the different individuals into 'a single schematic preference' (130). This reproduces *Hetero economicus* on a more general level as a complex system, but except for the added tagging system as an account of agent interaction, there is nothing really different in this view of the agent from our original Crusoe. All agents are homogeneous as sets of resources, algorithms, and (now) tags, and differ merely by having different combinations of these, which is the result of their different paths through a differentiated space. That is, there is nothing in the appearance of Friday as another individual that changes Crusoe (or Friday).

Non-Euclidian space and path-dependence, therefore, are not sufficient to produce real agent heterogeneity. Potts's Crusoes are not only defined all in the same way, but their contact with their Fridays does not change their nature. Indeed Potts's Crusoe does not meet a Friday as a different type of individual, but just another Crusoe. Individuals are still all defined in terms of their own characteristics, or atomistically, demonstrating that a non-Euclidian space joined to a standard view of the individual only ends up producing an essentially neo-Euclidian understanding of social space. I suggest, then, that if we are to develop a genuinely evolutionary-complexity-computational approach to social space and an adequate understanding of individuals as heterogeneous beings, we need to begin with the individual, and specifically with a relational conception of the individual. I further develop this conception in the following section by introducing an identity analysis of complex individuals which emphasizes how they are and are not affected by social interaction.

THE IDENTITY OF COMPLEX INDIVIDUALS

Since the relational conception defines individuals in terms of their relations to others, and since individuals have many different kinds of relations to others, they are complex in the first instance in virtue of having many different kinds of (incommensurable) connections to others, whether these connections are market relations, organizational ties, social relationships, etc. Individuals thus understood might be said to have multiple selves, a concept that was originally developed in connection with the atomistic individual conception and the idea that solitary individuals could conceivably have multiple utility functions (for example Elster, 1979; compare Davis, 2003, ch. 4). If we give up the utility function idea, and re-appropriate the multiple selves concept for the relational conception, individuals would then be understood to have multiple selves in virtue of their having multiple connections to others. This alternative understanding treats individuals' connections to others as connections they have to social groups, so that their multiple selves are then associated with their different social identities, thus linking their locations in different social networks to their being members of different social groups. Of course there are limitations to seeing individuals' social network locations as social group affiliations, and indeed also limitations to the idea of a social group itself, reflecting problems involved in determining what constitutes a social group and what constitutes membership in a social group. But I put these problems aside here to focus on how individuals having different social identities make them complex individuals.[4]

The idea of a 'social group' itself is a classification category differentially constructed in social science, public administration, and popular discourse, framed in third person object language, which orders individuals by sets of characteristics interpreted as shared, and which ascribes to individuals seen as having the characteristics appropriate to particular social groups the status of having membership in those groups. The idea of 'group membership', then, is simply that of being an item in a set or being an object with a certain characteristic that causes it and all other things having that same characteristic to belong to that set. Thus individuals' multiple selves understood as their social identities constitute different 'object characterizations' of individuals that on the relational conception of individuals must be part of their general definition as individuals. But it is also part of the idea of an individual that individuals are not only objects, but are in some undefined sense 'agents' as well, so that on the relational conception an individual is complex not just in having many social identities and relations to others, but also in being both an agent and an object (or an object in as many senses as the individual has social identities). I distinguish these two aspects of complex individuals in terms of the two ways the concept of identity can be applied to them.

The individual's object characterization as a group member – or object identity – as is reflected in all the different ways in which individuals are classified in social group taxonomies by social scientists, public authorities, and in the many forms of social discourse – thus rather their many object identities – may be referred to as a person's set of *individual identities*. The social grounds for the constitution of a person's different individual identities in the contemporary world are familiar and numerous: tax and social contribution requirements, legal responsibility determination, market contract compliance, pension and social services delivery, medical treatment, credit rating, rights elaboration, education and training evaluation, birth and death verification, experimental investigation, and so on in an essentially unbounded list. All explain individual identity (in different and often essentially incommensurate ways) by ascribing to individuals membership in categories constructed to represent different social group aggregates. Corresponding to these different forms of individual identity, moreover, there exists a variety of 'continuity' tracking technologies used to operationalize these different individual identities in the face of constant change in individual characteristics: names, number assignments, individualized records of all kinds, family descent, curriculum vitae, photographs, biometric measures (fingerprints, DNA identification, dental records, brain scans, iris scans), surveillance, and incarceration or institutionalization. As social group categories are tools designed for the management of heterogeneous populations of individuals according to functional relationships believed to obtain between them, the use of these tools requires there be practical working systems for their consistent application. Consistency in this regard is a matter of being able to continue applying a given category to individuals as long as they satisfy its requirements, especially when there is change in their other characteristics.

Discussions of individual identity in philosophy (traditionally thought to be the subject domain in which identity questions particularly concerning individuals are systematically investigated) usually explain the concept of individual continuity in terms of characteristics of ahistorical, socially isolated individuals (for example, continuity of psychological states), and not surprisingly frame this as a question of 'personal' identity. However, the relational conception of the individual, as formulated in terms of individuals having many social identities, naturally turns our attention to the numerous practical systems for addressing continuity of individual identity that have long been in place in the world. Here we find not only an established general principle for explaining individual identity as continuity through change, namely, sustained membership in a group that can be represented by a social category, but also a rich variety of social practices have been developed to operationalize this principle. Thus, in modern history at least, the origins of the concept of individual identity appear historically prior to the origins of the concept of personal identity. Indeed philosophers generally date the origin of 'personal identity' as a distinct question of investigation to the late seventeenth century work of John Locke, who is said to have given the first systematic account of personal identity (see Noonan, 1989; Locke 1975 [1694]). Thus, if we follow this historical progression, and emphasize the social practices model for labeling, categorizing, and tracking individuals, we ought to investigate and explain the concept of personal identity as an extension and development of the concept of individual identity.

How, then, should the concept of personal identity to be understood? If we assume that there is something more to individuals than just their many individual or object identities, given the discussion above, we might take it to arise in the form of personal principles of individual continuity which individuals themselves seek to implement as analogues to the tracking practices and individual identity categories they see applied to themselves in social group classification systems. From this perspective, the concept of *personal identity* emerges as a category that individuals themselves manage when there already exist systems of social categories constructed for managing people's various individual identities. A concern with personal identity is thus a relatively recent historical development that reflects the emergence of individual identity systems and their tracking technologies. But whereas social tracking technologies have multiplied, and have now become increasingly sophisticated, it is hard to say what tracking technologies analogous personal principles of individual continuity or personal identity might attempt to employ. Indeed individuals generally use social tracking technologies (their names, their family descent, curriculum vitae, etc.) to represent their personal identities or 'who' they think they are. Following Clark (1997), individuals appear to rely on these social tracking technologies as external scaffolding that they use to manage their personal identities. That is, they recognize the concept of their personal identity as distinct from their various individual identities, but they lack means of operationalizing the concept.[5]

What does this leave us to say, then, about how individuals manage their own personal identities? One thing that seems clear is that, if the concept of personal identity is taken to be an historical analogue to socially constituted individual identity systems, then it may also be distinguished from these systems by its being a self-referencing or reflexive type of activity. Social systems that manage different individual identities treat them as object identities distinct from the processes involved in the categorization, labeling, and tracking of individuals. In contrast, individuals who manage their personal identities treat these identities as identical with themselves, that is, as their 'own' personal identities that are different in their view from the individual identities that others create for them. More fully, the activity individuals engage in when managing their personal identities might be seen as a *self-organizing* or *self-reproducing activity*. Indeed, since the social practices that classify individuals into social groups fragment them as single individuals, the task of individuals if they are to act on a concept of themselves is to produce that concept for themselves. We may take this idea also to underlie the standard characterization of individuals as 'agents'. Agents are usually defined as entities whose behavior determines events rather than is determined by events. Since reflexive entities are in some sense self-determining, they cannot be fully determined by events, and this allows for the possibility (if does not guarantee) that their behavior determines events. Thus we may also associate the idea of the individual being an active agent with the historic emergence of the personal identity concept.

Individuals, then, organize their own personal identities, using tracking technologies that derive from different social constructions of their individual identities. To express this in terms of the relational conception of the individual set forth above, consider the market as one basis for the social construction of individual identities in terms of the individual identity categorizations assigned to market participants. In neoclassical economics, markets are everywhere the same as a single supply-and-demand process, and market participants are accordingly frozen in a single individual identity which the theory constructs in the atomistic terms it assigns to isolated rational maximizers. In contrast, consider Mirowski's evolutionary-complexity-computational approach to markets, the markomata conception (Mirowski, 2007). Since markets as markomata are everywhere diverse and complex, market participants – or the individual identities that participation in markets thus understood entails – must also be everywhere different and heterogeneous. Markets as markomata are linked and interrelated by the different kinds of information they accept from other markets as computational inputs, so that markets constitute nodes of a complex informational network that can be characterized in terms of different overlapping and hierarchical relationships. Accordingly individual market participants, or their individual identities, must also be related to one another in a complex informational network similarly characterized by different sets of overlapping and hierarchical relationships to other individuals. This is the same respect in which individuals are characterized as complex on the relational conception of the individual as set out above.

But if this provides an evolutionary-complexity-computational understanding of the individual identities of market participants, how do we understand the personal identity of market participants seen as what they themselves manage and produce? Note first that from the neoclassical view this question does not arise, because individuals are explained entirely in terms of their individual object identities. Since there is but one individual identity for market participants in but one kind of market form (the supply-and-demand model), there is no question of organizing a collection of plural individual identities for the individual to address. This is consistent with what I have previously argued on this subject (Davis, 2003), namely, that personal identity cannot be explained in neoclassical economics, either in terms of its earlier subjectivist individual conception or in terms of what later replaced that conception, the abstract individual conception. The abstract individual conception can be applied equally to individuals, groups of individuals, the different selves of individuals, animals, and non-living entities; thus it cannot refer to the single individual, and its adoption effectively eliminates the individual from economic theory.[6] In terms of the treatment of identity here, then, the only account of individuals neoclassical theory possesses is its individual object identity characterization of market participants.

However, the markomata evolutionary-complexity-computational view does provide an understanding of personal identity as a self-organizing or self-reproducing kind of activity in which individuals engage as an analogue to the market social process that continually constructs individual identities for them as market participants. That is, as markets proliferate, and as this social process multiplies market participants' individual identities, so individuals have an ever more tangible problem of constructing their personal identities. From Mirowski's view, markets as markomata are understood as a form of automata, as in von Neumann's theory of automata, where automata are self-reproducing entities whose evolution can generate more complex forms of themselves in terms of possessing greater computational capacity (see Mirowski, 2002). Parallel to this, individuals' self-organizing activity seen particularly in the sense of a self-reproducing kind of activity mimics and reinforces the self-reproduction process of markets, since an increasing complexity of markets in terms of greater computational capacity needs to be accompanied by an increasing capacity for complexity on the part of individuals as market participants able to self-organize themselves in such a market system. This is not to say that individuals in their personal identity construction processes are to be taken as Turing Machines or other types of artificial intelligence systems. As Clark (2005, 27) says, 'we shouldn't be fooled into mistaking the basic apparatus of the Turing Machine for an explanation (at any useful level of abstraction) of the way biological brains support rational thought'. Indeed, on the evolutionary understanding here of individuals and markets, both have essentially open-ended capacities for self-reproduction made additionally complex by their co-evolution.

This evolutionary-complexity-computational relational conception of the individual can be compared to Potts's view. Potts explains the heterogeneity of individuals in terms of the differentiated character of a non-Euclidian space, so that there is nothing in the interactions between individuals that contributes to their heterogeneity, and they are thus only incidentally differentiated from one another, and not differentiated in terms of their own characteristics. From this view, however, individuals' different interactions in markets produce different individual identities as market participants, which generate different self-organizing/self-reproducing activities in different individuals. Individuals are consequently different in themselves in a non-incidental sense. I have termed this conception a complex individual conception, because the characteristics that constitute different individuals are incommensurate and cannot be reduced to one another. Though individuals share a personal identity principle, it lacks a single content across individuals that would allow us to describe individuals all in the same way. This complex individual conception, I suggest, is the conception appropriate to a non-Euclidian view of space and an evolutionary-complexity-computational approach to individuals. Potts indeed reasons in terms of non-Euclidian space, but his adoption of an atomistic individual conception produces what might be termed a neo-Euclidianism that emphasizes path-dependency of well-formed atoms – a modest change in dynamical thinking that lacks real novelty and emergence.

COMMENTS ON SOCIAL ECONOMIC POLICY TOWARDS INDIVIDUALS

Here I make one comment regarding normative implications of the complex individuals conception. Just as the traditional atomistic individual conception supports a set of normative arguments, especially as associated with efficiency judgments, so the complex individuals conception supports a set of normative arguments, though ones that involve an altogether different conception of individual well-being. From the standard viewpoint, changes in markets are recommended that increase efficiency by enabling individuals to achieve higher levels of utility. This view is often associated with the idea that atomistic individuals possess determinate utility functions with which they are identified. In the complex individuals conception, however, individuals do not have given utility functions. At a given point in time and from the perspective of a particular individual identity, one might approximate individuals' interests with some such functional representation, but this would produce a partial representation of the individual better characterized as one of an individual's multiple selves. Yet as the multiple selves problem seen as a multiple utility function problem cannot be resolved in the standard framework, even partial representations of individuals in utility function terms are to be avoided.

The complex individuals account here represents individuals in terms of their self-organizing/self-reproducing activity. This 'production' understanding of the individual does not lend itself to the idea of satisfying some functional state, but rather underlies the idea of individuals as agents. What view of individual well-being does this then support? Since individuals are inescapably heterogeneous from this viewpoint, I suggest that it supports treating diversity and difference as a normative ideal along side other measures of well-being associated with fairness and equality as apply to shared individual identities. The social systems that categorize individuals in terms of their membership in social groups have as implicit normative principles equal and fair treatment of all individuals who fall within an established category. By its very nature, this object identity bureaucratization principle disregards differences between individuals. Moreover, as social categorization systems are often loosely integrated, there are few normative principles that apply to individuals across their multiple individual identities. As a principle of this sort falls outside the individual identity system, and is associated with individuals' analogue self-organizing concerns, it seems it accordingly constitutes a principle that makes individual diversity and difference a normative ideal.

Note that recent evolutionary-complexity-computational thinking in economics has yet to do much to formulate normative concepts and policy prescriptions. Indeed, that simulation methods create so many different possible world scenarios seems to undercut the entire idea of a normative stance toward the economy. At the same time, a principle of individual diversity and difference as an ideal plays no role elsewhere in contemporary economics. Oddly, outside of economics, diversity of individuals as a normative ideal is commonly defended. This chapter suggests that this ideal can play a role in economics in an evolutionary-complexity-computational type of approach that differentiates the different aspects of the identity of individuals, and recognizes personal identity as a central component of any account of individuals.

NOTES

[1] Debreu's (1959) assumption of a complete set of forward markets for all time is a paradigmatic expression of this. But others careful about their axiomatic foundations are also explicit about the real field as the space in which economic explanations occur. See the current leading advanced microeconomic text, Mas-Colell (1985, xiv-xvi).
[2] I argue in Davis (2003) that the neoclassical atomist conception of the individual does not satisfy reasonable criteria needed to identify individuals as distinct and relatively enduring entities, and accordingly fails as a conception of an individual.
[3] This is the normal or main case as exhibited in speech act behavior. Duplicitous we-intentions, in which the individual privately denies the shared quality of an expressed or known we-intention, are derivative from and depend on the existence of the main case.
[4] For three quite different ways in which the concept of social identity has been introduced into economic models, see Davis (2006a).
[5] Here I do not attempt to explain this apparent lacuna other than to say that it might be argued that first person singular speech, which is appropriate to a personal identity discourse, lacks the same systematic elaboration afforded by third person speech used to characterize individual identity.
[6] This conception of the individual is anticipated in prewar operations research theory, a mixed collection of decision-making tools meant to be used by experts in a wide range of applications that involve complex strategic coordination problems (see Mirowski, 2002, ch. 4).

REFERENCES

Blaug, M. (2003), 'The Formalist Revolution of the 1950s', in W. Samuels, J. Biddle and J. Davis, eds., *A Companion to the History of Economic Thought*, Oxford:

Blackwell: 395-410.

Clark, A. (1997), *Being There: Putting Brain, Body and World Together Again*, Cambridge, MA: MIT Press.

Clark, A. (2005), *Review, Alan Turing: Life and Legacy*, C. Teuscher, ed., London Review of Books, December 27.

Davis, J. (2003), *The Theory of the Individual in Economics*, London: Routledge.

Davis, J. (2006a), 'Social Identity Strategies in Recent Economics', *Journal of Economic Methodology*, Vol. 13 (3): 371-390.

Davis, J. (2006b), 'The Turn in Economics: Neoclassical Dominance to Mainstream Pluralism?' *Journal of Institutional Economics*, Vol. 2 (1): 1-20.

Debreu, G. (1959), *Theory of Value*, New York: Wiley.

Ellerman, D. (1984), 'Arbitrage Theory: A Mathematical Introduction', *SIAM Review*, Vol. 26: 241-261.

Elster, J. (1979), *Ulysses and the Sirens*, Cambridge: Cambridge University Press.

Fontana, W. (2003), 'The Topology of the Possible', in A. Wimmer and R. Koessler, eds, *Paradigms of Change*, Cambridge: Cambridge University Press.

Frenken, K. (2006), *Innovation, Evolution and Complexity Theory*, Cheltenham, UK and Northampton, MA, USA: Edward Elgar.

Gilbert, M. (1989), *On Social Facts*, London: Routledge.

Holland, J. (1995), *Hidden Order: How Adaptation Builds Complexity*, New York: Helix.

Kauffman, S. (1993), *The Origins of Order: Self-Organization and Selection in Evolution*, Oxford: Oxford University Press.

Kirman, A. (1987), 'Graph Theory', in J. Eatwell, M. Milgate and P. Newman, eds, *The New Palgrave: A Dictionary of Economics*, Vol. 2, London: Macmillan: 558-559.

Kirman, A. (1992), 'Whom or What does the Representative Individual Represent?', *Journal of Economic Perspectives*, 6: 117-136.

Kirman, A. (1997) 'The Economy as an Interactive System', in W.B. Arthur, S. Durlauf and D. Lane, eds, *The Economy as an Evolving Complex System II*, Reading, Mass: Addison-Wesley.

Locke, J. (1975 [1694]), *An Essay concerning Human Understanding*, ed. P.H. Nidditch, Oxford: Clarendon Press.

Mas-Colell, A. (1985), *The Theory of General Equilibrium: A Differentiable Approach*, New York: Cambridge University Press.

Mirowski, P. (1989), *More Heat Than Light: Economics as Social Physics*, New York: Cambridge University Press.

Mirowski, P. (1994), 'Arbitrage, Symmetries and the Social Theory of Value', in A. Dutt, eds, *New Directions in Analytical Political Economy*, Aldershot, UK and Brookfield, USA: Edward Elgar.

Mirowski, P. (2002), *Machine Dreams: Economics Becomes a Cyborg Science*, New York: Cambridge University Press.

Mirowski, P. (2007), 'Markets Come to Bits: Evolution, Computation and Markomata in Economic Science', *Journal of Economic Behavior and Organization*.

Noonan, H. (1989), *Personal Identity*, London: Routledge.

Potts, J. (2000), *The New Evolutionary Microeconomics*, Cheltenham, UK and Northampton, MA, USA: Edward Elgar.

Simon, H. (1959), 'Theories of Decision-making in Economics and Behavioral Science', *American Economic Review*, Vol. 49: 253-283.

Simon, H. (1962), 'The Architecture of Complexity', *Proceedings of the American*

Philosophical Society, 49: 253-283.

Tesfatsion, L. (2006), 'Agent-Based Computational Economics: A Constructive Approach to Economic Theory', in Leigh Tesfatsion and Kenneth L. Judd, eds, *Handbook of Computational Economics Vol. 2: Agent-Based Computational Economics*, Amsterdam: Elsevier.

Tuomela, R. (1995), *The Importance of Us: A Philosophical Study of Basic Social Notions*, Stanford: Stanford University Press.

7. The Importance of Ignorance: Non-Knowledge and the Limits of Bayesianism

Oliver Kessler

INTRODUCTION

There is an overall agreement that the rational approach to institutions is insufficient for understanding the complexity of economic practices. To escape the straightjacket of methodological individualism and its caricature of institutions, heterodox economists have over the last decades developed an entire semantic field of conventions, rules, and uncertainty (Hodgson 2004; Lawson 1997; Schlicht 1998). Within approaches ranging from pragmatism, Austrian economics to Keynes's economics, the notion of uncertainty has attracted particular attention where heterodox economists have convincingly pointed out that the argument uncertainty and risk could be treated as synonyms, an assumption on which contemporary rational expectations models are based, is based on too shallow a social theory. However, as important as heterodox approaches of 'genuine', 'radical' or 'strong' uncertainty for understanding economic institutions are, the literature focuses predominantly on how uncertainty is resolved or reduced. Less effort has been spent on understanding how and why uncertainty needs to be maintained and reproduced with the consequence that the debate between mainstream and heterodox economists is preliminary fought in terms of action theory. As deep as the differences between mainstream and heterodox economists are, both remain within the paradigm of individual choice when it comes to uncertainty: both take a knowing subject facing a decision problem as their vantage point. The difference is then often framed in terms of an agent's cognitive capabilities (Dequech 2004) and might be considered as an empirical rather than a conceptual problem. But to recast the intersubjective dimension of institutions in terms of individual cognitive capacity comes with certain limitations. Most importantly, this setting allows for only a limited understanding of institutions themselves as institutions can only work behind the backs of individuals as structural constraints and can only influence or regulate economic practices. Yet, if it is true that institutions both constrain and enable practices (Hodgson 2006: 2; Searle 2005: 21), their constitutive function is beyond the scope of these models.

That an interest in the constitutive quality of institutions cannot be fully pursued within the paradigm of constrained choice becomes visible when we ask how 'alternatives' emerge. When we start by assuming our future to be unstructured and 'open' (or non-ergodic), and if we focus on action over time, then the question becomes relevant how the (un)structuring of the future occurs. Of course, one answer could be to simply point to an individual moving forward in time: as we live our lives, the future is always the horizon of possibilities that seems to (re-)appear naturally. However, then the question arises how exactly the structuring of the present and the structuring of the future, how the present future and the future present, relate to each other. In other words, this simple answer would assume that how the present is structured would have no implications on what possible futures would look like. This might have the advantage of focusing on uncertainty reduction, but has the disadvantage that institutions do not play any significant role. It seems, as long as the paradigm of an individual choice is maintained, and as long as 'contingency' as the realm of the possible is seen as a natural product, the constitutive function of institutions for the individual level are beyond reach.

To leave behind the paradigm of individual choice and thus to see uncertainty and institutions as constitutive for economic practices, this chapter suggests a focus on the reproduction of non-knowledge. To focus on the things we do not know might seem strange at first sight. However we need only remember how the increase of knowledge does not lead to a reduction but can, in the face of new problems, risks, and unintended consequences, lead to an increase of non-knowledge: the more we know, the more we often become aware of what we do not know, especially in times of paradigmatic Gestalt shifts such as from Newton to Einstein's relativity theory. Relativity theory certainly increased our knowledge, but at the same time produced new paradoxes, new unresolved problems and a shadow of what is yet to be discovered. However, this non-knowledge is not reducible to individual lack of knowing but is inherently 'systemic'. As such, it cannot be resolved by looking harder at the facts. The sources of non-knowledge are not empirical but often conceptual and point to the generative power of intersubjectively constituted interpretations as the same data, the same phenomena are still there, but their meaning and interpretation has changed as they are relocated in different narratives or causal chains.

This example only seeks to point out that the conceptualisation of knowledge and non-knowledge as direct opposites, as the focus on individuals and the reduction of uncertainty implicates, is too narrow. Non-knowledge is not a problem of more or better data, but non-knowledge and knowledge are mutually implicating where their interplay results in an evolutionary process in which new risks, new non-knowledge, and new regulations interact. Central to this reconfiguration of 'uncertainty' is the idea of social contingency: that the future, present and past are not simply 'there', that change does not simply 'occur'. Change is not the result of an exogenously given impulse, but refers always back to the particular complexity of social systems.[1]

The purpose of this chapter is to explore the contours of such an approach interested in non-knowledge. The first section is conceptual and shows how various definitions of non-knowledge manifest themselves in the concepts of risk and uncertainty. By providing a topology of probability theories, an ontological as opposed to an epistemological concept of non-knowledge will be distinguished. The ontological concept starts from the assumption that the space of future possibilities can be characterised by probability theory, that is, a set of possible states of the world and security equivalents. Focusing on 'security' and 'necessity', knowledge and non-knowledge are treated as direct opposites. The epistemological concept, on the other hand, focuses on possibilities and risks beyond the confines of standard probability theory in order to analyse the construction of probabilities as functional equivalents of exactly those processes by which reality is structured and unstructured. Starting from this approach acknowledges a variety of different forms of knowledge where the 'knowledge about non-knowledge' is of a different kind from the knowledge about the world.

The second part explores some methodological consequences different notions of 'non-knowledge' imply. This part shows that epistemological and ontological approaches are built on a different logical footing where the boundary can be framed in terms of quantity/quality considerations. By replacing epistemology by ontology via the common prior assumption, Bayesianism for example reduces intersubjective constituted qualitative changes to quantitative considerations. This has the advantage that it allows for a falsifiable research design. But by hiding the problem of non-knowledge behind a third-person methodology of explaining, it redefines what and how actors do not know and evades questions of qualitative judgements and intersubjective processes such as paradigmatic shifts. In other words: it reduces the intersubjective quality of economic life to individual incentives or cost-benefit calculus.

But the alternative proposed by Austrian economists especially, to focus on Weberian first-person understanding (Lachmann 1971; Mises 1949) will lead to the same dead end. As long as it is attempted to locate the meaning of a situation in the individual's mind and reduce ideas to endogenous preference formation, that is as long as the focus on individual choice is maintained, it is assumed that intersubjective phenomena like conventions, rules and norms can be analysed by observing individual behaviour which assumes that norms or rules can determine behaviour. Taking seriously that conventions, rules and norms provide a condition of possibility for a variety of possible practices, which makes the attempt to 'test' the validity of rules or norms by measuring conformity or deviation highly problematic, requires a reconstructive method where meaning is defined as the difference between actuality and potentiality. So defined, meaning, evolution, and the constitutive function of institutions provide a framework where institutions not only reduce but also reproduce uncertainty.

A TOPOLOGY OF RISK, UNCERTAINTY AND PROBABALITY

The reference to different concepts of probability often serves as a vantage point for exploring different notions of uncertainty. Paul Davidson, for example, distinguishes epistemological uncertainty from ontological uncertainty to clarify his notion of 'ergodic vs. non-ergodic systems' (Davidson 1991); Tony Lawson (1988) discusses Keynes's concept of logical probability (1921) to open uncertainty for a critical realist reading; and David Dequech (2004) explores epistemology and ontology of probability by re-emphasising Hacking's distinction of aleatoric and epistemic probability. The notion of probability provides indeed an ideal entrance point for differentiating notions of uncertainty as it explains how a possible state of the world may manifest itself. As such, the concept inhabits crucial assumptions about how the world is organised, the importance of knowledge and experience in structuring the future, and in particular, about what is not known and how knowledge about the unknown can be acquired. To show how this relation between probability, knowledge and uncertainty has been arranged, this part of the chapter suggests a topology based on two distinctions. Apart from the aleatoric (frequency, de re) and epistemic (de dicto) distinction, I use the distinction of objective and subjective probabilities. If probabilities are assumed to be objectively given, probability is thought to be a property of a given problem or situation itself. Its existence is independent of any subjective estimation; it is to be 'discovered', 'learned' or 'known'. For proponents of subjective probabilities, on the other hand, probability is not to be discovered but 'ascribed', 'invented' or 'possessed'. Probabilities solely result from subjective judgements and do not 'belong' to the material situation itself. Combining these categories allows forming a two by two matrix (Figure 7.1).[2] To reduce complexity and not engage in detailed description of the internal tensions these approaches certainly inhabit, this discussion centres on the key figures of each quadrant: Richard von Mises, Frank Ramsey, John M. Keynes and Ludwig Wittgenstein.

	aleatoric	epistemic
objective	Relative Frequency	logical Probability
subjective	Subjective Probability	Social Probability

Figure 7.1: Four Approaches to Probabilities

Objective, Aleatoric Probabilities: Relative Frequency

This approach evolved from the work of famous figures such as Reichenbach (1949), Nagel (1933), and in particular Richard von Mises (1926, 1928) and is clearly driven by the revolutionary advancements of physics and mass production in the late 19th century to explain mass phenomena like games, gas behaviour or applications of Newtonian physics. The vantage point of this approach was the restricted applicability of classical approaches. To account for a greater variety of probability relation than classical approaches had to offer, Mises redefined probability as referring to an attribute within a given collective where probability is the relative frequency of that attribute in the infinite limit: $P(A|C) = lim_{n\to\infty} m(A)/n$, where $P(\cdot)$ is the probability relation, A the attribute, C the collective, m the number of observed elements with attribute A and n the number of observed elements of the collective (Mises 1928: 69). By defining probability as primarily a problem of measurement, he confined probability theory to an empirically dominated methodology based on experimentation and statistics (Mises 1939; van Fraassen 1988).

This symbiosis between measurement, probability and positivism is based on the assumption of well defined collectives (Mises 1928: 12). Before calculation of probabilities is possible, basic categories and concepts have to be well defined. That is: processes of categorisation are prior to probability theory itself. This understanding of categories as objectively given boxes can be found in the often held view that a trial, event, or experiment leads via random variables to a unique result which can be unambiguously ascribed to a class of possible results. There is simply no discussion about whether the six on the dice is 'really' a six. As trivial as this example might appear, it shows that the relative frequency approach presupposes a clearly defined separation of the perceiving subject and objectively given world to define probabilistic relations independent of time, space, or any notion of knowledge, subjective evaluation or subjectively felt duration. Rather, probability obeys universal and objective natural laws waiting to be discovered. Or as Mises formulated it: as long as the axioms and formal rules of probability theory are valid, all its problems can be regarded as already solved (Mises 1926: 79).

Subjective, Aleatoric Probability: Frank Ramsey's Partial Belief

The position of subjective-aleatoric probabilities is widely known as 'subjective probability theory' and emerged with Frank Ramsey (1926) and later most prominently with Bruno de Finetti (1964) and Leonard Savage (1954). All three authors would reject the idea that probability is 'out there' waiting to be discovered. Rather, probability is always and irreducible an expression of human ignorance, a degree of belief in a given proposition (Ramsey 1926: 174). This approach is interested in how individuals *ascribe* probabilities to situations according to their beliefs. Its main task and major challenge is the construction of a procedure or mechanism by which beliefs are monotonously transformed in probabilities (Ramsey 1926: 168). This challenge was taken up in two different approaches: the first avenue is located at the boundary of mathematics, psychology and economics and is associated with the 'psychometrical' studies of Kahneman and Tversky most notably (Kahneman et al. 1982). The other avenue seeks to bridge the subjective degree-of-belief with the objective relative frequency approach by providing a common framework based on Bayesian conditionality (Harsanyi 1967).

Without going into a detailed description of how these two avenues evolved over time, it is sufficient to see that both alternatives are based on a mathematical, averages oriented conceptualisation of expectations. This circle of quantitative beliefs, numerical probabilities and mathematical expectations is particularly visible in Ramsey's claim that he has to 'define degree of belief in a way which presupposes the use of the mathematical expectations' (Ramsey 1926: 174). Combined with a definition of rationality as internal consistency, mathematical expectations allow access to subjective assessments by an objective method. Without this definition of expectations, the claim that a logic of partial belief would adhere to basic axioms of probability theory and thus be open to an axiom-driven research design could not be sustained.

This link between subjective assessments and scientific method can be seen in the very definition of probability. For example Ramsey defines probability as 'p is m/n, then his [an actor's] action is such as he would choose it to be if he had to repeat it exactly n times in m of which p was true, and in the others false' (Ramsey 1926:174). This quote nicely shows that despite the unique character of the proposed bet, the probability relation itself is defined in aleatoric terms and thereby makes the same ontological and epistemological assumptions as its objective, relative frequency counterpart. From this perspective, it comes as no surprise that both experimental game and contract theory based on Bayesian reasoning and psychometric studies share many characteristics in the way they approach their empirical experiments. Most characteristically maybe is the necessity of decision problem to be well defined. Actors can move within a given setting and need no diagnostic capabilities in figuring out what the very rules of the game are. In other words: actors share a common signalling system whereby they can effectively communicate. This also allows the observer to stay outside the experiment and stay within the confines of a positivist philosophy of science. The justification for these assumptions is found in the famous Dutch book argument. Both the Dutch book argument and its counterpart of Ramsey's 'ethical neutrality' provide justification for applying the principle of insufficient reason: even in the presence of complete or unspecified uncertainty, a decision-maker can always make subjective probability statements which obey the normal axioms of probability theory. With this at hand, decisions under *uncertainty* can be treated as choice under *risk*. It is always possible to re-frame decision problems in probabilistic terms which allow for instrumental rational behaviour. Mathematical expectations, uncertainty as risk and a supreme ontological status to formal reasoning mutually support each other.

As a short summary: treating 'uncertainty as risk' is based on an aleatoric probability theory which inscribes iterability of events into the very definition of probability. But defining probability in aleatoric terms directs the focus to quantitative relations where probability is understood to name ex-ante contingency in an ex-post determined world: it might not be known which number the dice might show, but the result can be perfectly explained by the functions of probability theory. In this sense, the boundary of probability theory is determined by the boundary of number theory. To sustain this view, both approaches have to assume a well defined ontology. Quite analogously to the assumption of well defined categories in the relative frequency approach, psychometric experiments in game theory demand well defined problem settings or rules of the game. The game or problem setting is ontologically prior to the formulation and observation of expectations. In this sense, we can see the same subject-object distinction working in both approaches where the basic questions of probability theory require an objective and deductive method. This is a view that treats knowledge and non-knowledge as direct opposites as the focus can only be on propositional knowledge, that is the knowledge we find objectively given, and true functions, theorems and laws. On the other hand, quasi as counterpart, we always find an imaginary individual – or transcendental self – facing an objectively given decision problem. Probability is always referred back to the individual level to explain, in the realm of economics, the regulatory function of expectations. But expectations do not constitute or define the game, an assumption that will become problematic in the next section.

Objective Epistemic Probability: The Logical Theory of J.M. Keynes

The logical theory of probability flourished in turn-of-the-century Cambridge and references can be found in Russell and early Wittgenstein to address the limit of argumentation, semantics and ethics. The overall interest of the theory is not the modality of necessity, the realm of technical, deductive problems that might be solved through demonstration, but on practical, inductive problems where available data, evidence and indicators are unable to produce a clear picture and are thus open for multiple interpretations or possible worlds. The fullest account of this approach has been provided by John Maynard Keynes (1921). For Keynes, probability describes 'existence of a logical relation between two sets of propositions in cases where it is not possible to argue demonstratively from one to the other'. (Keynes 1921: 9). This refocus replaces epistemologically 'certainty' for 'uncertainty' and ontologically necessity by contingency. Thereby, probability is inscribed into the basic laws of logic where the previous quest for establishing irremediable links between certainty and necessity is abandoned. The change from deductive to inductive logic, from security to probability or uncertainty as the basic concept of logic itself, and the focus on practical problems go hand in hand. This puts the focus not on 'games' but on 'argumentation' theory.[3]

As has recently been pointed out by a number of scholars investigating the philosophical roots of Keynes's thoughts (Carabelli 1988; Lawson 1988; Lawson and Pesaran 1985; Runde and Mizuhara 2003), he defines an argument as consisting of premises (denoted by h), and a conclusion (a). Now 'between propositions there exists a relation, in virtue of which if we know the first, we can attach to the latter some degree of rational belief. This relation is the subject matter of the logic of probability' (Keynes 1921: 7). According to this definition, probability expresses a logical, constant and objective relation between a stock of knowledge entailed in premises and a conclusion. The expression $\alpha = a/h$ represents the degree α to which a can be partial inferred from h as well as the rational degree of belief α in a given h. Probability is thus the degree of rational belief to support conclusion a given h.

This relation is further developed by Keynes in his discussion on plurality of knowledge structures which is based on the two distinctions of direct and indirect knowledge and primary and secondary propositions.[4] Keynes argued further that all objects of knowledge, propositions, are acquired either directly by intuition or indirectly by argument. Direct knowledge results from contemplating about the objects of acquaintance. Objects of acquaintance, according to Keynes, 'are our own sensations, which we may be said to experience, the ideas or meanings about which we have thoughts and which we may be said to understand, and facts or characteristics or relations of sense data or meanings, which we may be said to perceive; experience, understanding and perception being three forms of direct acquaintance' (Keynes 1921: 12). Indirect knowledge of propositions, on the other hand, is obtained by argument, that is by perceiving the probability relation of secondary propositions about a. Placed in this context, intuition allows for a temporal fusion of subject and object and thus allows for partaking of objective, direct knowledge of logical relations. Via intuition, probability relations, related to secondary propositions, partake with direct knowledge and are thus objectively given, as Keynes explains:

> Although it is with knowledge by argument that I shall be mainly concerned in this book there is one kind of direct knowledge, namely of secondary propositions, with which I cannot help but be involved. In the case of every argument, it is only directly that we can know the secondary proposition which makes the argument itself valid and rational. When we know something by argument this must be through direct acquaintance with some logical relation between the conclusion and the premises. In *all* knowledge, therefore, there is some direct element; and logic can never be made purely mechanical. (Keynes 1921: 15)

Unfortunately, a deeper discussion of Keynes's epistemology would require more space than is available here. At this point, it might be sufficient to see the differences to previous definitions. First, in contrast to both objective and subjective aleatoric approaches, Keynes is not interested in establishing a propositional logic based on logical atoms. Probability is not defined as either relative frequency or degree of belief in a *given* proposition, as the subjective-aleatoric position maintains, but as the logical relation *between* propositions. As the change of the basic metaphor from 'bet' to 'argumentation' indicates, this definition is framed in singular terms and explicitly incorporates reference to the 'amount' of available knowledge.

Keynes is thereby in the position to inquire into the processes that allow for repetition of events in the first place and consequently, as he emphasises in his foreword, to disconnect probability from expectations and distributions.

As a consequence, the conditions of possibility for numerical representation of probability might not be given as it is 'not possible to say of every pair of conclusions, about which we have some knowledge, that the degree of our rational belief in one bears any numerical relation to our degree of rational belief in the other ... [nor is it] always possible to say that the degree of our rational belief in one conclusion is either equal to, greater than, or less than the degree of our belief in another' (Keynes 1921: 37). Indeed, Keynes admits, 'if every probability was necessarily either greater than, equal to, or less than any other, the principle of indifference would be plausible' (1921: 45). But as Keynes emphasises throughout the book, to ascribe the principle of insufficient reason universal validity, that is independent of any prior qualitative, contextual considerations would necessarily leads to paradoxes and inconsistencies (1921: 45).

To open probability theory up for context determining, qualitative judgements, Keynes had to treat the possibility for numerical probabilities in much more restrictive terms than aleatoric probability approaches would suggest. The incorporation of qualitative judgements into probability theory opens the system for a multiplicity of different models or meta-languages in which probability may take on a different meaning. For example, the principle of insufficient reason cannot be applied to organic systems where the addition of a new part alters not just the value of the whole, but the value of the existing parts as well. Consequently, in contrast to the subjective-aleatoric approach, the model is not given but has to be chosen. Keynes incorporates self-reflective and diagnostic processes and thereby alters the problem of practice: whereas Ramsey requires problem settings to be well defined before individuals engage with the world, for Keynes the very choosing of a particular perspective already belongs to probability theory. Probability belongs not to the world, but is a result of our engagement with the world. Therefore, probability is not outside a deductive, necessity-oriented logic, but an inherent part of it. Consequently, while the concept of rationality in subjective-aleatoric probability theory is moulded to suit methodological individualism, Keynes includes the trail and error process of invoking different models or interpretation. In contrast to subjective approaches, rational belief is not related to the event of a choice, but to a process. Of course, the choosing of a model is the subjective element in Keynes's theory, but that is surely not the same subjectivity as choosing numerical probabilities within a given model as it actually transcends the subject-object divide.[5]

Subjective Epistemic Probability

The turn from objective to subjective epistemic probability theory has to be understood in the context of Wittgenstein's linguistic turn. While Wittgenstein in the *Tractatus* took a logical theory perspective, the *Philosophical Investigations* and the *Remarks on the Foundations of Mathematics* place probability now in the context of his language philosophy where he still supports the metaphor of 'dialogue' but now rejects an assumed objectivity of logic. What that means might be exemplified by a short example: usually, it is assumed that probabilities, like proportions, are finitely additive. The necessity of this logical operation is assumed to derive from the objective logical system. What Wittgenstein emphasises is that logical necessity cannot be derived from logic itself. For example, the basic truth that $1 + 1$ equals 2 is taken to be an unshakable truth. A short reflection, however, shows that different languages change the truth-value of this statement. In every machine language $1+1$ equals zero; if this equation describes a fusion of two entities, it might equal 1.5, sometimes $1+1$ even makes 11. This critique is not solely directed at the 'finite additive' assumption to call for non-additive probabilities, but is located at the level of logical operation itself. As there is a plurality of language games with each having its own constitutive rules, the meaning of logical operations can vary between them. As Wittgenstein (1956: §65) notes: 'When language games change, concept, and notions change, and with them the meaning of words.' Consequently, the meaning of logical operations is contingent to the language game one is in. This, however, implies that Boolean algebra is only one out of many possible 'languages' and its claim of universal validity and its ascription of necessity to logical operations is unwarranted. Taking this critique seriously would require a new algebra, a new foundation of mathematics itself. However, any foundations of mathematics cannot be grounded in logic itself (Wittgenstein 1953: 64).

To see why, we need to remember that Wittgenstein's calling into doubt of logical necessity a priori is based on the proof that the third axiom of classic logic, the *tertium non datur*, the background of aleatoric probability theory, cannot be established completely from first principles if the underlying system is sufficiently complex (Nagel and Newman 2002). Consequently, any query into the foundations of mathematics does not point to mathematics or logic, but to the social, contextual conditions of cognition. It points to societies and language games, to institutional settings within which mathematics are embedded and give meaning to the mathematical semantics. Consequently, this approach to probability asks for the 'probability of probability'. It sees its own conditions of possibility, its own probability as contingent. Recognising these limitations makes the truth-conditional theory of meaning, on which Ramsey's process is founded, obsolete to give way to Wittgenstein's use theory of meaning and the analysis of interdependence of social and semantic change.

Thus, the basic question of probability theory is still an epistemological one but linked to his concept of language game. He thereby changes the basic question of probability theory: of relevance is not what probability *is* but how it is conceptualised. The 'what' is to be replaced by the 'how' question: how do societies think/have thought about probability? What are the societal preconditions of its semantic evolution? What were the functional equivalents across various models? Put in this perspective, probability is not a problem of representation but one of drawing boundaries: what rules are followed, what paths are not taken, how they are set apart, which distinctions are invoked, etc. From a subjective-epistemological view, the conception of probability changes with changing dimensions of meaning and thus life-forms and discourses. As social and semantic change is a mutually dependent process, there is no possibility to provide one historic definition of probability. The historicity of mathematical concepts, shown for example by Niklas Luhmann (1995) or Ian Hacking, leads us to challenge their timeless nature. As Ian Hacking once directed against Keynes:

> Many modern philosophers claim that probability is a relation between an hypothesis and the evidence for it. This claim, true or false, conceals an explanation as to the late emergence of probability: the relevant concept of evidence did not exist beforehand. (Hacking 1975: 31)

According to Hacking, one of the preconditions of modern probability theory was a semantic shift of 'evidence'. But '[u]ntil the seventeenth century, there was no concept of evidence with which to pose the problem of induction. Although concepts of authority and testimony were clearly available, what was lacking was a concept of internal evidence of things' (Hacking 1975: 31). Consequently, the notion of probability in the modern sense could not exist. Equally, the assumed objectivity of logical probability crucially depended on the objectivity of evidence and processes of truth-finding. This is as relevant for probability theory in particular as for theory of science and logic in general. But what counts as evidence, its criteria and possible conclusions, is part of the same processes that allowed for the emergence of 'probability'.[6] Questions of evidence and scientific proof are not objectively given – they have a history. Hacking refers to a broader debate concerning the 'nature of evidence' in the philosophy of science through the paradigms debate of Thomas Kuhn's *The Structure of Scientific Revolution* (Kuhn 1964) and Paul Feyerabend's *Against Method* (Feyerabend 1996) and the *incommensurability debate*. They showed how revolutions in science paradigm shifts transcend the linear process that Karl Popper suggested in

Conjectures and Refutations (Popper 1974) but take on the dynamics of *Gestalt Shifts*. Changes in the scientific vocabulary cannot be understood as a linear process towards an objectively given truth, as both Keynes and Popper would suggest, but need to be understood in terms of the drawing of boundaries between stages of normal science.

To summarise the epistemic approaches and draw some insights for the issue of non-knowledge, this discussion showed that qualitative judgements precede measurement as they point to the particular way in which situations are defined. But these processes of problem definition cannot be reduced to individual levels. The speaking of a language is never just a private enterprise as being in the world is always already being with others. If probability theory seeks to incorporate the 'choice' of the right model, the constitutive function of rules, then it needs to take seriously this intersubjective dimension. Of course, Keynes and Wittgenstein would differ substantially in how this intersubjective realm is structured. However, both would agree that the subject-object distinction finally needs to be abandoned. Both share the basic conviction that the relevant knowledge cannot be found in deductive, formal reasoning but in the capacity to follow rules. Knowledge is not only what we receive as an answer to our questions, but the knowledge we have while acting, questioning, threatening, promising etc.

Acknowledging these different kinds of knowledge shows that any incorporation of qualitative, contextual judgements into probability theory changes the relationship between knowledge and non-knowledge. By placing epistemology before ontology, epistemic positions stress the importance of context for understanding probability or risk assessments. The vantage point of this understanding is not a given game with objective categories, but the observer dependence of knowledge. This necessitates abandoning the assumption there could be only one 'true' model to leave space for a variety of possible worlds. In this setting, it is not nature that provides the truth conditions for the meaning of variables, but theories are tested always against other theories. Observing the world is never just a passive description, but always part of the observed object. It is an activity where actors do not act within a given game, but where inter-subjective processes define it. This redefines the basic problem of epistemology: the basic problem is not 'representational' as propositional knowledge indicates. Rather, the problem is to make visible the boundaries by which perspectives, worlds or knowledge and non-knowledge are created. However, this knowledge about non-knowledge is of a different kind than the knowledge of 'propositions'. The remaining question is of course how this difference between functions and rules lead to different methods and subsequently different concepts of institutions.

NON-KNOWLEDGE AND INSTITUTIONS

The last part argued that it matters crucially whether one starts from an ontological-aleatoric or from an epistemological definition of uncertainty. Conceptualising uncertainty in terms of probability distribution and possible states of the world, where uncertainty is reduced to risk and probability and is a property of the coin or dice, focuses on quantities where only structural breaks and qualitative changes need to be introduced exogenously. One can often hear the consequence when statisticians have to admit that the context of their model has changed and therefore past correlations have no information value for the present situation at hand. By upholding the idea of models being a true representation of the world, this setting treats knowledge and non-knowledge as direct opposites: the more we know, the more data we have, the less we do not know.

The epistemological concept of uncertainty conceptualises non-knowledge exactly in terms of an absence of probability relations (Lawson 1988) to inquiry into how situations and probabilities are constructed. This approach emphasises the knowledge we find in the following of rules. Of course, that is not to be confused with a conservative interpretation that we should follow pre-existing rules and shall not demand any changes. This interest in rules has to be understood in juxtaposition to functions. Rules inherently have an intersubjective dimension which is the *condition of possibility* for phenomena to emerge. Rules point to the social construction of institutions and their constitutive, enabling function. But before this point is addressed in detail, some potential criticism should be addressed. At least, arguing that the 'intersubjective' dimension of rules escape propositional knowledge could raise some eyebrows as one could now argue that subjective-aleatoric probability theory has solved this problem by deriving a quantitative from a purely qualitative probability measure. In the end, is not game theory all about 'intersubjectivity'? If that is true, then empiricism prevails and my discussion is meaningless. However, as I will now argue, Savage, for example, derives his quantities not deductively but by an analogy. What he needs is a notion of equal probability, or as Ramsey called it, ethical neutrality, that is he needs to establish a symmetry argument independent of any context that allows locating probability into the realm of gambling and betting. This, he thinks, is provided by the principle of insufficient reason as it allows him to use quantitative measure even in a state of complete ignorance.

Traditionally, the equality of the probabilities was supposed to be established by what was called the *principle of sufficient reason*, thus: Suppose that there is an argument leading to the conclusion that one of the possible combinations of ordered scores, say {1,2,3} more probable than some other say {6,3,4}. Then the information on which that hypothetical argument is based has such symmetry as to permit a completely parallel, and therefore equally valid, argument, leading to the conclusion that {6,3,4} is more probable than {1,2,3}. Therefore, it was asserted, the probabilities of all combinations must be equal. (Savage 1954: 64)

This measure is justified by convention: 'This definition, or something very like it, is at the root of all ordinary mathematical work in probability' (Savage 1954: 33). I think Savage is quite aware that he is introducing something substantial not endogenously but exogenously as he tries to hide his failure by a discussion on potential objections. However, this discussion remains surprisingly vacuous and does not even attempt to legitimise the previous step. However, I would hold that given the importance of this move, a justification on the basis of 'that is how we always have done it' is not sufficient as it leaves the prior question unanswered, namely: on what basis can one assume that epistemic probability obeys basic mathematical laws? On what basis can epistemology be replaced by ontology? As soon as we know that probabilities add up to one, we are in the position to calculate with counter-probabilities. In a setting with two alternatives, *either A or ¬A have to* manifest. If *A* does not materialise, then we know at the same time something about ¬*A*. *That is, however, a different problem setting than the original degree of belief definition of probability*, where such an inference is not possible.

To see why, consider an actor who finds himself in a state of complete ignorance. Now an interrogator asks for his degree of belief that the fair coin will show 'tails'. Ignorant as he is, the actor provides an answer in line of the principle of insufficient reason: ½. After 10 000 throws, the interrogator repeats his question. Again, the person's answer is ½. If, however, the player now evinces a probability of ½ in both cases is there not a qualitative difference between these two identical assessments? Obviously, the same numerical presentation has a different meaning as the confidence in the proposition, or what Keynes has called the 'weight' of argument, has substantially increased.

According to Ramsey and Savage, the question 'more probable' is translated into 'higher betting quotients'. As the relevance of data is translated into the vocabulary of 'stochastic independence', they need to fuse both the degree of belief and weight of argument into one numerical value. Consequently, in Bayesian terms, this increase cannot be analysed as the information value of the repetition, the learning by experience, cannot be accounted for. Savage explicitly denies this problem. If probabilities should be uncertain, one should take an average value of 'probabilities of probabilities' to arrive at new estimates. The altered estimate will then represent the uncertainty or relevance/weight in its entirety. But this argument nicely shows the misunderstandings involved. Within Savage's approach, actors orient themselves by statistical average values. The degree of belief is derived from a quantitative definition of probability where information, evidence and signals are endowed with a *given* information value that allows for conditional updating of one's belief. This assumption of 'given' information or signalling values cannot be sustained when there is a multiplicity of possible worlds where signals change their meaning and actors have to figure out where a signal actually belongs. Was the late delivery of goods due to opportunistic behaviour, a mistake or to a higher force?

According to Keynes, this increase of the 'weight' is due to an increase of the stock of knowledge *h*. Although the probability of an argument may prevail or even decrease, the weight of argument always increases with new evidence. Analogously, Ellsberg (1956: 657) thinks that: '[w]hat is at issue might be called the *ambiguity* of this information, a quality depending on the amount, type, reliability, and "unanimity" of information, and giving rise to one's degree of "confidence" in an estimate of relative likelihoods'. 'This judgement of the ambiguity of one's information of the over-all credibility of one's composite estimates, of one's confidence in them, cannot be expressed in terms of relative likelihoods or events' (ibid). What the weight tries to get at – and what consequently Savage tries to hide – is that there are different forms of knowledge. The weight of the argument raises issues about relevance and significance of data. In other words: to answer questions of the weight of arguments, questions of authority, legitimacy and the social and institutional context or conventions emerge. Which data is seen as relevant or legitimate depends on the social context one finds oneself in. But any answer to this question is – at least in social contexts – the result of an intersubjective process that points to knowledge of different kind than knowledge of the data itself. That is: confidence *in* data and their contextually defined 'relevance' and 'significance' points at 'uncertainty' in an epistemological sense and not to uncertainty in an ontological sense. As Ellsberg confirms by quoting Frank Knight: 'This action which follows upon an opinion depends as much upon the amount of confidence in that opinion as it does upon the favorableness of the opinion itself. Fidelity to the actual psychology of the situation requires, we must insist, recognition of these two separate exercises of judgement, the formation of an estimate and the estimation of its value' (Knight 1921: 227 quoted in Ellsberg 1961: 660).

Consequently, intersubjective processes determine what the actual rules of the game are, who an actor is, what expectations are legitimate and what norms and conventions apply. These processes are not answered by looking harder at the facts but by providing an interpretation and description of their meaning. Institutions are such intersubjective phenomena that fulfil exactly these functions. They provide a context, define situations and constitute actors and actions. The meaning institutions have for actors thus needs to be described in terms of these shared understandings. A naturalistic framework where knowledge and non-knowledge are opposites is consequently inappropriate. But going back to the plurality of possible worlds, the meaning of the actual is only given in contrast to these further alternatives. Including qualitative judgements recognises that the actual present materialised from one set of alternatives and the very act of materialisation opened further alternatives. Meaning, in other words, is the constant reproduction of the actual and the possible. But in contrast to *probabilistic* statements, the possible is not defined from the perspective of the actual – as Savage would claim – but the actual is understood and set in context to *the possible*.

From this perspective, institutions provide a particular way in which the set of alternatives is structured and complexity reduced. But every complexity reduction instantly reproduces complexity, the reduction of knowledge produces at the same time new non-knowledge. Institutions do not only allow for 'rational' decisions, but determine what is known, how it is known and what is not known. The rise of new financial instruments like derivates as a form of knowledge has also produced new non-knowledge in the form of unknown opportunities, the opening of the space for new contingencies and possibilities, but also new problems and unintended consequences. No one can calculate the systemic risks arising from derivatives at the moment.

The appropriate method to make visible this boundary of the known and the unknown can focus exactly on the very constitutive boundaries of these institutions that are rooted in semantic distinctions like risk and uncertainty, or labour and capital. These boundaries are not natural givens but have a history, and to reveal how their productive and performative capacity structured institutions allows for the constitution of actors and the production of social facts. For example, if I refer to institutions by saying 'this is money' or 'this is a contract', I am not only passively describing something, but I am performing an act, I am reproducing these institutions. And whoever claims that saying 'I do' during a marriage ceremony is only a description and not part of getting married might learn rather quickly the opposite. But to say 'I do' or 'this is a contract' or 'hereby I entitle you' does not 'cause' the existence of an institution like a stone causes glass to break. That would involve some serious category mistakes just because institutions have no existence outside our shared understandings about these institutions.

This shows that simple data does not explain social facts. Social facts cannot be explained in the strict sense, but only be understood. Methodologically speaking, this directs our focus to *reconstructive methods* that reconstruct the 'meaning' of distinctions and their change over time. Reading the social systems theory of Niklas Luhmann from this perspective might provide an avenue to use his ideas on complexity and communication, selection and evolution, and boundaries and social differentiation for analysing economic institutions. For example, the knowing how to follow the rules of economic institutions shows that knowing the particular rules of the game results from a wider set of alternatives. Equally, there is a difference in how labour unions, employers' associations, accountants and finance managers see the world, what arguments are seen as relevant, what norms apply, what kind of knowledge is relevant etc. New actors like Hedge Funds or NGOs redefine the rules of the game and thus the way in which actors observe themselves and others. At the same time, institutions structure the particular way in which actors form expectations, observe themselves and form identities and thus shape the form in which communication and interaction occurs.

CONCLUSION

This chapter explored how a focus on the *reproduction* of uncertainty could shed a different light on the study of economic institutions and questions of *structure formation*. This readjustment may allow us to see economic institutions not only as devices for 'rational' decisions, but to see their constitutive function, that is how they structure practices by determining what and how something is not known. As the attempt to acquire new knowledge leads at the same time to more non-knowledge, the reduction of uncertainty by institutions at the same time opens the door for new uncertainties. Consequently, issues of non-knowledge cannot be reduced to some 'lack' of knowledge that could be solved by looking harder at the facts or processes of conjecture and refutation. The chapter showed that a focus on non-knowledge in ontological terms is biased, but that an epistemological approach demands bringing epistemology and ontology in line. To approach intersubjective phenomena like institutions with a positivist method assumes that conventions can determine actions. But that would reproduce the paradigm of individual choice with the consequence that the intersubjective quality will be lost. Instead of looking into the heads of actors, the chapter proposed a reconstructive method that avoids naturalistic fallacies. Following this path allows both to see that observation is always an activity and institutions both constrain and enable action. Institutions provide a means of structuring unorganised complexity but at the same time produce new non-knowledge. Tracing the interplay of knowledge and non-knowledge over time allows us to see how new regulations always open new space for crises to emerge. Every attempt to fix the heterogeneous interpretation of actors by providing 'standards' will always produce new heterogeneity as numbers and economic facts never speak for themselves but are produced by actors on the basis of current regulations that attempt to bend and possibly break the given framework to produce expected numbers. In the same vein, accounting rules structure the way companies observe and know themselves. At the same time, regulations can be circumvented by bending some loop holes. The attempt to fix the loophole by introducing new regulation opens the door for new contingencies.

NOTES

[1] I refer here to Luhmann's (1995) notion of complexity and social change. See also Byrne (1998).

[2] However, what surely needs to be developed further, and where this matrix can only be a first step, is to dismantle different concepts of 'subjectivity' and 'objectivity'. See for example Searle (2005).

[3] Now one could argue that Ramsey too established probability as logic of partial belief. Though this is partially correct, there are some differences which will be discussed in this section: first, Ramsey defines probability in aleatoric terms and then derives its logical qualities. Keynes defines probability as a logical term first and then derives conditions under which repetition and the principle of insufficient reason is applicable. Secondly, Keynes acknowledges a variety of knowledge structures that Ramsey is not able to see. See below.

[4] Primary propositions refer to the proposition   independent of any probabilistic reasoning and as such is called knowledge *of a*. Secondary propositions (a/h) entail probability relations and are knowledge *about a*. As a corollary, all direct knowledge is certain by assumption. 'All knowledge, that is to say, which is obtained in a manner strictly direct by contemplation of the objects of acquaintance and without any admixture whatever of argument and the contemplation of the logical bearing of any other knowledge on this, corresponds to *certain* rational belief and not merely probable degree of rational belief' (Keynes 1921, p. 17).

[5] In my opinion, the term 'belief' is ambiguous as it automatically suggests a pre-existing individual that 'holds' them. The crucial step is thus is the move to treat 'subjectivity' identically to 'individuality'. Where the subjective element is to be found within different approaches is not given by just pointing to 'belief'. Here, it is possible to locate the subjective element differently within different approaches. Moreover, subjectivity could only mean 'observation-dependent'. Nowadays it is common knowledge that self-referential systems 'observe' their environment without presupposing a knowing individual or person.

[6] See the parallel discussion of Galilei in Feyerabend (1996).

REFERENCES

Bergson, Henri (1913), *Introduction to Metaphysics*, London: Knickerbocker.

Byrne, David (1998), *Complexity Theory and the Social Sciences*, London: Routledge.

Carabelli, Anna (1988), *On Keynes's Method*, London: Macmillan.

Davidson, Paul (1991), 'Is Probability Theory Relevant for Uncertainty? A Post Keynesian Perspective', *Journal of Economic Perspectives*, 5, 129-143.

de Finetti, Bruno (1964), 'Foresight: its Logical Laws, its Subjective Sources', *Studies in Subjective Probability*, 93-158, edited by H.E. Kyburg and H.E. Smokler, New York: John Wiley.

Dequech, D. (2004), 'Uncertainty: Individuals, Institutions and Technology' *Cambridge Journal of Economics*, 28, 365-378.

Ellsberg, Daniel (1961), 'Risk, Ambiguity and the Savage Axioms', *Quarterly Journal of Economics*, 75, 643-669.

Feyerabend, Paul (1996), *Against Method*, London: Verso.

Harsanyi, John C. (1967), 'Games with Incomplete Information Played by "Bayesian" Players I-III. Part I. The Basic Model', *Management Science*, 14, 159-182.

Hodgson, Geoffrey Martin (2004), *The Evolution of Institutional Economics: Agency, Structure, and Darwinism in American Institutionalism*, New York: Routledge.

Hodgson, Geoffrey Martin (2006), 'What are Institutions?', *Journal of Economic Issues*, 40, 1-25.

Kahneman, Daniel, Paul Slovic and Amos Tversky (1982), *Judgment Under Uncertainty: Heuristics and Biases*, Cambridge: Cambridge University Press.

Keynes, John Maynard (1921), *A Treatise on Probability*, London: Macmillan.

Kuhn, Thomas S. (1964), *The Structure of Scientific Revolutions*, Chicago: Chicago University Press.

Lachmann, Ludwig (1971), *The Legacy of Max Weber*, Berkeley: The Glendessary Press.

Lawson, Tony (1988), 'Probability and Uncertainty in Economic Analysis', *Journal of Post-Keynesian Economics*, 11, 38-65.

Lawson, Tony (1997), *Economics and Reality*, London; New York: Routledge.

Lawson, Tony and M. Hashem Pesaran (1985), *Keynes' Economics: Methodological Issues*, Armonk, NY: M.E. Sharpe.

Luhmann, Niklas (1995), *Social Systems*, Stanford: Stanford University Press.

Mises, Ludwig von (1949), *Human Action: A Treatise on Economics*, New Haven: Yale University Press.

Mises, Richard von (1926), *Wahrscheinlichkeit, Statistik und Wahrheit*, Berlin: Springer.

Mises, Richard von (1928), *Probability, Statistics and Truth*, London: George Allen and Unwin.

Mises, Richard von (1939), *Kleines Lehrbuch des Positivismus: Einführung in die empiristische Wissenschaftsauffassung*, The Hague: W.P. van Stockum und Zoon.

Nagel, Ernst (1933), 'A Frequency Theory of Probability', *The Journal of Philosophy*, 30, 533-554.

Nagel, Ernest and James R. Newman (2002), *Gödel's Proof*, New York: University of New York Press.

Popper, Karl (1974), *Conjectures and Refutations*, London: Routledge and Kegan Paul.

Ramsey, Frank Plumpton (1926), 'Truth and Probability', in *The Foundations of Mathematics and Other Logical Essays*, London: Routledge.

Reichenbach, Helmut, (1949), *The Theory of Probability*, Berkeley: University of California Press.

Runde, Jochen and Sohei Mizuhara (2003), 'The Philosophy of Keynes's Economics: Probability, Uncertainty and Convention', in *Economics as Social Theory*, London: Routledge.

Savage, Leonard (1954), *The Foundations of Statistics*, New York: John Wiley.

Schlicht, Ekkehart (1998), *On Custom in the Economy*, Oxford: Oxford University Press.

Searle, John (2005), 'What is an Institution?', *Journal of Institutional Economics*, 1, 1-22.

van Fraassen, B.C. (1988), *Laws and Symmetry*, Oxford: Clarendon Press.

Wittgenstein, Ludwig (1953), *Philosophical Investigations*, Oxford: B. Blackwell.

8.   Strong Uncertainty and How to Cope With It to Improve Action and Capacity

Paul Davidson

INTRODUCTION

The entrepreneurial system that most people call capitalism, though imperfect, is the best system humans have yet devised for promoting economic growth, development and prosperity. In fact, classical economic theory in its 19th and early 20th century version and its modern Walras-Arrow-Debreu interpretation that is the foundation of 21st century mainstream economic theory can 'demonstrate' that free market capitalism is the most efficient engine possible for propelling our society towards an economic Utopia here on earth. In such a system, a free market coordinates the decisions of self-interested agents without any need for government interference.

After the experience of the Great Depression and the Second World War, however, a myriad of institutional arrangements for regulating product, labor, exchange rate and financial markets were installed. Today's mainstream conventional wisdom tells us that these welfare state institutions are now barriers to economic progress. To improve economic action and growth capacity, we are told, all markets must be liberalized.

Logically consistent classical theory ideologues urge immediate dismantling these regulatory institutions (the equivalent of the shock therapy recommendations for nations pursuing a transition to capitalism). The common sense of mainstream 'Keynesian' economists breaks into their classical logical consistency when they urge a longer time horizon for complete liberalization. For these economists the only question is: 'how long before complete liberalization'? All mainstream economist theorists agree that in the long run governments should adopt a laissez-faire stance that encourages globalized free trade and unfettered international financial capital mobility. Perhaps for political reasons, these advocates of unhampered capital mobility often remain silent regarding the question of should government encourage free international labor mobility.

When asked what specific market needs most to be liberalized, especially in the more developed nations, the response is typically the domestic labor market. It is my understanding that economic advisers to German politicians believe that Germany's labor market is especially sclerotic. Consequently, they recommend removal of legislation that (1) protects labor unions, collective bargaining and high minimum wages, (2) provides significant unemployment insurance, (3) restricts working hours per week, (4) encourages 'long' annual vacations for workers, (5) causes exorbitant firing costs, and (6) provides other social safety net protections. The removal of these institutional arrangements will reduce, if not eliminate, the intransigence of workers to accept the free market conditions that lead to classical theory's Utopia.

In our world of experience, the entrepreneurial system is not as perfect as the one classical theory describes primarily because the future can not be as reliably predicted as classical theory postulates. In our world where the economic future is uncertain, there are two 'outstanding faults of the economic society in which we live ... its failure to provide full employment and its arbitrary and inequitable distribution of income and wealth' (Keynes, 1936, p. 372).

Keynes's *General Theory* focused on the unemployment fault as his analysis explained why labor and product market rigidities were not to be blamed for economic maladjustments. Supply side constraints on prices, wages, exchange rates, etc. are neither necessary nor sufficient conditions to cause persistent unemployment, recessions, depressions and overall poor economic performance. Instead, these economic ills are inevitably tied to the question of liquidity.

Keynes limited his discussion of the inequality fault to a few side comments in the last chapter of *The General Theory*. At the end of this chapter I will spend a few moments to provide potential recommendations regarding reducing existing inequalities, while explaining why classical theory assumes that whatever inequalities exist are an inevitable outcome of our progress towards economic Utopia.

WHAT WAS REVOLUTIONARY ABOUT KEYNES'S ANALYSIS?

On New Year's Day in 1935 Keynes wrote a letter to George Bernard Shaw stating:

> To understand my new state of mind, however, you have to know that I believe myself to be writing a book on economic theory which will largely revolutionize not I suppose at once but in the course of the next ten years the way the world thinks about economic problems. When my new theory has been duly assimilated and mixed with politics and feelings and passions, I cannot predict what the final upshot will be in its effect on actions and affairs, but there will be a great change and in particular the Ricardian Foundations of Marxism will be knocked away.
>
> I can't expect you or anyone else to believe this at the present stage, but for myself I don't merely hope what I say. In my own mind I am quite sure.

Classical theory attributed unemployment and recessions to built in labor market institutional rigidities. Keynes (1936, p. 259) demonstrated that this classical argument that rigidities cause unemployment is an ignoratio elenchi, that is, a fallacy in logic of offering a proof irrelevant to the proposition in question. Specifically in chapter 19 of *The General Theory* and even more directly in his published 1939 *Economic Journal* response to Dunlop and Tarshis, Keynes argued that unemployment equilibrium could still occur even if the world was one possessing flexible wages and prices. In other words, Keynes's general theory showed that wage and price rigidities are neither necessary or sufficient conditions for demonstrating the existence of involuntary unemployment equilibrium.

Keynes (1936, p. 3) called his analysis a general theory and stated that the axioms underlying 'classical theory are applicable to a special case and not to the general case .... the characteristics of this special case ... happen not to be those of the economic society in which we actually live, with the result that its teaching is misleading and disastrous if we attempt to apply it to the facts of experience'. In the preface to the German language edition of *The General Theory* (1936, p. ix) Keynes noted 'This is one of the reasons which justify my calling my theory a general [emphasis in the original] theory. ... it is based on fewer restrictive assumptions [weniger enge Voraussetzungen stützt] than the orthodox theory' (second emphasis added). Keynes here is claiming that what makes his analytical system more general than the classical (today's Walrasian-Arrow-Debreu general equilibrium) analysis is that Keynes's theory requires a smaller common axiomatic base (fewer restrictive axioms). In contrast, Debreu has argued that 'a good general theory does not search for the maximum generality but for the right generality' (Weintraub, 2002, p. 113). Thus Debreu's general equilibrium theory is a special case that imposes additional restrictive axioms to Keynes's axiomatic foundation to get the 'right generality'[1].

Keynes compared those economists whose theoretical logic was grounded on the classical special case additional restrictive axioms to Euclidean geometers living in a nonEuclidean world:

> who discovering that in experience straight lines apparently parallel often meet, rebuke the lines for not keeping straight- as the only remedy for the unfortunate collisions which are taking place. Yet, in truth, there is no remedy except to throw over the axiom of parallels and to work out a non-Euclidean geometry. Something similar is required today in economics. (Keynes, 1936, p. 16)

To throw over an axiom is to reject what the faithful believe are 'universal truths'. The Keynesian revolution in economic theory required economists to 'throw over' three restrictive classical axioms from its theoretical foundation.

Keynes's biographer, Lord Skidelsky [1992, p. 512] wrote "that mainstream economists after the Second World War treated Keynes's theory as a 'special case' of the classical theory, applicable to conditions where money wages and interest were sticky. Thus his theory was robbed of its theoretical bite".[2]

As explained below, post war mainstream Keynesians believed the Walrasian classical theory to be the foundation of economic analysis. In the 1960s and early 1970s, classical monetarists led by Milton Friedman (and later by Robert Lucas), were able to emphasize the inconsistencies of the synthesis of mainstream Keynesian macroeconomic policies with its neoclassical (Walrasian) microtheory. As a result, by the 1970s, orthodox policy recommendations had regressed to reiterating the misleading and potentially disastrous prescriptions of classical theory.

Today, 70 years after Keynes wrote of his hopes that his revolutionary analysis would effect economic actions and affairs, we find a majority of economists and political leaders are prisoners of classical theory in their choice of economic policies. This classical foundation is especially obvious in the orthodox justification for outsourcing as merely an aspect of the Ricardian law of comparative advantage. Yet, in the United States the real income of those without a university degree has actually declined significantly in the last half dozen years as a result of outsourcing to China and other Asian nations with their almost unlimited supply of unskilled, but easily trained, workers willing to work at a fraction of the costs of comparable labor in the United States. The affected US workers have not been re-employed to work in some other more productive activity where the US supposedly has a comparative advantage. Instead these workers are either long-term unemployed, or have accepted part time low wage service industry jobs that can not be outsourced, or have dropped out of the labor force entirely. These workers are unlikely to be re-employed until their wage approaches that paid to Chinese unskilled workers.

CLASSICAL THEORY VS KEYNES

A sage once defined a 'classic' as a book that everyone cites but no one reads. In this sense, John Maynard Keynes's book *The General Theory of Employment, Interest and Money* (1936) is truly a classic for mainstream professional economists.

For most students who studied economics in a university in any OECD nation during the last half of the 20th century, Paul A. Samuelson's neoclassical synthesis Keynesianism epitomized revolutionary analysis of Keynes. In a paper (Davidson, 2006) I explain, given the virulent anti-communist political atmosphere (McCarthyism) that existed in the United States in the later 1940s and early 1950s, economic textbooks that tried to provide an analysis of Keynes's *General Theory* were 'politically incorrect' and banished from University campuses. Samuelson, by using clever 'lawyer-like' writings (to use Samuelson's own phrase) in his textbook and by claiming classical microfoundations, avoided this textbook witch hunt. Consequently, Samuelson dominated the US economic textbook world with a politically correct classical foundation Keynesianism that is logically incompatible with Keynes's *General Theory*. The result was that Samuelson aborted Keynes's revolutionary theory from being adopted as mainstream macro economics.

In a telling interview with Colander and Landreth (1996, pp.158-159), Samuelson admits that when he read *The General Theory* while a student at Harvard in the 1930s he found the *General Theory* analysis 'unpalatable' and not comprehensible (ibid. p. 159]. Samuelson finally indicated that 'The way I finally convinced myself was to just stop worrying about it [about understanding Keynes's analysis]. I asked myself: why do I refuse a paradigm that enables me to understand the Roosevelt upturn from 1933 till 1937? ... I was content to assume that there was enough rigidity in relative prices and wages to make the Keynesian alternative to Walras operative' (ibid. pp.159-160). In 1986, 30 years after reading *The General Theory* Samuelson was still claiming that 'we [Keynesians] always assumed that the Keynesian underemployment equilibrium floated on a substructure of administered prices and imperfect competition' (ibid. p. 160). When pushed by Colander and Landreth as to whether this requirement of rigidity was ever formalized in his work, Samuelson's response was 'There was no need to' (ibid. p. 161).

It should not be surprising therefore that, in the academic literature of the

1970s, the Monetarists easily defeated Samuelson's neoclassical synthesis Keynesianism on the grounds of logical inconsistency between its classical microfoundations and its macroeconomic analysis and policy prescriptions. The effect was, in the mid-1970s, to shift the emphasis for developing domestic and international choice of policies from prescriptions founded on Keynes' *General Theory* to the age-old laissez-faire policies promoted by classical theory that had dominated 19th and early 20th century thought. Consequently, socially acceptable policies to prevent unemployment, to promote economic development, and even the method to finance government social security systems have regressed, with the result that the 'golden age of economic development' experienced by both OECD nations and LDCs during the more than quarter century after World War II has disappeared[3] despite the technological changes in the study of economics.

As a result of the Monetarist victory over Samuelson's neoclassical Keynesianism in the 1970s, economic advisors encouraged policy makers to dance to the Panglossian siren song that 'all is for the best in the best of all possible worlds provided we let well enough alone' and let liberalized markets work.

The classical axioms that Keynes threw out in his revolutionary economic theory equivalent to non-Euclidean geometry general analysis were (1) the neutrality of money axiom, (2) the gross substitution axiom, and (3) the axiom of an ergodic economic world.

In 1933 Keynes explicitly noted that in his analytic framework money matters in both the long and short run, that is, money is never neutral (Keynes, 1933, pp. 408-9). Keynes developed his theory of liquidity preference late in his evolving analysis when he recognized that his theory of involuntary unemployment required specifying 'The Essential Properties of Interest and Money' (1936, ch. 17). These 'essential properties' clearly differentiated his theory from the classical theory and. assured that money and all other liquid assets are never neutral. These essential properties (Keynes, 1936, pp. 230-231) are:

(1) the elasticity of production associated with all liquid assets including money is zero or negligible, and

(2) the elasticity of substitution between liquid assets (including money) and reproducible goods is zero or negligible. The gross substitution axiom is not universally applicable to all demand functions and, therefore, as Arrow and Hahn (1971, p. 361) have demonstrated, in the absence of ubiquitous gross substitution all existence proofs of general equilibrium are jeopardized.

A zero elasticity of production means that money does not grow on trees and consequently workers can not be hired to harvest money trees when the demand for money (liquidity) increases. Or as Keynes wrote: 'money ...

cannot be readily reproduced; labour cannot be turned on at will by entrepreneurs to produce money in increasing quantities as its price rises' (Keynes, 1936, p. 230). Thus, when income earners, instead of spending their entire income on the products of industry, save in the form of money and/or other nonproducible liquid assets, effective demand for goods declines.

The zero elasticity of substitution, assures that portion of income that is not spend on by the products of industry, that is, savings, will find, in Hahn's (1977, p. 31) terminology, 'resting places' in the demand for nonproducibles. Some 40 years after Keynes, Hahn rediscovered Keynes's point that a stable involuntary unemployment equilibrium could exist even in a Walrasian system with flexible wages and prices whenever there are 'resting places for savings in other than reproducible assets' (Hahn, 1977, p. 31).

Hahn rigorously demonstrated what was logically intuitive to Keynes. He showed that the view that with 'flexible money wages there would be no unemployment has no convincing argument to recommend it .... Even in a pure tatonnement in traditional models convergence to [a general] equilibrium cannot be generally proved' if savings were held in the form of nonproducibles. Hahn (1977, p. 39) argued that 'any non-reproducible asset allows for a choice between employment inducing and non-employment inducing demand'. The existence of a demand for money and other liquid nonreproducible assets (that are not gross substitutes for the products of the capital goods producing industries) as a store of 'savings' means that all income earned by households engaging in the production of goods is not, in the short or long run, necessarily spent on the products of industry. Households who want to store that portion of their income that they do not consume (that is, that they do not spend on the products of industry) in liquid assets are choosing, in Hahn's words 'a non-employment inducing demand' for their savings.

Just as in non-Euclidean geometry lines that are apparently parallel often crash into each other, in the Keynes-Post Keynesian non-Euclidean economic world an increased demand for 'savings', even if it raises the relative price of nonproducibles, will not spill over into a demand for producible goods and hence when households save a portion of their income they have made a choice for 'non-employment inducing demand'.

UNCERTAINTY AND THE ERGODIC AXIOM

To explain why utility-maximizing individuals would desire to store savings in the form of nonproducible durables requires the rejection of the classical ergodic axiom. Classical theory presumes that all income earners make optimum time preference decisions regarding allocating income between current and future consumption over their lifetimes. This requires each income earner to 'know' exactly what they will want to consume every day in the future and by their resulting market actions today inform entrepreneurs about their future consumption demands.

If one conceives of the economy as a stochastic process, then future outcomes are determined via a probability distribution. Logically speaking for income earners to make statistically reliable forecasts about future parameters that will affect their future consumption activities, each decision maker should obtain and analyze sample data from the future. Since that is impossible, the assumption that the economy is an ergodic stochastic process permits the analyst to assert that samples drawn from past and current data are equivalent to drawing a sample from the future. In other words, the ergodic axiom implies that the outcome at any future date is the statistical shadow of existing market data.

In contrast, Keynes viewed the economic system as moving through calendar time from an irrevocable past to an uncertain, not statistically predictable, future where income spending decisions are made by people who know that they do not know what the future will bring. This required Keynes to reject the classical ergodic axiom, for the latter specifies that all future events are actuarially certain, that is, the future can be accurately known or reliably forecasted from the analysis of existing market data. (The ordering axiom plays the same role in classical deterministic economic models.)

Keynes never used the term 'ergodic' since ergodic theory was first developed in 1935 by the Moscow School of Probability and it did not become well known in the West until after World War II and Keynes was dead. Nevertheless Keynes's main criticism of Tinbergen's econometric 'method' (Keynes, 1939, p. 308) was that the economic data 'is not homogeneous over a period of time'. This means that economic time series are non-stationary, and non-stationarity is a sufficient (but not a necessary) condition for a nonergodic process. Consequently, Keynes, with his emphasis on uncertainty had, in these comments on Tinbergen, specifically rejected what would later be called the ergodic axiom.

Nevertheless Samuelson (1970, p. 11-12) has declared the ergodic axiom must be invoked if economics is to be considered a science. Samuelson indicated that ergodic scientific models will settle 'down to a unique equilibrium position independently of initial conditions'. Consequently, Samuelson notes, invoking the ergodic axiom means that if, in order to reduce income inequalities, 'the state redivided income each morning, by night the rich would be sleeping in their comfortable beds and the poor under the bridges' (Samuelson, 1970, p. 12). If one uses theory based on the ergodic axiom, then Keynes's inequality fault is really not a defect in our economic system; it is a result of the entrepreneurial system's relentless efficient drive to Utopia. Given the ergodic axiom, the unequal distribution of income and wealth cannot be changed by an act of government, anymore that the legislature can change the law of gravity.

In an ergodic system (or in a deterministic model based on the ordering axiom), today's income earners can reliably forecast when, and for what, every dollar of savings will be spent at each and every future possible date. Income earned today will be entirely spent either on produced goods for today's consumption or on buying investment goods that will be used to produce specific goods for the (known) future consumption spending pattern of today's savers. There can never be a lack of effective demand for things that industry can produce at full employment. The proportion of income that households save does not affect total (aggregate) demand for producibles; it only affects the composition of demand (and production) between consumption and investment goods. Thus, savings creates jobs in the capital-goods-producing industries just as much as consumption spending creates jobs in the consumer-goods-producing industries. Invoking the ergodic axiom means that since more capital goods means more productive capacity, savings is to be preferred over consumption.

When Nobel Prize laureate Samuelson claims that the ergodic assumption is necessary for economists to be hard-headed scientists, it is not surprising that Keynes's revolutionary analysis has been ignored by mainstream economic theory since World War II. If we could resurrect Keynes, or at least his theory, the argument would be that, in an uncertain (nonergodic) world, it is the desire of income earners to save in the form of nonproducible liquid assets that is the basis of the economic problems of the 21st century global economy. In such a world, encouraging the savings propensity will not be desirable if the economy is operating with unemployed workers.

In Keynes's theory, as opposed to the classical theory and the scientific approach of Professor Samuelson, people recognize the future is uncertain. Consequently, people decide on how much of current income is to be spent on consumer goods and how much is not to be spent on consumption goods but is instead saved by purchasing various liquid assets that can be used to transport this store of wealth to an indefinite future time period.

Keynes devised a two stage spending decision-making process for those who save out of current income. At the first stage the income-earner decides how much of current income will be spent today on produced goods and how much of current income will not be spent on currently produced goods and services, that is, how much of current income will be saved in the form of nonproducibles. Classical economists call this first stage saving decision process the time preference decision for it supposedly reflects consumers' preference for putting off buying some pleasure-yielding consumer goods today to obtain pleasure-yielding producibles at some specific time in the future. In the real world, however,

> an act of individual savings – so to speak – is a decision not to have dinner to-day. But it does not necessitate a decision to have a dinner or buy a pair of boots a week hence or a year hence or to consume any specified thing at any specified date. Thus it depresses the business of preparing to-day's dinner without stimulating the business of making ready for some future act of consumption ... it is a net diminution of such demand. (Keynes, 1936, p. 210)

Keynes called this first stage decision of the allocation of income between spending and saving the propensity to consume. In contrast to the time preference of classical theory Keynes's propensity to consume implied that income earners are willing to commit some portion of current income to purchase consumer goods today but are uncertain about the future and therefore do not want to commit all their income (claims) on real resource use. Keynes's propensity to consume and save indicates that 'He who hesitates [to consume] is saved to make a decision [regarding consumption] another day!'

Savers are required to make a second stage decision, the liquidity preference decision where each saver must choose among the many liquid assets available which ones to utilize for moving current savings into the indefinite future.[4] To carry forward their saved (unused) spending power of current income, savers have to decide on one or more vehicles (time machines) for transporting this unspent income into the future. If the future is uncertain and cannot be reliably predicted, then savers can never be sure as to the future specific date(s) when they shall want to utilize the spending power of these savings. Consequently savers will look for durable time machines that possess a minimum of carrying costs (for example, maintenance, repair, insurance, and warehousing costs) for the indefinite period that this saving will be held and not spent.

In a monetary economy where 'Money buys goods and goods buy money; but goods do not buy goods' (Clower, 1969, pp. 208-9), if at some unspecified future date a saver decides to use her savings to purchase some products of industry, if the saver has not stored his saving in the form of money, he/she will have to sell her time machine for money in order to finance this future purchase. Thus, savers will look for time machines that not only have negligible carrying costs, but also incur a minimum of transactions costs of buying and reselling liquid assets that can be easily offset by income flows received while holding the assets plus any capital gains (or net of capital losses). In sum, savers will use as time machines for their savings only things that have small or negligible carrying and transactions costs.

Real assets such as plant and equipment, consumer durables, etc. have relatively high carrying and transaction costs – especially transaction costs of reselling these durables, if these second-hand durables can be sold at all. Real producible durable goods, therefore, are not very useful time machines for savings, especially in a monetary economy with a developed financial system where savers have a plethora of liquid assets to choose from. Liquid assets are preferable time machines for carrying savings into the future in any economy as long as people have trust in their government's monetary system.

A PERMANENT ROLE FOR GOVERNMENT

Since it is the desire for liquidity that can create the major faults of an entrepreneurial system the permanent role for government is (1) to provide whatever liquidity is necessary to maintain orderly financial markets and (2) to assure that the effective demand necessary to assure full employment is never lacking.

Keynes wrote suggesting (1930, ii, p. 220) that bank 'credit is the pavement along which production travels, and the bankers if they knew their duty, would provide the transport facilities to just the extent that is required in order that the productive powers of the community can be employed at their full capacity'.

This 'paving stone' aspect requires government to install a well understood institutional arrangement that guarantees that financial markets will always operate in a well-organized and orderly fashion that encourages employment hiring and economic growth. As long as individuals abide by the civil law of contracts, governments have the power to maintain orderly domestic financial markets even when an unexpected event creates a tremendous fear of the uncertain future in the minds of the public.

For example, the events in New York on 11 September 2001 created great uncertainty about the future of financial markets in the United States. When the symbols of the great New York financial markets, the World Trade Towers, collapsed, there was the potential for a massive fast exit of US resident and foreigners from US bond and stock markets. Despite its ideological bias for the liberalized laissez faire efficient financial markets of classical theory, the pragmatic side of the Federal Reserve management flooded the financial system with liquidity immediately after the 9/11 terrorist attacks. In the two days following the attack, the Federal Reserve pumped $45 billion into the banking system. Simultaneously, according to the *Wall Street Journal* (18 October 2001, p. 1) 'to ease cash concerns among primary dealers in bonds – which include investment banks that aren't able to borrow money directly from the Fed – the Fed on Thursday [13 September 2001] snapped up all the government securities offered by dealers, $70.2 billion worth. On Friday it poured even more into the system, buying a record

$81.25 billion of government securities'.

The *Wall Street Journal* also reported that just before the stock market opened the following Monday for the first time since the terrorist attack, investment banker Goldman Sachs, loaded with liquidity due to Fed activities, phoned the chief investment officer of a large mutual fund group to tell him that Goldman was willing to buy any stocks the mutual fund managers wanted to sell.

The post 9/11 activities of the Federal Reserve flooding the banking and financial system with liquidity vividly demonstrate that the Monetary Authority can assure stable, orderly financial markets whenever the public's fast exit propensity threatens financial crisis. Does anyone seriously believe that laissez-faire financial markets that rely on private sector market makers to maintain orderliness could have achieve the results that the Fed did on the days following 9/11?

After the East Asian currency crisis and the Russian bond default, President Clinton called for a 'new financial architecture' to avoid future international financial panics. Classical theorists' response was that all that is required is a faster liberalization of exchange rate markets until exchange rates freely float without any government or central bank interference in the exchange rate market.

To permit exchange rates to become objects of speculation without any government institution to promote orderliness and organization is to flirt with potential disaster.

Currently the globalized economic community faces a growing dilemma in the currency markets that may have even more serious repercussions than the terrorist strike on 9/11. Given the huge and growing US current account deficits, a decline in the market value of the dollar sufficient to make a significant reduction (even if it does not eliminate) the US trade deficit can be a weapon of mass destruction. Can we muddle through on the hope that, despite the uncertainty about the future, speculators in our liberalized international financial markets 'know' what is good for the global economy as the classical theory implies? Or should we wake up our policy makers and insist that they develop contingency plans for a new financial architecture based on Keynes's general theory principles is an absolute necessity to avoid this potentially devastating bursting of the dollar standard?

Orthodox economists are almost unanimous in preaching the virtues of floating – and its logical inevitability. Yet many, perhaps most, countries remain attached to some form of fixing. Is this a case of economists being out of touch with reality? Or is it that reality is out of touch with economists?

The post-Bretton Woods world has never been one of pure, generalized floating. There is a kaleidoscope of currency arrangements ranging from 'hard' fixers to 'pure' floaters, and almost anything in between. Conventional wisdom claims floaters are gaining over the currency fixers and currency rate managers and that soft pegs are unsustainable. Are we moving towards a bipolar world where most currencies float freely and a minority, such as the Euroland nations, adopt hard pegs (see Fischer, 2001)?

Conventional wisdom assumes that the motives of the 'fixers' always has been predominantly economic. For decades after World War II, however, fixers were motivated in large part by geopolitical, rather than purely economic, reasons. The Western European countries accepted the dollar standard in return for military protection against communism. Today, the willingness of the Euro countries to float against the dollar can be viewed as an assertion of political independence.[5]

Nevertheless, the growing financial maturity and the reduction of trade barriers in Euroland did not lead the European countries to float against each other. Rather it led them towards the most extreme version of hard fixing. The Euro-nations have recognized that fixed, but not necessarily undervalued, rates should be preferred both for macroeconomic stability and to facilitate interregional trade expansion. If this is true for Euroland, is it not true for the globalized economy of the 21st century? But politics make it almost certain that a supranational global central bank is not possible. Elsewhere I (Davidson, 2002) have suggested an alternative arrangement that promotes a stabilizing new international financial architecture that can assure full employment without workers in the US or Euroland being required to accept wages approaching those in China, India, etc.

It should be clear that the most vocal advocates of floating are predominantly Americans – operating under the ideological spell originally cast by Milton Friedman's classical theory Monetarist approach that is founded on the long-run neutral money axiom[6] where only relative prices are important in determining the composition of output of a fully employed economy. But as Frank Hahn (1973, p. 14) noted 'practical men and ill-trained theorists everywhere in the world do not understand what they are claiming ... when they claim a beneficent and coherent role for the invisible hand' of a market with freely flexible prices and exchange rates.

The desire of nations such as China, India, Japan, and other Asian rim countries to maintain a competitive fixity of exchange rates against the dollar reflects the desire of these nations to pursue export-led growth – with the US economy the ultimate primary marketing target for these Asian nations' export industries. Of course this Asian decision to pursue export-led growth permits the consumers in the US to live well beyond their means. At the same time it means that these export-oriented nations are pursuing policies that encourage significant savings on their rapidly growing international accounts.

Taking advantage of the world's appetite for dollars, the US has accepted the view that other nations should bear the onus for American's exuberant consumption spending patterns. These other nations have a choice on how they accept this responsibility. They can either (1) revalue their currencies but to do so would mean they would have to accept lower rates of real growth or (2) they can accept dollars almost without limit to maintain their real economic growth and movement to prosperity. Given these options, it is not difficult to understand why the imbalance between the Asian creditors and the world's largest international debtor tends to persist despite a declining dollar. Asiatic nations recognize that their rapid export-led economic growth policies success relies on encouraging the United States to 'overspend' on its international account. The Euro nations, on the other hand, perhaps in their desire to demonstrate their geopolitical independence from the US, apparently prefer to impose overall lower real economic growth on their residents.

What generalization regarding economic growth policies can we draw from this current world situation? In essence there exists today two roads to real economic growth. Most of the world relies on export-led growth for achieving significant rates of real economic growth.[7] On the other hand, the road that the US travels (and Euroland apparently desires to tread on) requires significant labor productivity growth to generate real output growth. Under the Bush Administration, despite a slight recession, there has been a respectable rate of economic growth, while total employment is still less than the employment levels in January 2001 when President Bush took office. Higher real GDP with less workers signifies a strong rate of productivity growth associated with the real economic growth experienced by the US in the 21st century.

To assure that there is never a persistent lack of effective demand, the government must develop institutional arrangements that encourages some decision makers to spend in excess of their current income so that aggregate spending on the products of industry will offset any excess savings propensity at full employment. Years ago, when Hyman Minsky would hear me express this idea he would say Davidson never saw a deficit he did not love.

The second important permanent role for governments in our entrepreneurial system is to 'love deficits' that assure that if income recipients tend to save more out of income, then others are encouraged to increase spending in excess of their income.

In the analysis of a less than fully employed, closed economy – or an open economy where the nation does not have to worry about current account deficits – this love of deficits means a cheap money policy that lowers interest rates until, if possible, the private sector deficit spends itself to full employment. If this cheap money policy does not induce sufficient aggregate effective demand then the federal government should either directly, or with the cooperation of the private sector, deficit spend sufficiently on capital account to provide additional productive capacity and stimulate growth at full employment. Unfortunately given free trade and the current international payments system, most governments find that any deficit stimulating domestic policy induces additional spending on imports that ultimately results in a current account deficit problem.

At the next Bretton Woods conference, hopefully nations will agree on a new financial architecture such as my IMCU (Davidson, 2002) plan. Under my IMCU proposal nations that have persistent and significant unemployed resources can promote domestic spending growth without fearing they will be burdened with unmanageable current account deficits. Each nation can operate as if it were a closed economy (while reaping whatever benefits of trade that exists) where the size of the government deficits (or total government debt) relative to its gross national income is only an accounting problem – and should not act as a barrier towards fully and profitably employing its labor force.

THE INEQUALITY FAULT

Finally we should say a word about reducing if not eliminating the second major fault of entrepreneurial economies – the arbitrary and inequitable distribution of income and wealth. Since many of the world's poor are unemployed or underemployed, actively pursuing the paving stone and deficit loving in tandem with a new financial architecture, will propel the world closer to a global full employment position. Full employment will increase significantly the income of the previous unemployed and underemployed, thereby contributing substantially to reducing income inequalities. Moreover a cheap money policy should provide constraints on the income of wealthy rentiers. As we approach full employment, however, we may experience aggressive rent-seeking activities on the part of sellers of goods and labor services, leading to a phenomena that in the mid 20th century was labeled wage-price inflation. To avoid inflation at less than full employment because of these rent-seeking actions, nations should adopt a socially acceptable form of an incomes policy such as Sidney Weintraub's (2002) Tax-based Incomes Policy or TIP.

Finally, even if we approach full employment and avoid inflation via an incomes policy, the resulting distribution of income and wealth may still exhibit levels of inequality that the majority of the citizens of a nation may find socially undesirable. At that point fiscal policy via more progressive income and estate tax rates should be considered for possible reduction in the existing inequalities of income and wealth. The additional revenues obtained from this increase in rate progressivity can be used, for example, to provide free public education through the university level for all those having sufficient intelligence to qualify. Provision of such educational opportunities can further enhance the income-earning power of the children of lower income classes who are at a disadvantage vis-à-vis the children of higher income groups in obtaining a good education.

CONCLUSION

I have not presented a comprehensive program for solving all the possible economic problems facing a 21st century global entrepreneurial economic system. I hope, however, I have provided some enlightenment on how we can mitigate the two major faults of our economic system and thereby transform it to something that more closely approaches the results that the special case classical theory presumes already exists.

NOTES

[1] The onus is, therefore, on those who add the restrictive axioms to the general theory to justify these additional axioms. Those theorists who invoke only the general theory axiomatic base are not required, in logic, to prove a general negative, that is, they are not required to prove the additional restrictive axioms are unnecessary.

[2] Mainstream economists called this sticky interest rate argument the 'liquidity trap' where at some low, but positive, rate of interest the demand to hold money for speculative reasons was assumed to be perfectly elastic (that is, horizontal). After World War II, econometric investigations could find no empirical evidence of a liquidity trap. Had mainstream economists read *The General Theory*, however, they would have known that on page 202 Keynes specifies the speculative demand for money as a rectangular hyperbola – a mathematical function that never has a perfectly elastic segment. Moreover eyeball empiricism led Keynes (1936, p. 207) to indicate that he knew of no historical example where the liquidity preference function became 'virtually absolute', that is, perfectly elastic. In sum, from both an empirical and theoretical view, Keynes denied the existence of a liquidity trap.

[3] For almost a quarter of a century after World War II, governments actively pursued the types of economic policies that Keynes had advocated in the 1930s and 1940s. The result was that per capita economic growth in the capitalist world proceeded at a rate that has never been reached in the past nor matched since. The average annual per capita economic growth rate of OECD nations from 1950 until 1973 was almost precisely double the previous peak growth rate of the industrial revolution period. Productivity growth in OECD countries was more than triple (3.75 times) that of the industrial revolution era. The resulting prosperity of the industrialized world was transmitted to the less developed nations through world trade, aid, and direct foreign investment. From 1950-1973, average per capita economic growth for all less developed countries (LDCs) was 3.3 per cent, almost triple the average growth rate experienced by the industrializing nations during the industrial revolution. Aggregate economic growth of the LDCs increased at almost the same rate as that of the developed nations, 5.5 per cent and 5.9 per cent respectively. The higher population growth of the LDCs caused the lower per capita income growth (see Davidson, 2002, pp. 1-3).

[4] In essence, liquid assets are efficient time machines that savers use to store and transport savings to the future. Unlike savers in the classical system, real world savers do not know exactly what they will buy, and what contractual obligations, they will incur at any specific future date. As long as in the world of experience money is that thing that discharges all contractual obligations and money contracts are used to organize production and exchange activities, then the possession of money (and liquid assets that have small carrying costs and can be easily resold for money) means that savers possess the ability (a) to demand products whenever they desire in the uncertain future and/or (b) to meet a future contractual commitment that they have not foreseen. Liquid assets are savers' security blanket protecting them from the possibility of hard times in the future. For as Nobel Price winning economist, Sir John Hicks (1977, p. vii) stated, income recipients know that they 'do not know just what will happen in the future'. Without sufficient liquidity, today's income earners fear they may face insolvency, or even bankruptcy sometime in the future. In contradiction to classical theory that claims people maximize their happiness when spending everything they earn, in Dickens's *David Copperfield*, Mr Micawber, recognizing that happiness involves not spending all one's income, said 'Annual income twenty pounds, annual expenditure nineteen six, result happiness. Annual income twenty pounds, annual expenditure twenty pounds ought and six, result misery'. Mr Micawber's misery result could only come in a world where future expenditures and income were not known with certainty. In a classical world, Mr Micawber's dictum would be declared 'irrational' behavior.

[5] If the Euro was pegged to the dollar, would European support for President Bush's intervention in Iraq be different?

[6] An axiom is a doctrine that is accepted as a 'universal truth' for which no proof is required.

[7] I have explained why export-led growth is such an attractive option in Davidson (1996).

REFERENCES

Arrow, K.J. and Hahn, F.H. (1971), *General Competitive Analysis*, San Francisco, Holden-Day.

Clower, R.W. (1970), 'Foundations of Monetary Theory' in *Monetary Theory* edited by R.W. Clower, Baltimore, Penguin Books Inc.

Colander, D.C. and Landreth, H. (1996), *The Coming of Keynesianism to America*, Cheltenham, UK and Brookfield, USA, Edward Elgar.

Davidson, P. (1996), 'The General Theory in an Open Economy Context', in *A Second Edition of the General Theory*, vol. 2, edited by G.C. Harcourt and P. Riach (London, Routledge); reprinted in *Uncertainty, International Money, Employment and Theory* (vol. 3 of the Collected Writings of Paul Davidson) edited by Louise Davidson, (London, Macmillan, and New York. St. Martins Press).

Davidson, P. (2002), *Financial Markets Money and The Real World*, Cheltenham, UK and Northampton, USA, Edward Elgar Publishing.

Davidson, P. (2006), *Samuelson and the Keynes/Post Keynesian Revolution: The Evidence Showing Who Killed Cock Robin*.

Fischer, Stanley (2001), 'Exchange Rate Regimes: Is the Bipolar View Correct?', *Journal of Economic Perspectives*, 15, 3-24.

Hahn, F. H. (1973), *On the Nature of Equilibrium in Economics*, Cambridge, Cambridge University Press.

Hahn, F.H. (1997), 'Keynesian Economics and General Equilibrium Theory: Reflections on Current Debates', in *The Microeconomic Foundations of Macroeconomics*, edited by G.C. Harcourt, London, Macmillan.

Hicks, J.R. (1977), *Economic Perspectives*, Oxford, Oxford University Press.

Keynes, J.M. (1930), *A Treatise on Money*, Vol. 2, London, Macmillan.

Keynes, J.M. (1933), 'A Monetary Theory of Production', in *a Festschrift fur Arthur Spietoff*, reprinted in *The Collected Writings of John Maynard Keynes*, vol. 13, edited by D. Moggridge (1973), London, Macmillan. All references are to reprint.

Keynes, J.M. (1936), *The General Theory of Employment Interest and Money*, New York, Harcourt Brace.

Keynes, J.M. (1939), 'Professor Tinbergen's Method', *The Economic Journal*, September, reprinted in *The Collected Works of John Maynard Keynes*, Vol. 14, edited by D. Moggridge (1973), London, Macmillan. All references are to reprint.

Samuelson, P.A. (1970), 'Classical and Neoclassical Theory', in *Monetary Theory*, edited by R.W. Clower, Baltimore, Penguin Books Inc.

Weintraub, E.R. (2002), *How Economics Became a Mathematical Science*, Durham, Duke University Press.

9. Strategy, Innovation and Entrepreneurship: An Evolutionary Learning Perspective

Carl Henning Reschke and Sascha Kraus

INTRODUCTION

Strategy is a useful starting point for extending the reach of evolutionary learning approaches as it is directly related to issues in technical change, innovation and diffusion which also matter for and are interlinked with entrepreneurship. Moreover, evolutionary approaches have already been discussed before in relation to strategy (Barnett and Burgelman 1996; Lovas and Ghoshal 2000; Rumelt 1991; Van de Ven and Garud 1994). Furthermore, evolutionary concepts and frameworks offer a potential approach to integrating elements and parts of these different approaches. Therefore, it can be argued to be characterized by conditions that allow application of evolutionary concepts.

In strategy and innovation, reality is standing on more shaky ground than in disciplines like engineering and (natural) sciences, where principles can be measured comparatively to form firmer benchmarks of quality. Communication and cognition play an important role in strategy and innovation. The process of strategy evolution is far more self-referential than in other areas of economic research (see for example Weick 1993). Therefore, the concepts developed in the fields of evolutionary economics and in the economics of technical change and innovation need to be extended to include these characteristics. In so far as strategy is related to other areas of social sciences such as, for example politics, culture and international management, it offers a further entry point for concepts developed in evolutionary economics.

We argue that social processes in organizations and between organizations can be captured and analyzed with an ecological-evolutionary framework based on perspectives from evolutionary economics, psychology and sociology. This framework posits the interaction between mental representations, actions, perception and feedback as an evolutionary learning process. The framework can be applied on a multitude of layers from capturing intra-organizational processes to industry evolution. This offers the advantages of parsimony and generality. Generality is balanced by openness to many theories and the need to adapt the framework to the requirements of each level. Therefore, our framework can be used to guide research on social processes as well as systems. One area where those processes are analyzed from various competing disciplines and perspectives is the field of strategies, which are closely linked with innovation and entrepreneurship. Thus the power and relevance of the framework can be evaluated here. On the micro-level of individual actors, strategy involves creativity, whereas it gives rise to a competitive evolutionary learning process on the macro-levels of groups of actors. Strategy, innovation and entrepreneurship are all based on the knowledge actors have gained from historical examples. Furthermore, it is a psychological, cognitive, sociological, political and economic phenomenon.

A TOUR D'HORIZON OF RELEVANT PERSPECTIVES

Strategy

Strategy is seen here as an evolutionary process of partly pre-planned action and re-action of (groups of) social actors, in situations characterized by an 'open future' in the sense of Popper, where novelty and emergent effects occur in social systems. Mintzberg (1994) has argued along the following lines: a realized strategy is the outcome of the interaction between an intended and an emergent strategy resulting from the tension between the deliberate (planned) strategy and the impact of environmental forces. Thus, we argue, strategy is based on a twofold interacting approach, namely (1) a process of probing, experimentation and learning which leads to the conception of a vision of how the future will unfold, and (2) the implementation of a plan to realize a purpose or goal, by means of resources and capabilities under possibly changing conditions, which offer opportunities and constraints[1] for the attainment of the goal and the implementation of the measures. To a certain degree, this may involve changes in strategy as original goals may prove unattainable. It certainly involves learning on what to do and how to do it. Strategy can be conceived as the outcome of actions in response to changing requirements directed by a vision – which maps into Mintzberg's view of strategy.

Thus, there is a certain similarity to the conceptions in (evolutionary) game theory in that equivalents to 'states of the world', 'pay-off structures' and 'behavioural strategies' are dealt with. However, it is also assumed that the elements of strategic interactions occur and evolve as the 'strategic players' go along, rendering the process of strategy-making more open than amenable to the definitional 'closure' of game theory 'worlds'. In Mintzberg's worlds game theory would describe the deliberate, planned and intended strategies, while the residual between our view and game theory's view on strategy is the equivalent to Mintzberg's emergent strategy.

Strategy research has often though not always focussed on the connections between the elements of strategy, structure and performance (see for example Chandler 1962; Rumelt 1974). This approach has been criticized because of the limited causal proof of the links between the elements (see for example Miller 1979). Thus Rumelt (1991) has called for an evolutionary approach to the analysis of the development of industries. If such an analysis is not to stay on phenomenological levels just 'correlating' changes in several areas, a causal micro-story of how strategy comes about and how this links into the development of larger patterns is needed These larger patterns are the prime focus of this chapter; how they can be based on a causal micro-story is shown in a cursory fashion.[2]

In contrast, Grant claims that a transfer of evolutionary principles to human strategy processes is not useful. He argues that competitive processes in biological systems and economics differ, since human actors can anticipate actions (Grant 1991). We argue that there is modeling-wise not a sufficiently large difference to justify a rejection of evolutionary processes. Both evolutionary processes and human learning are structurally similar if seen over several biological generations and several 'rounds' of human interaction, because human actions are usually varied, anticipation is limited and recedes in relative importance over longer time frames. Mutations and human hypotheses are hypotheses which are tested in their respective environments. Interestingly, Grant (1991) accepts a 'derivation' of strategy as a process of differentiation and discovering of niches, quoting an ecologic analogy to strategy by Henderson (1989). Complexity and uncertainty lead to imitation in economic actors, such as enterprises (Alchian 1950), which results in similar strategies and actions. This suggests searching for similar patterns and processes in the evolution of economic entities.

Evolution

Strategy research is often based on the theoretical perspective of neo-classical micro-economics, assuming rational utility-maximizing actors. An evolutionary perspective to strategy needs to be built on (a modification of) evolutionary economics based on a cognitive perspective (Reschke 2001, 2005).

Evolutionary economics aims to analyze particularly the developmental, dynamic aspect of economic processes based on a framework of evolutionary processes and assumes myopic, error-prone but learning, satisficing actors influenced by traditions, habits and norms (see for example Veblen 1898; Nelson and Winter 1982). Evolutionary economics differs from mainstream economics by its focus on cultural, organizational and institutional contexts and endogenous factors of change. With respect to variation, evolutionary economics is largely characterized by an effort to transfer the concept of *random* variation to social systems, based for example on Campbell's (1960) conception of evolutionary epistemology as a process of variation, selection, and retention of knowledge. With respect to actors it is largely characterized by Nelson and Winter's (1982) claim to offer a *Lamarckian* theory of economic evolution. Both conceptualizations are somewhat at odds. We argue that this contradiction can be resolved on the basis of an evolutionary economics that is based on systemic evolutionary epistemology (Riedl 2000). This school argues that constraints imposed by the existing system matter in the generation of variation, such that changes in a given system are only possible if they match into the existing configuration of the system, which leads to largely local variation. The same should be true for social systems.

Evolutionary Biology

The Neo-Darwinian synthesis (NDS) is based on the assumption of undirected, random mutation on the genetic level, while systemic evolutionists argue that change is not completely random but constrained, if not 'directed' by the existing structural make-up (on the genetic and morphological level) of organisms and its limited freedom for change (for an overview of these issues see Riedl (1990 [1975])) or Maynard Smith and Szathmary (1995) who argue coming from a mainstream biology point of view). NDS models can explain processes of differentiation (speciation) through random variation (by mutation) and selection (by competition and fit). These types of models have trouble with analyzing and explaining system-transforming, structural changes. Conceptually this leads to the postulation of emergence (see for example Lorenz 1973; Mayr 1989). The NDS model therefore probably does not constitute a sufficiently rich structure for explaining creative and social – possibly evolutionary – processes.

The distinctive focus of the systemic evolutionary school is about selection processes internal to the organism (Riedl 1990 [1975]), the relevance of functional interaction of (organic) systems and their parts for the evolution of adaptations (Hass 1970). A prevalent characteristic of systemic evolutionary biology is the trial to deal with feedback effects from 'the environment' on the medium that carries information over generations. These feedback effects are obvious in social systems but are usually rejected in evolutionary biology, with some notable exceptions (see for example Riedl 1990 [1975]; Wagner 1983). To prevent misunderstandings, it should be noted that they do not argue for a Lamarckian theory of evolution, but for a feedback effect on the level of the population via successfully selected structures, which are built up cumulatively and the effect this has on further selection. Systemic evolutionary theory therefore does not reject standard NDS theory, but rather claims the NDS theory needs to be extended.

Psychology

Reschke (2005) proposes using mental representations from personaling construct theory (Kelly 1955) as equivalent to the role of the genotype and routines as the translation apparatus between the mental and real world. Eden has developed a particular version of Kelly's concept and methodology applied to strategy (see for example Eden et al. 1992). Here is not the place to discuss the intricacies of variants of the general approach. Fiol and Huff (1992) provide an overview and discussion of several of the approaches to integrating mental representations and research on strategy.

Mental representations are concepts, which actors use to structure their environment in cognitive maps. These can be measured and compared to the structure of reality and action of actors. This is the basis for a 'systemic' evolutionary concept of selecting and characteristics-changing feedback between the perception of actors on the one hand and reality on the other. Perception of actors guides actions and results affect perception in a later time interval. Thus evolution in social systems is a type of learning process, where mental representations are updated and selected based on experience of actors. Experience involves the perception of 'feedback' effects from the environment. Schlicht (1997) as well as Kubon-Gilke and Schlicht (1998) suggest, based on systemic evolutionary theory and gestalt psychology, that human psychological characteristics lead to a process of local search and improvement in behaviour, which leads to a process of patterned variation instead of a random distribution of variation (as assumed in standard evolutionary biology). This is indirectly confirmed by Silverberg and Verspagen (2003), who claim that variation in innovations is ordered a bit more than a Poisson distribution. Similar, patterns variation can be observed on the level of industries in industry development (see for example Klepper 1997) which is discussed in the fourth section.

ENTREPRENEURSHIP AND INNOVATION

Innovation and entrepreneurship cannot be separated cleanly, as innovation involves acts of entrepreneurial behavior as well as an entrepreneurial mindset, while entrepreneurship is often concerned with bringing new ideas, services and products to an economic market or social arena where they compete for attention and inclusion in existing systems.

Entrepreneurship

According to Schumpeter, the entrepreneur is characterized by a vision of how the future will unfold. His role lies in the combination of some or all of the following elements: ideas, technologies, services, people, knowledge, to form a workable product and organization selling it. In the 'Theory of Economic Development' (1993 [1934]), written before WWI and translated into English afterwards, Schumpeter analyzes the function of the entrepreneur in economic change. Entrepreneurs further innovation as new combinations of (sometimes new) elements that lead to the 'competitive elimination of the old' (Schumpeter 1993 [1934], 66-7). Entrepreneurs perceive opportunities, combine ideas, resources, and production factors into new products and entrepreneurial ventures that, if successful, lead to innovations and the creative destruction of established enterprises and industries. Schumpeter (1993 [1934], 66) distinguishes between five cases of innovation:

(1) the introduction of a new good,
(2) the introduction of a new method of production,
(3) the opening of a new market,
(4) the opening of a new source of supply, and
(5) the organization of a new organization of any industry.

The last 15 years have provided the prevalent insight that entrepreneurship is one of the most important driving factors of economy and society of every modern nation (Brock and Evans 1989; Carree and Thurik 2000; OECD 2002). In these days, entrepreneurship is considered as the tool to cope with the new competitive landscape and its enormous speed of changes (Hitt & Reed 2000).

The word 'entrepreneurship' is derived from the French 'entreprendre' which can be translated by 'to undertake' or 'to take in one's own hands' (Schaper and Volery 2004, 4). The real entrepreneurial work is about bringing new ideas into actual ventures that exploit market opportunities by better serving the customers' needs The entrepreneur does not necessarily have to be the inventor of the new product, service, or business – but he is the one introducing this innovation to the market place. An entrepreneur is thus somebody who takes something (for example an opportunity or a business venture) in his own hands, at his own risk (Brazeal and Herbert 1999).

A powerful movement of academic entrepreneurship research emerged from this (Kuratko 2003). However, entrepreneurship is not necessarily just about new ventures or start-ups. It can also be found in existing small and medium-sized enterprises (SME), large companies, or in the public sector. Organizations regardless of type and size are required to be innovative and entrepreneurial in order to survive in these days. Nevertheless, the fact that small firms and start-ups build the majority of enterprises throughout the world has drawn attention to the academic field of entrepreneurship especially in the last decade. All of today's successful businesses exist because of the entrepreneurial endeavours of yesterday's founders.

Thus, entrepreneurial behaviour is not just possible in new ventures or SME, but also in established/larger organizations. Entrepreneurial managers seek new technology, products, services, or business models inside an organization. The terms 'intrapreneurship' or 'corporate entrepreneurship' apply synonymously. An intrapreneur is somebody working from within an organization (and being on its payroll), but in an entrepreneurial way, having an entrepreneurial mindset including adventuring himself of being creative and innovative; in short: daring new ideas or procedures. Entrepreneurial behaviour inside an organization requires an internal culture encouraging innovation and entrepreneurial activities (Douglas 2001). An entrepreneurial mindset and the search for high potential opportunities is required for firms to compete successfully in the new competitive landscape of uncertain business environments (Hitt et al. 2002). All in all, entrepreneurship can be described as the commercialisation of innovations.

Innovations are thus central to the concept of entrepreneurship, lying at its very heart. Innovations are based on creativity leading to an insight or invention. According to some authors, an innovation can be described as the 'successful implementation of creative ideas within an organisation' (Schaper and Volery 2004, 5). An innovation is thus more than just a good idea, it also has to be a potential problem-solver that fills the customers' needs and wants, at the speed the market demands (Kuratko and Hodgetts 2004). Hence, an innovation is the turning of an invention into a marketable product or service (Ellyard 2001). Only those innovations that create or add value for their buyer can become a competitive advantage for the company and thus allow significant profit and growth potential (Timmons 2004). In order to survive, an enterprise has to be at least as innovative as its competition (MacKenzie 2001).

Creativity forms the foundation of innovation, which forms the foundation for entrepreneurship. Innovations originate from ideas, which are the results of creative thinking of employees, customers, suppliers, or others (Boeddrich 2004). Creativity and innovation can therefore be regarded as the key ingredients for entrepreneurial work. Obviously innovation is not always the one and only prerequisite for entrepreneurship. There is no doubt that there are numerous ventures worldwide which cannot really be described as innovative, but that are nevertheless successful. Thus creativity and innovation are without a doubt usually positively related to entrepreneurship, and will in consequence be valuable for the promotion of entrepreneurial endeavour. This relation can be shown in Figure 9.1:

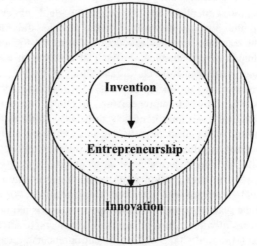

Source: Own illustration.

Figure 9.1: Layers of Entrepreneurship

The relation between invention, which involves creativity, and entrepreneurship, which is one (major) element in the process of innovation, needs to be discussed in more depth than is possible here. However, it can be stated that entrepreneurship and innovation are referring to processes that run partly parallel and are partly interlinked, and can thus be regarded as two sides of the same coin. Both concepts are equal as far as promoting and accepting something novel is concerned. Entrepreneurship is about identifying the relevant markets and framing the product in a form that is acceptable by market participants. Innovation is about similar activities, although the focus on the market is less strong and can be concerned with adaptation and adoption of novel methods, products and the like in any social setting. Likewise, innovation with specific market focus needs to be carried out also by managers in large organizations. Lately, this is often labelled as 'intrapreneurship' in the management literature.

Creativity is about destruction in the Schumpeterian sense (Schumpeter 1993 [1934]), the rejection of established methods, assumptions or precepts and construction of a new beginning (Morris and Kuratko 2002; Gettler 2003). Being creative always requires the ability to broaden your horizon, destroy the old, and create the new in your mind. Creativity is 'the ability to develop new ideas and to discover new ways of looking at problems and opportunities' (Zimmerer and Scarborough 2002, 37). Morris and Kuratko describe creativity as 'the ability to relate or connect, to put things together in a novel way' and as 'the capacity to develop new ideas, concepts, and processes' (2002, 104). In short, creativity is 'what makes something better or new' (DeGraff and Lawrence 2002, 2). Creative ideas are not only novel, but also valuable (Sternberg et al. 2004). Thus, creativity in itself is of little value for an organisation. It needs to be turned into innovation in order to be beneficial. As we see, innovation cannot exist without any form of creativity. In consequence, creativity and innovation often build the foundation of a company's ability to compete successfully (Zimmerer and Scarborough 2002). Therefore, companies have to become more responsive and flexible to be able to react quickly in rapidly changing environments (Mauzy and Harriman 2003). The basis for this is creativity. Accordingly, strategy, innovation, and entrepreneurship are all fuelled to some degree by creativity, trial-and-error (Campbell 1960) and learning by doing (Arrow 1962), and can therefore all be seen as examples of an interlinked learning process.

LINKING MICRO AND MACRO THROUGH SOCIAL EVOLUTION

The Evolutionary Learning Process

As we have seen in the preceding section, differing perspectives are at the root of creativity, innovation and strategy. Ultimately, this spills over into economic competition. The systemic evolutionary perspective links to punctuated equilibrium, respectively predicts such patterns. In addition to technological developments, industry development shows patterns that seem to conform to this expectation. This will be discussed in the fourth section. But first, we focus on linking perception to evolution.

A true evolutionary account of social phenomena requires the researcher to juxtapose the perception of actors with its effects in the real world over longer periods. Perception could play an analogous role to the biological genotype while the role of the phenotype is taken by artefacts, designs and documents. Such a conceptualization allows capturing the perception of an actor in a cognitive architecture, based on dichotomous separation between the defining characteristics of concept.

Usually routines (Nelson and Winter 1982) are seen as an organizational analogue to biological replicators (genes). In Reschke (2005a) it is argued that this view is problematic. Rather, mental representations are to be seen as analogues to biological replicators and routines are to be seen as having a transmission function between replicators and interactors, for example human actors. The application of the systemic evolutionary approach on the organizational level is discussed more deeply in Reschke (2005d). In general, it is assumed that the development of social evolutionary processes depends on the perceived characteristics, their interpretations and associated actions. Perceived characteristics depend on the individual elements of mental representations and the structure of cognitive maps. Structurally, the process looks like this:

(9.1.) $MR//CM^t \rightarrow p_x^t \rightarrow D/A \rightarrow p_x^{t+1} \rightarrow MR//CM^{t+1}$
with
MR: mental representation,
CM: cognitive map
p: perception,
D / A: decision or action.
$MR // CM$: mental representation given a certain cognitive map

Thus social evolution is – much like biological evolution – a process of learning where pieces of information and their links to other pieces of information are updated to form a network of knowledge. The process of knowledge growth is based on the interaction of hypotheses and the real world (see Riedl 1990 [1975], 2000). In the course of social evolution, a population of entities is (perceived to be) associated with certain characteristics, which leads to decisions and actions. This affects the population of entities in terms of types of entities and the set of characteristics they comprise, as well as the perceptions of actors. So there are feedback effects from perception to entities that make up a population, the characteristics these entities possess and the decisions/actions that actors take. In turn, decisions/actions affect the population of entities and actors. In the formula (9.1.) actions can be seen as elements of a cybernetic, signals-based concept of communication as espoused by Luhmann (1995). Communication affects mental representations – possibly without the need to transform mental representations into real world actions – and could in the above equation thus take the role of decisions or actions, or play an 'orthogonal' role to the latter. However, that is a story for another paper.

A Model for Social Evolution

The same type of reasoning can be applied to evolutionary processes in populations of organizations that possess and change certain characteristics which are relevant to competition and strategy-making. The evolutionary learning process can be captured by the model type used in population ecology (Hannan and Freeman 1989). The framework presented in this section is based on Pistorius and Utterback's (1997) transfer of the population ecology approach to technology interactions. It provides a formalization of the relationships and effects that should occur, given an evolutionary view of strategic processes in industry development. The link between strategy and industry patterns is provided by the beta parameter, which describes interaction between actors that also require similar resources as competing actors or provide needed resources for 'symbiotic' actors.

A population p of for example strategy elements, products, technologies or organisational (sub-) systems i is defined by a set of objects (or processes) O with particular technical, social and economic characteristics c of value x:

(9.2.) $\qquad p_i := \{O_i\{c_{xi}\}\},$

where x identifies the relevant characteristics for an issue. Which characteristics are relevant is the starting point for strategic thinking and the formulation of goals. Therefore the specific issue at hand and the formulation of goals determines how populations of products and organizations are to be delimited. The differing views of young and established companies are often the basis for an attacker's advantage and the realization of disruptive innovations (Christensen 2004).

The development of a population over time depends on the number of individuals n_i in the preceding period and the statistic distribution D of relevant characteristics c_x:

(9.3.) $\quad p_i^{t+1}\big(D_{\mu,\sigma}^{t+1}(c_{xi}^{t+1}), n_i^{t+1}\big) = p_i^t\big(D_{\mu,\sigma}^t(c_{xi}^t), n_i^t\big) + \Delta_i^{t \to t+1}(D, c, n),$

with $\Delta_i^{t \to t+1}$ as change operator, which affects the distribution and emergence of characteristics and the population size. We assume that the variance of characteristics fluctuates depending on technical progress, intensity of competition, fashions, and managerial and societal attention to issues. Breakthroughs in research allow the application of new technologies and the development of new products. Societal and political acceptance is often important too, as the example of 'gene-manipulated' food shows. The intensity of competition can have a negative or positive influence on the development of products and technologies. It may stimulate competing enterprises to develop countermeasures on the same level or force them to retreat. If one considers the perception of consumers and purchasers, the model structure allows reflecting competition on the basis of technical quality and marketing/differentiation measures. Even though technical characteristics are similar, social characteristics may be (perceived) to be widely differing.

Strategies are based on the artful combination of these variables and adaptation to changing requirements.

Based on the literature on economic and social change (Pistorius and Utterback 1993; Hannan and Freeman 1989), we assume that the population size n_i follows a logistic Lotka-Volterra system:

$$(9.4.) \qquad n_i^{t+1} = n_i^t + r_i * n_i^t \left(1 - \frac{n_i^t}{k_i^t}\right),$$

where k refers to the carrying capacity (measured in terms of sales or application numbers) of a social system for products, organisations or technologies i in a period t.

Carrying capacity k is variable over time and depends on social acceptance, competition by substitutes, image and marketing expenditure.

Competition can be described as follows:

$$(9.5.) \qquad n_i^{t+1} = n_i^t + r_i * n_i^t \left(1 - (\frac{n_i^t}{k_i^t} - \Sigma_{j \neq i}^J \beta_{ij}^t n_j^t)\right),$$

where $\beta_{ij}^t n_j^t$ describes the effects of the interaction between product i and one or more other products j on the carrying capacity for i.

Considering the effects and evolution of 'Weltbilder' in actors, the statements about the principal possibilities of evolution of such a system can be compared to the environment (as it is perceived by actors), which allows the identification hidden elements of their strategies and potential points of attack. This is particularly relevant in newly emerging business fields and situations of change where no clear 'models' of how to act and how to interpret the world exist. Extending the model towards the potential development of actors allow it to be connected to the evolution of industries (Klepper 1997; McGahan 2000). Applying the model structure on the organizational level allows integrating competitive analysis as described above to change processes and performance measurement (see Reschke 2005d).

APPLICATION OF SOCIAL EVOLUTION TO STRATEGY

Industry Evolution

The model structure described above should give rise to specific patterns, depending on the values the variables take. We argue in the following that the universe of possible values can be restricted by identifying patterns in the history of industries. Systemic evolutionary theory can be linked to patterns of punctuated equilibrium (Riedl 1990 [1975], Crutchfield and Nimwegen 1999). Given the argument of Schlicht (1997) that psychological characteristics lead to channelling, and constrained patterns of variation in human action and decision-making, we should expect similar patterns not only in innovations (see Reschke 2005c), but also on the next-higher level involving the commercialization of innovations, namely in industrial development. The framework of industry evolution laid out here combines standard neoclassical and Schumpeterian or evolutionary perspectives on economics. It is based on concepts taken from economics and management and tries to fuse them into one coherent set of ideas that can account for phenomena on a variety of levels by supposedly similar mechanisms.

In the areas of innovation management and technical change, we have been influenced in developing this framework by the concept of dominant designs - developed by Utterback and Abernathy 1975; by Tushman and Anderson 1986; Anderson and Tushman 1990; by Schumpeter's (1993 [1934]) concept of creative destruction, the extension of Schumpeter's ideas in Andersen (1996).

The pattern of industry evolution is based on observations taken from the already mentioned population ecology perspective (Hannan, Freeman, Carroll) and especially the community perspective (Astley 1985; Barnett 1990). This has been complemented by research on industry life cycle patterns in economics (Klepper 1997). In partial refutation of the population ecology perspective, we are of the opinion that legitimation is only a proxy for more basic processes going in the evolution of an industrial system. Legitimation is important with regard to consumer perception of the viability and usefulness of products as described below. In fact these are factors that depend on the match of the new product and its producing industry in existing political, social and legal institutions, and economic and especially cultural structures.

Another important building block is the concept of the product evolutionary cycle developed in the marketing literature that indicates that the product life cycle hypothesis is valid for only a subset of industries (Tellis and Crawford 1981; Hunt 1997). It generally claims that only the early and late stages of the product life cycle are correct descriptions of reality, while the others are subject to the influence of economic variables and managerial discretion. This is extended in the later article to general contentions on market evolution processes.

Generally, we claim that this framework allows combining neoclassical and Schumpeterian perspectives on industry evolution, in which both are special cases of a general evolutionary framework. The evolution of an industry over time is governed by six differing change operators that describe six different regimes. This is in contrast to Andersen (1996), who identifies three change operators based on an extension of Schumpeter (1987 [1942]) and Anderson and Tushman (1990) who identify two regimes of change. The analysis of patterns in the form of two aggregates reduces a far more complex pattern consisting of qualitatively different subregimes. This leads to confusion and invalid theoretical predictions in economic theory respectively practical prescriptions in the management area.

A Framework of Industrial Development

The logic of the application of the evolutionary approach to strategies and historical developments – integrating modern and postmodern perspectives – is discussed further in Reschke (2005b).

Subsequently we describe a generic model that is meant to work as a baseline model for patterns in industry evolution. It is separated into six different stages of change operators. In the description below we will focus mainly on the number of firms in the different stages – in keeping with the population perspective. It should be noted, though, that this is only one facet and another important variable is the volume of products actually sold.

The *first stage* describes the inception of a new industry with a wide variety of production approaches and product characteristics. Product competition does not play a decisive role, because demand limitations do not matter greatly. Resource constraints are important with respect to funding and human resources, for instance. The interaction between the different producers is assumed to be mutualistic, since the product or product system still has to gain legitimacy in the eyes of consumers. This justifies the focus of population ecology on legitimation issues. This variable is also of overwhelming importance in obtaining funds from banks or venture capitalists. The same is true for attracting capable personnel. A minimum of secure perspectives for the future is required even for the most entrepreneurial minded employee. These limitations pose difficulties for all new enterprises in an emerging industry and lead to a slow initial development of the number of firms. Firms produce according to widely differing specifications. Consumers can choose from a variety of design approaches and product characteristics. Once the initial difficulties have been overcome, the number of industry participants should start to rise with an accelerating pace. Basically the process can be described by a logistic equation as for example in diffusion processes. Both increase and rate of increase in the number of firms are positive. We would want to call this first regime mutualistic inception.

We would locate the transition to the *second stage* of industry development at the point where the increase in the number of firms in an industry starts to decline. Perceived or real limitations on resources and demand slow down entrepreneurial founding activities. Exit rates of firms should increase due to increasing competition among competing design alternatives. The product/system has gained basic legitimation and focus shifts towards competition between different solutions. The beginning limits of carrying capacity for the number of firms and different approaches promoted by them are to be felt. This stage might be called mutualistic competition to account for the dichotomous character of competition under high degrees of variety.

The *third stage* is characterized by the emergence of stable product characteristics, an industry wide dominant design, or a small number of these for different subsets of application areas as a process of lock-in (Arthur 1988). This shift marks the switch from the resource-abundant regime to the more competitive, limited one. It means that the carrying capacity for non-dominant design solutions goes towards zero, resulting in a shakeout. These may survive as specialty niche producers but need not necessarily. The 'dominant design'[3] need not be the direct cause of the shakeout. The research of Klepper and Simmons (1997) and suggests that it might be associated more with production technology and organization matters. Furthermore they throw doubts on the distribution of product versus process innovation over time. In any case the legitimation of dominant design products/producers increases, the carrying capacity is likely to increase and thus also the overall volume of production sold. This stage could be called competitive destruction or competitive selection.

The *fourth stage* is characterized by the competitive processes after the dominant design has emerged This implies a greatly reduced number of competitors. The volume of production for each of these may increase over time. The particular development of firm numbers and production volume depends on the particular circumstances of demand and competitive manoeuvring in this stage and the influence of institutional factors on the development of carrying capacity. The number of competitors is more likely to decrease than to increase – apart from small volume specialty producers. This stage is most accurately described by the concepts of the literature on industrial organization – product differentiation, advertising wars, increasing concentration. It is the economic period which most closely resembles the concepts of mainstream economics. Concentration is likely to increase; advertising wars and product differentiation prevail as most important strategic measures. This stage could be called the mainstream stage. In terms of innovation management and technical change literature this can be described as the regime of incremental change.

The *fifth stage* is characterized by the emergence of a second, new industry which interacts with the first one, now definitely mature. It is related to the processes of niche opening and demise of paradigms. According to Andersen (1996) and Schumpeter (1993 [1934]) this leads to the 'tail' and possibly also to an increase in production volume in the manner observed by Klepper (1997) and Barnett (1997). Andersen and Schumpeter argue that the new industry's product increases the demand for the old industry's product. They use the example of railroad transport increasing the demand for short-distance travel and horse carriages. This would in sum be a symbiotic relationship. We propose to call this regime competitive interaction.

The *sixth stage* is characterized by competition between the first traditional and the second newly emerged industry. Their relationship takes a predator-prey character in the terminology of ecology. The old industry is likely to decline sharply in this stage either in absolute terms or at least in relative economic importance. The new industry is – depending on its precise circumstances – to be found in stages one to three, though we would judge stage two to be the most likely case. This interaction between new and old industries describes what can be truly labelled creative destruction.

It has to be noted that the first two stages and the last two stages overlap for the case where an old and new industry exist at the same time. Thus the number of different stages reduces to three, if a succession of 'dominant designs' is observed while there are no new entrants in the concerned industries. It has to be noted as well that there are cases deviating from the patterns described above particularly in science-based industries and complex products. There are obviously several issues that could be discussed in more depth. The view does not cover all possible patterns of industry development (see particularly Klepper 1996, 1997; Klepper and Simmons 1997; McGahan 2000). Possibly innovation diffusion curves and product life 'cycles' (for example Lambkin and Day 1989), and technology cycles (Anderson and Tushman 1986; Anderson and Tushman 1990) have effects on industry development that need to be discussed and modelled more explicitly.

Strategic Management

Strategic management is connected inseparably to change and develops concepts to create competitive advantage and to control the enterprise in the long run. This has led to a transfer of concepts from non-linear systems theory to management issues. For instance, Downs et al. (2002) and Stacey (1993) describe organizations as complex adaptive systems which are most creative and function best when they are located at the border of chaos. In rapidly changing environments, survival and success depend on the ability to adapt quickly. This ability of enterprises is strongly determined by top-management's institution of conditions and boundaries for strategy formulation and implementation (Sachs 2002). Strategic management can favour dynamic, open structures. Strategy is a learning process that is characterized by interdependent links, similar to the chain-linked model of Kline and Rosenberg (1986). Since it is a learning process, it integrates with the evolutionary approach/point of view. Evolutionary strategic management results from:

- high degrees of novelty,
- open-ended processes of change,
- emergence of new structures, or
- if the right structure develops only during processes of change,
- if there are high degrees of openness and many lateral relations in the organisation.

Strategic management is based on interdependent internal and external success and control factors (Baaij 1996). The internal rate of evolution in an enterprise depends on the number of product variations and new products in a given period. This number depends on processes of adaptive learning, performance and feedback processes from the product markets. Obviously, it is important that an enterprise does not rest on its successes, but adapts its activities, knowledge base and resources to external and internal requirements. In the long run strategy can be seen as a learning process which results in strategic initiatives or inertia (Miller and Friesen 1980), dependent on the 'Weltbild' of its actors, particularly the top management. An evolutionary approach to strategic management sees the procedure as a circular process of creation, selection and implementation of ideas and actions based on the elements of strategy-making shown in Figure 9.2.

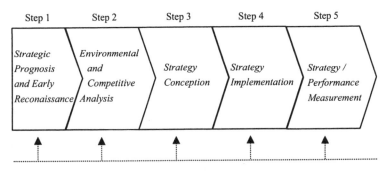

Systemic Evolutionary Learning

Source: Model based on Kline and Rosenberg (1986).

Figure 9.2: An Evolutionary Approach to Strategic Management

This sequence and delineation of process steps is to be seen as a first approximation. The underlying reality is more difficult to describe in a solely linear fashion because it is highly interlinked, which has been discussed with respect to innovation processes and management already before (Kline and Rosenberg 1986). Consequently, management must not try to implement too strict linear models and programs of action in the exploration phase. It also needs to consider the need for adaptation and further learning that needs to be allowed in the exploitation phase of business opportunities however seductive easy step-by-step routines may seem. This advice presumes a certain minimum level of cognitive competence and ability to make value judgements in the workforce. These capabilities might be more easily found in research and development, as well as strategic planning departments. However, the answer is clear: if you want the possibility of adaptation, you need to school your workforce accordingly, which is costly and may be better done by society – which forms a case for public education in general and cognitive abilities.

(1)   *Strategic Prognosis and Early Reconaissance:* The evolutionary learning approach can add value to strategic prognosis and early reconnaissance by creating a frame for putting observations about competitors' actions and environmental changes into a coherent framework and emphasizing variation which can lead to changes relevant for the enterprise. Thus effects of changes can be better identified and evaluated.

(2)   *Environmental and Competitive Analysis:* Competitive analysis, as a dynamic comparison of the position of a company relative to its competitors, can be based on the population ecology approach which serves either as a mental framework for orientation or, given enough data, as a basis for the formalization via Lotka-Volterra type models. This then suggests integration with financial and controlling data and combination with balanced scorecard approaches (Kaplan and Norton 1992) used in the performance measurement step below. The effects of cultural values and economic demand both make up what has been covered by the concept of carrying capacity. This offers a possibility to overcome the barriers of disciplinary focus on either side in sociology and economics. For instance, it can capture and integrate changes accumulating behind the mask of either demand or changes in values favouring or disfavouring products, technologies and services. For the area of environmental analysis dealing with the legal framework, institutions and culture, a dynamic analysis is possible on the basis of established methods in evolutionary and institutional economics. The situation of the company situation depends on its resources, (dynamic) capabilities, and core competences (Wernerfelt 1984; Hamel and Prahalad 1994). The analysis of strengths and weaknesses, opportunities and threats (SWOT) amounts to a

profile of the company versus the 'requirements' of the environment, which both underlie change in a nonlinear and evolutionary way.

(3)   *Strategy Conception:* Strategy is based on the development of a vision of the future and the company's role in it. This necessarily includes interactions between actors and environmental conditions as well as the change resulting from it. The vision is to help the organization develop a sustainable and advantageous position in competition with other actors under possibly radically changing conditions. Strategy conception requires input from competitive analysis, the results of prognosis exercises and feedback from the implementation and performance measurement steps in order to assess the feasibility and practicality of a strategy concept as well as to change the concept accordingly if need be.

(4)   *Strategy Implementation:* To implement the strategic conception, the organization and its members often need to be persuaded and empowered to reach the goals. On the other hand, implementation also has to be supervised and adapted to changing environmental conditions.

(5)   *Strategy/Performance Measurement:* The implementation of a strategy needs to be measured in order to provide feedback to the employees and managers about their situation. The model outlined above can be used to structure and evaluate competitive actions as well as product and organizational characteristics against the measurement standards developed for a strategy (Kaplan and Norton 1992).

STRATEGY, GLOBALIZATION, POLITICS AND EVOLUTION

There are further areas where strategy and evolutionary perspectives can complement each other. For instance the definition of economic sub-populations based on (perceived) characteristics allows integration with the strategic group (see for example Cool and Dierickx 1993; Reger and Huff 1993) and configuration (see for example Miller 1979) research streams. The research and particularly the results flowing from those endeavours may be employed in politics and management productively. Dealing with uncertainty, complexity and the search for novelty are becoming increasingly important. At the same time, it is widely acknowledged that the linear and mechanistic extrapolations of the 1960s and 1970s are of less importance in a world of evolutionary dynamic change, particularly with respect to managing and dealing with entrepreneurial ventures (Kraus and Reschke 2004). Positioning advice and value chain analysis (Porter 1980, 1985), re-engineering (Hammer and Champy 1993) and 'learning' perspectives (Hamel and Prahalad 1994) may be a short-term help to managers facing new competitors, new technologies and cost pressures, but do not convey information on where to go and how to get there in dynamic, uncertain environments that nevertheless seem to follow historic patterns.

Economies of scale and scope favor globalization of business activities. At the same time resistance to what is seen as cultural domination by the western world and large companies increases (Castells 1996-1998; Kingsnorth 2003). This poses a problem for strategy and innovation on a global scale. Similarly, innovative projects are often rejected in their home organizations and countries. It seems that the two 'forces' of economic innovation associated with globalization and cultural identity are irreconcilable at first sight. Paraphrasing Adam Smith (1998 [1776]), the reach of economic forces towards globalization is only limited by the extent of the market. This gives rise to a question of judgement where to limit the reach of the market which ultimately depends on value judgements. Accordingly, Smith had also put emphasis on the importance of moral values in his 'Theory of Moral Sentiments' (Smith 1998 [1759]). Similarly, List (1841, arguing against Ricardo), and Veblen (1899) emphasized the role of cultural differences in economic theory and practice. This tension is re-entering the political and strategic management scene with the downfall of economic barriers after the end of the 'cold war' and economic opportunities due to new technologies.

Cultural and social systems themselves are subject to a tension between integration and disintegration. Thus, the tension between economic 'global homogenization' and 'cultural differentiation' as well as the antagonism between cultural stability and innovative change reflects a fundamental conflict at the basis of both small social systems and large societies which applies to differing cultural and innovating systems. This same tension has accompanied the emergence of modern societies. Various theoretical systems have been developed in sociology to deal with aspects of the question, for example Simmel, Parsons, and lately Luhmann, Beck, Giddens and Habermas. Thus, managing economic units as well as global businesses requires balancing forces between homogenization and differentiation. Or to rephrase the issue: the management of the trade-off between integration and variety (for example cultural responsiveness) can be informed by an evolutionary account of how social systems unfold.

The contrasting tendencies for individual as well as social differentiation and integration can be explained on the basis of different theories of human and social systems' characteristics (for example Miller 2000: Luhmann 1995). The tension of differentiation versus homogenization and maintenance of social order or integration thus seems to be a driving force at the basis of our life-world. Taking a larger perspective, one can argue that also social processes show evolutionary characteristics. A similar argumentation structure as in sociological systemic theories can be found in systemic evolutionary theories (see for example Riedl 1990 [1975]). The emergence of stable 'structures' requires a balance between traditional structures and variation. Analogous arguments can be made on the basis of psychological gestalt theory and cognitive perspectives for social and economic systems (Schlicht 1997; Reschke 2005). A systemic evolutionary theory of economic processes may thus be able to better deal with the tension between homogenization and diversity than neoclassical economics alone. This theory can be used to inform strategy and management practice.

CONCLUSION

This chapter shows that an evolutionary view on strategic issues from relevant areas can be used for the integration of traditional perspectives. As we have shown in this chapter, evolutionary viewpoints promise to add value to all relevant steps of strategic management, beginning from entrepreneurship and innovation over environmental and competitor analysis, strategy development and implementation towards strategy/performance measurement and control to globalization. Such evolutionary viewpoints open room for a wide field of new problems and approaches. The evolutionary view of strategy described in this chapter links to the results of existing schools of strategy, integrating them and emphasizing the dynamic and long-term aspects. Strategy-making thus involves a learning process about where the enterprise fits into its current environment and where it needs to adapt (see for example Lewin and Volberda 2003), and how this situation can be changed in favour of the enterprise. This involves design and execution as well as process and learning perspectives. Strategy-making is the task to develop and implement a vision and the steps necessary to achieve it, to protect it and to adapt it to changing conditions in the long run. In environments that exhibit certain degrees of stability, short-term optimization and constant reorientation are usually inferior to long-term adaptation on the basis of a strategy which is stable but flexible.

In addition, goals and strategies inevitably differ from enterprise to enterprise. Hence it follows that also the necessary measures and methods must be different. New ventures on the basis of new technologies, product ideas and business models in young, growing markets offer the opportunity to develop into a successful and growing enterprise. The identification, development and protection of niche opportunities should be regarded as the strategic goal of small and young enterprises. The strategy goal of larger and/or established enterprises should on the other hand be oriented at the protection of these market niches, while these larger companies may be interested in 'conquering' other markets at the same time. To describe such processes, models and concepts from ecology and evolution theory seem useful.

Ecology and evolution offer theories and tools that have been developed to precisely analyze such situations of change. Therefore they also offer a foundation for scenario analysis, planning, competitive analysis and strategic advice in changing business situations in an integrated, quantitative framework. This framework is based on psychological concepts which nevertheless allow linking the framework to more qualitative approaches. It gives the entrepreneurial strategist and the planners and managers in large enterprises a qualitative as well as quantifiable, flexible framework to deal with dialectics of strategic thinking in economic competition. Strategy researchers are provided with a framework that may resolve the conflicts about too little or too much paradigmatic freedom in the field of strategy by integrating the different perspectives and giving them a place in larger picture. This situation calls for integrating theoretical perspectives into a coherent framework and testing thereof on the basis of old and new data.

NOTES

[1] In scientific studies on innovation, these issues have been covered under heading of the exploitation - exploration trade-off (Cohen and Levinthal 1989, 1990; Smith and Tushman 2005).

[2] The causal micro-story is examined elsewhere more explicitly (Reschke 2005d). A potential perspective filling the need for a causal micro-story has been proposed by 'strategy-as-practice' researchers (for example Whittington 1996, Hendry 2000). The strategy-as-practice approach to strategy aims to develop a micro-perspective on strategy-making. Thus it operates on the micro-level of managerial actions. A combination of the strategy-as-practice approach and an evolutionary perspective can deliver an integrative approach to strategy that manages to span the different layers from the micro- to the macro-level. To make strategy amenable to an evolutionary analysis also requires integration with an evolutionary perspective on economic behaviour (Nelson and Winter 1982) and organisational ecology (Hannan and Freeman 1989).

[3] We use dominant design as a catch-all phrase for different concepts of stable product configurations (see Reschke 2005 for an overview).

REFERENCES

Addams-Webber, J.R. (1979), *Personal Construct Theory. Concepts and Applications*, Chichester and others: John Wiley.

Alchian, A. (1950), 'Uncertainty, Evolution, and Economic Theory', *Journal of Political Economy*, 58, 211-221.

Andersen, E.S. (1996), *Evolutionary Economics: Post-Schumpeterian Contributions*, London: Pinter.

Anderson, P. and M.L. Tushman (1990), 'Technological Discontinuities and

Dominant Designs: A Cyclical Model of Technological Change', *Administrative Science Quarterly*, 35, 604-633.

Arrow, K. J. (1962), 'The Economic Implications of Learning by Doing', *Review of Economic Studies*, 29, 155-173.

Arthur, W.B. (1988), 'Self-Reinforcing Mechanisms in Economics', Stanford University discussion paper series, 111, 9-31.

Astley, W.G. (1985), 'The Two Ecologies: Population and Community Perspectives on Organizational Evolution', *Administrative Science Quarterly*, 30, 224-241.

Baaij, M.G. (1996), *Evolutionary Strategic Management - Firm and Environment, Performance over Time*, Delft Eburon.

Bannister, D. (1985), *Issues and Approaches in Personal Construct Theory*, London and others: Academic Press.

Barnett, W.P. (1990), 'The Organizational Ecology of a Technological System', *Administrative Science Quarterly*, 35, 31-60.

Barnett, W.P. (1997), 'The Dynamics of Competitive Intensity', *Administrative Science Quarterly*, 42, 128-160.

Barnett, W.P. and R.A. Burgelman (1996), 'Evolutionary Perspectives on Strategy', *Strategic Management Journal*, 17, 5-19.

Bauer, B. (2002), *Kleine und mittlere Unternehmen - Übersicht über Bedeutung, bereits getroffene und mögliche weitere Maßnahmen auf EU-Ebene und in Österreich*, Vienna: Federal Ministry for Finance.

Boeddrich, H.-J. (2004), 'Ideas in the Workplace: A New Approach Towards Organizing the Fuzzy Front End of the Innovation Process', *Creativity and Innovation Management*, 13(4), 274-85.

Boyd, R. and P.J. Richerson (1980), 'Sociobiology, Culture and the Economic Process', *Journal of Economic Behavior and Organization*, 1, 97-127.

Brazeal, D.V. and T.T. Herbert (1999), 'The Genesis of Entrepreneurship', *Entrepreneurship: Theory & Practice*, 29(3), 29-45.

Brock, W.A. and D.S. Evans (1989), 'Small Business Economics', *Small Business Economics*, 1, 7-20.

Campbell, D.T. (1960), 'Blind Variation and Selective Retention in Creative Thought as in Other Knowledge Processes', *Psychological Review*, 67, 380-400.

Carree, M.A. and A.R. Thurik (2000), 'The Impact of Entrepreneurship on Economic Growth', in D.B. Audretsch and Z.F. Acs (eds), *Handbook of Entrepreneurship*, Boston, MA: Kluwer Academic Publishers.

Castells, M. (1996-1998), *The Information Age: Economy, Society, and Culture, I-III*, Oxford: Blackwell.

Chandler, A.D. (1962), *Strategy and Struture: Chapters in the History of the Industrial Enterprise*, Cambridge, MA: MIT Press.

Christensen, C. (2004), *Seeing What's Next: Using the Theories of Innovation to Predict Industry Change*, Harvard: Harvard Business School Press..

Cohen, W. and D. Levinthal (1989), 'Absorptive Capacity: A New Perspective on Learning and Innovation', *Administrative Science Quarterly*, 35, 128-152.

Cohen, W. and D. Levinthal (1990), 'Innovation and Learning: The Two Faces of R&D', *The Economic Journal*, 99, 569-596.

Cool, K. and I. Dierickx (1993), 'Rivalry, Strategic Groups and Firm Profitability', *Strategic Management Journal*, 14, 47-59.

Crutchfield, J.P. and E. van Nimwegen (1999), *The Evolutionary Unfolding of Complexity*, Santa Fe, NM: Santa Fe Institute.

Csikszentmihalyi, M. (2001), 'A Systems Perspective on Creativity', in J. Henry (ed.),

Creative management, London: Sage, 11-26.

D'Aveni, R.A. (1999), 'Strategic Supremacy through Disruption and Dominance', *Sloan Management Review*, Spring 1999, 127-135.

David, P.A. (1994), 'Why are Institutions the "Carriers of History"?: Path Dependence and the Evolution of Conventions, Organizations and Institutions', *Structural Change and Economic Dynamics*, 5, 205-220.

DeGraff, J. and K. Lawrence (2002), *Creativity at Work: Developing the Right Practices to Make Innovation Happen*, San Francisco: Jossey-Bass.

Douglas, E. (2001), 'Entrepreneurship: the Link Between Invention, Innovation and Success', in Australian Institute of Management (ed.), *Innovation and Imagination at Work*, Sydney: McGraw-Hill, 60-86.

Downs, A., R. Durant and A. Carr (2002), 'Emergent Strategy Development for Organizations', *Emergence*, 5(2), 5-28.

Eden C., F. Ackermann and S. Cropper (1992), 'The Analysis of Cause Maps', *Journal of Management Studies*, 29, 309-324.

Ellyard, P. (2001), 'Imagining the future and getting to it first', in Australian Institute of Management (ed.), *Innovation and Imagination at Work*, Sydney: McGraw-Hill, 152-73.

Fiol, M. and A.S. Huff (1992), 'Maps for Managers: Where are we? Where do we go from here?', *Journal of Management Studies*, 29, 269-285.

Foster, R.N. (1986), *Innovation: The Attacker's Advantage*, New York: McMillan.

Friedman, D. (1996), *Hidden Order. The Economics of Everyday Life*, New York: Harper Business.

Frenken, K. and P. Windrum (2000), *Product Differentiation and Product Complexity. A Conceptual Model and an Empirical Application to Microcomputers*, Maastricht: Merit.

Goertzel, B. (1992), 'Self-Organizing Evolution', *Journal of Social and Evolutionary Systems*, 15, 7-54.

Grant, R.M. (1991), *Contemporary Strategy Analysis. Concepts, Techniques, Applications*, Cambridge, MA : Blackwell.

Hamel, G. and C.K. Prahalad (1994), *Competing for the Future*, Boston, MA: Harvard Business School Press.

Hammer, M. and J. Champy (1993), *Reengineering the Corporation - A Manifesto for Business Revolution*, New York: Harper Business.

Hannan, M.T. and Freeman, J. (1989), *Organisational Ecology*, Cambridge, MA, London: Harvard University Press.

Hass, H. (1970), *Energon. Das verborgene Gemeinsame*, Vienna: Fritz Molden.

Henderson, B.D. (1989), 'The Origin of Strategy', *Harvard Business Review*, 67(6), 139-143.

Hendry, J. (2000), 'Strategic Decision-making, Discourse, and Strategy as Social Practice', *Journal of Management Studies*, 37, 955-977.

Hitt, M.A. and T.S. Reed (2000), 'Entrepreneurship in the New Competitive Landscape', in G.D. Meyer and K.A. Heppard (eds), *Entrepreneurship as Strategy*, Thousand Oaks: Sage Publications, 23-48.

Hitt, M., R. Ireland, M. Camp and D. Sexton (2002), 'Strategic Entrepreneurship: Integrating Entrepreneurial and Strategic Management Perspectives', in M. Hitt, R. Ireland, M. Camp and D. Sexton (eds), *Strategic Entrepreneurship: Creating a new mindset*, Oxford: Blackwell, 1-13.

Hunt, S.D. (1997), 'Resource-Advantage Theory: An Evolutionary Theory of Competitive Firm Behavior', *Journal of Economic Issues*, 31, 59-77.

Kaplan, R.S. and D.P. Norton (1992), 'The Balanced Scorecard - Measures that Drive Performance', *Harvard Business Review*, 1, 71-79.

Kelly, G.A. (1955), *The Psychology of Personal Constructs*, 2 Vols, New York: Norton.

Kingsnorth, P. (2003), *One No, Many Yesses. A Journey to the Heart of the Global Resistance Movement*, London: Free Press.

Klepper, S. (1996), 'Entry, Exit, Growth and Innovation over the Product Life Cycle', *American Economic Review*, 86, 560-581.

Klepper, S. (1997), 'Industry Life Cycles', *Industrial and Corporate Change*, 6, 145-182.

Klepper, S. and K.L. Simmons (1997), 'Technological Extinctions of Industrial Firms: An Inquiry into their Nature and Causes', *Industrial and Corporate Change*, 6(2), 379-460.

Kline, S.J. and N. Rosenberg (1986), 'An Overview of Innovation', in R. Landau and N. Rosenberg (ed.), *The Positive Sum Strategy: Harnessing Technology for Economic Growth*, Washington, DC: National Academy Press, 275-304.

Kogut, B. and U. Zander (1992), 'Knowledge of the Firm, Combinative Capabilities, and the Replication of Technology', *Organization Science*, 3(3), 383-397.

Kraus, S. and C.H. Reschke (2004), *Evolutionäres Strategisches Management von Gründungsunternehmen*, Lohmar, Cologne: Eul.

Kubon-Gilke, G. and E. Schlicht (1998), 'Gerichtete Variationen in der Biologischen und Sozialen Evolution', *Gestalt Theory*, 20, 48-77.

Kuratko, D.F. (2003), *Entrepreneurship Education: Emerging Trends and Challenges for the 21st Century*, Madison, WI: USASBE.

Kuratko, D.F. and R.M. Hodgetts (2004), 'Innovation and the Entrepreneur', in D.F. Kuratko and R.M. Hodgetts (eds), *Entrepreneurship*, Ohio, Thomson, 138-150.

Lambkin, M. and G.S. Day (1989), 'Evolutionary Processes in Competitive Markets: Beyond the Product Life Cycle', *Journal of Marketing*, 53(July), 4-20.

Leonard, D. and W. Swap (2002), 'How Managers can Spark Creativity', in F. Hesselbein and R. Johnston (eds), *On Creativity - a Lead to Leader Guide on Creativity, Innovation and Renewal*, San Francisco: Jossey Bass, 55-65.

Lewin, A.Y. and H.W. Volberda (2003), 'Co-evolutionary Dynamics Within and Between Firms: From Evolution to Co-evolution', *Journal of Management Studies*, 40, 2105-2130.

List, F. (1841), *Das nationale System der politischen Ökonomie* (The National System of Political Economy), Stuttgart, London: Cotta, Longmans, Green and Co.

Luhmann, N. (1995), *Social Systems*, Stanford: Stanford University Press.

MacKenzie, K. (2001), 'Survival in the Corporate Jungle: Innovate or Perish', in Australian Institute of Management (ed.), *Innovation and Imagination at Work*, Sydney: McGraw-Hill, 17-34.

Margulis, L. (1992), *Symbiosis in Cell Evolution: Microbial Communities in the Archean and Proterozoic Eons*, 2nd edn, New York: Freeman.

Mauzy, J. and R. Harriman (2003), 'Becoming Creatively Fit as an Individual', in J. Mauzy and R. Harriman (2003), *Creativity, Inc: Building an Inventive Organization*, Boston: Harvard Business School Press, 35-54.

Maynard Smith, J. and E. Szathmary (1995), *The Major Transitions in Evolution*, Oxford: Freeman.

Mayr, E. (1989), 'Speciational Evolution or Punctuated Equilibria', *Journal of Social and Biological Structures*, 12, 137-158.

McGahan, A.M. (2000), 'How Industries Evolve', *Business Strategy Review*, 11(3), 1-

16.

Miller, D. (1979), 'Strategy, Structure and Environment: Context Influences upon Some Bivariate Associations', *Journal of Management Studies*, 16, 294-316.

Miller, D. and P.H. Friesen (1980), 'Momentum and Revolution in Organizational Adaptation', *Academy of Management Journal*, 23, 591-614.

Miller, G.F. (2000), *The Mating Mind. How Sexual Selection Shaped the Evolution of Human Nature*, New York: Doubleday.

Mintzberg, H. (1994), *The Rise and Fall of Strategic Planning*, New York: Free Press.

Mirowski, P. (1989), *More Heat than Light. Economics as Social Physics, Physics as Nature's Economics*, Cambridge: Cambridge University Press.

Mokyr, J. (1997), *Innovation and Selection in Evolutionary Models of Technology: Some Definitional Issues*, Evanston, IL: Northwestern University.

Mokyr, J. (2002), *Useful Knowledge as an Evolving System: The View from Economic History*, Evanston, IL: Northwestern University.

Morris, M.H. and D.F. Kuratko (2002), *Creativity and the Corporate Entrepreneur*, in Corporate Entrepreneurship, Orlando, FL: Hartcourt, 103-17.

Nelson, R.R. and S.G. Winter (1982), *An Evolutionary Theory of Economic Change*, Cambridge, MA: Harvard University Press.

OECD (2002), *The New Economy - Beyond the Hype: The Growth Project*, Paris: Organisation for Economic Cooperation and Development.

Pantzar, M. and V. Csanyi (1991), 'The Replicative Model of the Evolution of the Business Organization', *Journal of Social and Biological Structures*, 14(2), 149-163.

Porter, M.E. (1980), *Competitive Strategy: Techniques for Analyzing Industries and Competitors*, New York: Free Press.

Porter, M.E. (1985), *Competitive Advantage: Creating and Sustaining Superior Performance*, New York: Free Press.

Pistorius, C.W.I. and J.M. Utterback (1997), 'Multimode Interaction among Technologies', *Research Policy*, 26, 67-84.

Reger, R.K. and A.S. Huff (1993), 'Strategic Groups: A Cognitive Perspective', *Strategic Management Journal*, 14, 103-124.

Reschke, C.H. (2001), 'Evolutionary Perspectives on Simulations of Social Systems', *Journal of Artificial Societies and Social Simulation*, Vol. 4, No. 4.

Reschke, C.H. (2005a), *Routines, Economic Selection and Economic Evolution: Critique and Possibilities*, Paper presented at the DRUID Tenth Anniversary Summer Conference 2005 on Dynamics of Industry and Innovation: Organizations, Networks and Systems, Copenhagen: CBS.

Reschke, C.H. (2005b), *Strategy, The Path of History and Social Evolution*, Paper accepted for CMS '04 - 4th Critical Management Studies Conference, Cambridge.

Reschke, C.H. (2005c), *Evolutionary Processes in Economics. The Example of Strategy and Research in the Bio-Pharmaceutical Industry*, Witten/Herdecke, Cologne: mimeo.

Reschke, C.H. (2005d), *Strategy, Action, Perception and Performance: An Evolutionary Learning Perspective on Organizations*, Oxford: British Academy of Management.

Reschke, C.H. and S. Kraus (2005), 'An Evolutionary Approach to Innovation and Strategy in Small and Medium-Sized Enterprises', in M. Rebernik, M. Mulej, M. Rus and T. Kroslin (eds), *Shaping the Environment for Innovation Transfer*, Maribor: IRP, 175-186.

Riedl, R. (1990 [1975]), *Die Ordnung des Lebendigen. Systembedingungen der*

Evolution, München: Piper.

Riedl, R. (2000), *Strukturen der Komplexität. Eine Morphologie des Erkennens und Erklärens*, Berlin: Springer.

Rumelt, R.P. (1974), *Strategy Structure and Economic Performance*, Boston, MA: Harvard Business School Press.

Rumelt, R.P. (1991), 'How Much does Industry Matter?', *Strategic Management Journal*, 12, 167-185.

Sachs, S. (2002), 'Strategischer Wandel auf mehreren Ebenen. Eine intraorganisationale evolutionäre Perspektive', in M. Lehmann-Waffenschmidt (ed.), *Studien zur Evolutorischen Ökonomik VI. Ein Diskurs zu Analysemethoden der Evolutorischen Ökonomik*, Berlin: Metropolis, 173-196.

Schaper, M. and T. Volery (2004), *Entrepreneurship and Small Business: A Pacific Rim Perspective*, Milton: Wiley.

Schlicht, E. (1997), 'Patterned Variation: The Role of Psychological Dispositions in Social and Institutional Evolution', *Journal of Institutional and Theoretical Economics*, 153, 722-736.

Schumpeter, J.A. (1987 [1942]), *Kapitalismus, Sozialismus und Demokratie (translation of: Capitalism, Socialism and Democracy)*, 6th edn, Tübingen, New York: Francke, Harper and Bros.

Schumpeter, J.A. (1993 [1934]), *The Theory of Economic Development*, New Brunswick, London: Transaction Publishers.

Silverberg, G. (1997), *Evolutionary Modeling in Economics: Recent History and Immediate Prospects*, MERIT working paper, first revision, dated July 1997.

Silverberg, G. and B. Verspagen (2003), *Brewing the Future: Stylized Facts about Innovation and their Confrontation with a Percolation Model*, Paper prepared for the EMAEE Conference, Augsburg, April 10-12, 2003, dated March 2003.

Smith, A. (1790 [1759]), *The Theory of Moral Sentiments*, 6th edition, London: A. Millar.

Smith, A. (1998 [1776]), *An Inquiry into the Nature and Causes of the Wealth of Nations*, Oxford World's Classics, Oxford: Oxford University Press.

Stacey, R.D. (1993), *Strategic Management and Organisational Dynamics*, London: Pitman.

Sternberg, R.J., J.C. Kaufman and J.E. Pretz (2004), 'A Propulsion Model of Creative Leadership', *Creativity and Innovation Management*, 13(3), 145-153.

Szathmary, E. and J. Maynard Smith (1995), 'The Major Evolutionary Transitions', *Nature*, 374, 227-232.

Tellis, G.J. and M. Crawford (1981), 'An Evolutionary Approach to Product Growth Theory', *Journal of Marketing*, 45, 125-132.

Timmons, J.A. (2004), 'Opportunity recognition', in W. Bygrave and A. Zacharakis (eds), *The Portable MBA in Entrepreneurship*, New Jersey: John Wiley, 29-70.

Tushman, M.L. and P. Anderson (1986), 'Technological Discontinuities and Organizational Environments', *Administrative Science Quarterly*, 31, 439-465.

Utterback, J.M. and W.J. Abernathy (1975), 'A Dynamic Model of Process and Product Innovation', *Omega*, 6, 639-656.

Van de Ven, A.H. and R. Garud (1994), 'The Coevolution of Technical and Institutional Events in the Development of an Innovation', in J.A.C. Baum and J.V. Singh (eds), *Evolutionary Dynamics of Organizations*, Oxford: Oxford University Press.

Veblen, T. (1898), 'Why is Economics not an Evolutionary Science', *Quarterly Journal of Economics*, 12, 373-397.

Wagner, G.P. (1983), 'On the Necessity of a Systems Theory of Evolution and its Population Biologic Foundation. Comments on Dr. Regelmann's Article', *Acta Biotheoretica*, 32, 223-226.

Weick, K.E. (1987), 'Substitutes for Strategy', in D.T. Teece (ed.), *Competitive Challenge Strategies for Industrial Innovation and Renewal*, Cambridge: Ballinger, 221-233.

Whittington, R. (1996), 'Strategy as Practice', *Long Range Planning*, 29, 731-735.

Zimmerer, T.W. and N.M. Scarborough (2002), *Essentials of Entrepreneurship and Small Business*, 3rd edition, New Jersey: Prentice Hall.

10. The Problem of Knowledge in Economics: Prices, Contracts and Organizations

Stavros Ioannides

INTRODUCTION

Ever since the 'marginal revolution' and the advent of methodological individualism, the issues of information and knowledge have figured prominently in economics. On the whole, however, economists have relied upon a very narrow understanding of the two concepts, as illustrated by the fact that they have usually employed them as perfect substitutes. Both were thought of as describing unambiguously codifiable – and, thus, decodifiable – signals about states of the world, which agents could use merely as inputs in their maximizing calculations. As a consequence, issues like learning processes, ambiguous signals, socially shared knowledge, uncodifiable (that is tacit) knowledge, and so on, were excluded from the analysis.

Economics has begun to acknowledge the distinction between information and knowledge and to address the above issues only in the last quarter of the previous century. A useful conceptualization of the various concepts has been introduced by Hodgson (1999). First of all, Hodgson (p. 46) distinguishes between sense data, the various signals received by human senses, from information, which he describes as 'data to which some meaning has been attributed'. In order for meaning to be attributed to sense data, the agent must be assumed to already possess some knowledge relevant to the data she receives through her senses. Importantly, therefore, different people may attribute different meanings to the same data – that is treat them as different pieces of information.

Hodgson then describes knowledge as the product of information use. The information the agent receives, together with the meaning she attributes to it, allow her to obtain *knowledge*. Therefore, while information is an input for the acquisition of knowledge, the latter is a wider and deeper concept, for it constitutes both the prior endowment needed to make sense of any information, as well as the final outcome of a process of learning – that is the creation of a new knowledge endowment. [1] Finally, both knowledge itself as well as the process leading to it can be either codifiable or tacit.[2] Codifiable knowledge can be transferred – at a cost – whereas tacit knowledge is not easily alienable from its, individual or collective, bearer.

Even today, however, few economists would agree on the need for a taxonomy of concepts like the one proposed by Hodgson. Thus, although the issues that these concepts reflect have kept returning to the forefront of investigations for the whole of the previous century, they have never succeeded in replacing the dominant view of knowledge and information that I described above. And yet, there seems to be a shift in the last couple of decades, away from this dominant view and towards more sophisticated accounts of knowledge. This shift does not reflect a general refinement of the conceptual framework of modern theory, but it is instead focused on specific subfields. I argue that economists have increasingly sought more sophisticated accounts of knowledge the more they were involved in a sort of economics that tended to distance itself from price theory.

Of course, it is not possible to survey here the whole of 20th century economics, or even to highlight all the important ideas on knowledge and information that various economists put forward at various instances. My account will be highly selective, as it will focus on those debates and theoretical strands that, from the author's view, have exercised the greatest influence on the discipline, and will attempt to bring out the views on knowledge and information implicit in each one of them. Hopefully, however, a clear pattern will emerge: that we find consistently more elaborate contributions to the problem of knowledge as theory moved away from prices towards contracts and then towards institutions and organizations.

The chapter is organized as follows. The second section briefly describes the view of knowledge of standard neoclassical microeconomics. The third section discusses the 'socialist calculation debate' of the 1930s. Although this is almost an entirely forgotten episode in the history of the discipline, its importance for the analysis here is that it brought out some crucial issues regarding the nature and the management of knowledge, which were formally addressed by economics only decades later. The fourth section discusses a debate 'that never was', between Stigler and Arrow on the nature of knowledge and information. Arguably, the opposing views of the two theorists introduce a significant distinction between information as a commodity and knowledge as something different from information. The fifth section analyzes briefly the views on knowledge of New Classical Economics and of Endogenous Growth Theories. It is argued that both strands revert to the dominant view of knowledge, as they treat it as an entirely codifiable entity. The sixth section discusses the importance of the concept of asymmetric information and shows that the solution to the problems that it raises led theorists to the notion of contracts. The seventh section discusses various strands of New Institutional Economics and shows how the various contractual theories of economic organization explain the emergence of the capitalist firm as an institution. The eighth section discusses briefly the 'Resource-Based' or 'Capabilities' approach to economic organization and argues that it is here that we find the most sophisticated – on the basis of the benchmark inspired by Hodgson's conceptualization – treatment of knowledge in economic theory. Finally, the ninth section sums up the chapter's conclusion.

THE PROBLEM OF KNOWLEDGE IN STANDARD NEOCLASSICAL MICROECONOMICS

For whole generations of students of economics, the diagram of supply and demand[3] has been the entry point to the discipline. This is true even today, as is evident from a cursory inspection of most contemporary microeconomics textbooks. It is in that sense that I refer to 'standard' neoclassical microeconomics in the title of this section. What I wish to show here is that, in the context of that conceptualization of the workings of a typical market, knowledge is not – indeed, it *cannot* be – approached as a problem for theory.

The demand and supply schedules are supposed merely to reflect the intentions of agents,[4] about what quantities of goods to trade at each specific price. Obviously, if there is an issue of knowledge here, it merely refers to the agent's knowledge of her own preferences, which she is supposed to possess given the rationality assumption. Of course, things are more complex in the case of the supply schedule, which does not stem from the preferences of consumers but from the profit-maximizing decisions of firms.[5] Still, the fact that both schedules reflect simply the intentions of agents may allow us to treat them as inward-looking concepts that simply reflect what, from the agents' point of view, is already given.

The problem of knowledge emerges the moment we stop treating the two schedules as isolated phenomena and we use them jointly in order to explain the outcome of market interaction. The point of intersection of the two schedules defines the state of market equilibrium, as any disturbance of that state will automatically – and instantaneously – tend to reinstate equilibrium. The consistency of the model requires, therefore, the existence of some mechanism that ensures the constant existence or, more generally, the constant tendency towards the state of equilibrium. Not surprisingly, no such mechanism has ever been proposed. The protagonists of the 'marginal revolution' tried to overcome the problem by proposing either a fictitious 'auctioneer' (Walras 1874/1954) or the idea that no trading takes place before the establishment of equilibrium (Edgeworth 1881/1932). However, even more modern research has not been able to explain the process towards equilibrium, as it was already evident in Arrow's (1959) attempt to explain the convergence of prices.[6]

Given these difficulties, standard neoclassical microeconomics chose to focus instead on the end state of that process, the state of equilibrium. To be conceptualized as a truly end state, theorists had to assume that any tendency to disrupt it has already ceased to operate. The assumption that provided the basis for such an approach was *perfect competition*: the hypothesis that all competitive moves by agents have already been made so that no further gains from trade are possible.[7] However, it was only late in the interwar years[8] and especially in the post World War II period that the concept of perfect competition came to be fully accepted by the profession as an analytical tool, mostly as a result of the abandonment of Marshallian partial equilibrium analysis in favor of general equilibrium. The former, by offering the possibility to approach market phenomena in terms of consecutive stages, allowed the partial investigation of the effects brought about by the cancellation of various conditions of perfect competition.[9] By contrast, in the state of general equilibrium all effects of competition are assumed to have worked themselves out.

The concept of perfect competition has not, of course, escaped criticism. The suppression of time, implied by the static nature of the analysis, is one such criticism. Second, it precludes any possibility of standard microeconomics to theorize issues like entrepreneurship, innovation and technological change – that is the major instances in which the emergence of new knowledge impacts on the development process – as it inevitably depicts agents as constantly having to choose among a given array of fully known alternatives.

More importantly, however, the condition of perfect competition that is of special relevance here is that of *perfect knowledge*.[10] For perfect competition to hold, agents are assumed to know fully the technological alternatives, the prices of inputs and outputs, the best way to go about achieving their objectives, and so on. Moreover, agents are assumed to possess a stock of knowledge that has been piled up historically – that is its existence lies beyond the scope of theory – and which is common to all. It is assumed that all new information that the system produces is immediately – and costlessly – available to all market participants and that it is interpreted and evaluated in the same way by all. Therefore, and in contrast to the title of this section, for standard neoclassical economics knowledge is not a problem at all; it is simply assumed away.

KNOWLEDGE AND THE 'SOCIALIST CALCULATION' DEBATE OF THE 1930S

The problem of the neoclassical treatment of knowledge came forcefully to the fore in the 1930s, in a debate on the feasibility of socialism. One side in the debate, which Karen Vaughn (1980) has labeled as 'neoclassical socialists', argued that a system of comprehensive central planning was perfectly viable and that its operation could be understood on the basis of general equilibrium. Their opponents from the liberal side of the political divide argued that socialism would be an inherently inefficient form of social organization that would not be viable in the long run.[11] Interestingly, although my analysis will show that the issue of knowledge was the central problem around which the debate revolved, few of the protagonists realized it at the time.

Ludwig von Mises (1920) opened the debate with an attack on the conception of socialism put forth in the Marxian tradition. According to Mises, the abolition of private property in the means of production would abolish all markets for such goods, so their prices would have to be set by a central authority (the Central Planning Board: CPB). Thus, nothing could ensure that they would reflect the 'true scarcities' of means of production; they would inevitably disseminate misinformation to the managers of socialist firms and, as a consequence, the latter would mis-*calculate* – hence the term by which the debate came to be known – the true costs of production. Thus socialism would be an inherently inefficient system of social organization.

The rebuttal of Mises' criticism from the socialist side came from a number of economists (Dickinson 1933, 1939; Lerner 1934-5, 1937; Durbin 1936), who claimed that the solution to the problems he raised could be established by mathematical means, thus prompting Hayek to label this approach as the 'mathematical solution'. The core of this approach was perhaps best expounded by Dickinson (1933, p. 239), who demanded that all firms of the socialist system operate within 'glass walls', that is that they be obliged to publish all information relating to their operation. The public nature of this knowledge would allow the CPB to collect all the data required in order to build a mathematical model of the economy. By solving this system, the CPB would establish the market clearing prices and quantities, thus ensuring general equilibrium.

The protagonist in the next stage of the debate was Friedrich Hayek (1935), who pointed out that the knowledge requirements of the mathematical solution would make it impracticable. The accurate specification of the model's equations requires the CPB to obtain knowledge about the most effective use of every factor of production. However, this knowledge will inevitably change through time, which means that the CPB would have to be engaged in a continuous process not just of solving the system but also of respecifying its parameters. According to Hayek, the sheer volume of this information makes its centralization impracticable.

The neoclassical socialists took Hayek's point about the practical difficulty of the centralization of knowledge very seriously, as reflected in Oscar Lange's (1938) model of a 'competitive' socialist system, in which socialist enterprises are allowed to compete amongst themselves on two conditions. The first is that they must minimize average cost and determine production levels at the point that the marginal cost equals the price. The second condition is that prices and production levels for each industry are set be the CPB. However, in contrast to the mathematical solution, prices are to be set empirically rather than mathematically. In effect, Lange proposes that the CPB operates as a Walrasian auctioneer: lowering prices in the markets with excess supply and raising them in those with excess demand.[12]

It was again Hayek (1940), who fired the final shots in the debate. In his view, what makes the centralization of knowledge impracticable is not just its volume but, more importantly, the fact that a large part of this knowledge is uncentralizable because of its *tacit* character (Hayek 1963, p. 61). To this he added a further argument, which was based on an idea that was later to become prominent in economics under the name of *opportunism*. By its very nature, Lange's price-setting method cannot adjust prices to changing conditions as speedily as when private entrepreneurs are allowed to negotiate prices independently of any central direction. However, the question is how managers will behave while waiting for the CPB to change prices. The logic of Lange's proposal is that managers continue to trade at current prices. But how can it be ensured that the managers will loyally obey the CPB rather than attempt to take advantage of their own knowledge opportunistically?

Therefore, although not initially on the agenda, the issue of knowledge kept coming to the forefront as the debate evolved.[13] However, the socialist side remained trapped in a view of knowledge exclusively as codified information, thus the continued revision of their models addressed only the practical aspects of the problem. By contrast, and with hindsight, Hayek seems to have made the most innovative contribution, introducing the concepts of *tacit* knowledge and *opportunism*.[14] Opportunism was to be rediscovered decades later and to begin a prominent career in economics. Tacit knowledge had to wait longer and it remains much more controversial even today.

ON THE COMMODITY CHARACTER OF INFORMATION

Of course, the 1930s have marked the development of economics in the last century in a much more fundamental way with the advent of Keynesianism. Keynes (1936/1973) built his theory on the founding block of the notion of *uncertainty*. Even assuming that the agent knows fully all that is relevant at the current moment, she still is uncertain about the situation that will actually prevail the moment in the future that the results of her action will materialize. Therefore, no matter how complete her knowledge of the present may be, her action will always be guided by the *expectations* she holds about the future.[15]

The concept of expectation clearly encompasses the agent's prior knowledge, as it is on that foundation that expectations are constructed. For Keynes, however, the important thing about the formation of expectations is not so much this prior knowledge, as the general form of the decision problem faced by the agent. Keynes's famous simile is of a beauty contest, where the agent must choose not the person she considers more beautiful but the one that most of her competitors will believe, that most of their competitors will believe, to be so. O'Driscoll and Rizzo (1985, pp. 72-75) show that the agent's expectations are entirely time-dependent, thus we have an unending revision of expectations. Precisely because this process in which each agent tries to outguess her competitors has no end, the system never settles to an equilibrium. Inevitably, therefore, agents trade at 'false prices', which fuels further the endogenous creation of expectations and thus further false trading. Thus, prices do not embody all the knowledge that they would if they were equilibrium prices, which means that the knowledge they convey is open to interpretation by the agent.

Despite the novel ideas on knowledge that the *General Theory* introduced, it was obviously the undermining of the concept of equilibrium that was potentially much more damaging for established theory. The backlash was soon to come in the form of the 'neoclassical synthesis' initiated by Hicks (1937), which cancelled the anti-optimization thrust of Keynesian economics. Although not among the early anti-Keynesian targets, the notion of uncertainty was progressively neutralized, especially in the 1950s and the focus on stochastic modeling. The 1950s have been the decade that the 'General Equilibrium' (GE) paradigm became established as *the* dominant paradigm in economics. In fact, as many historians of the discipline have pointed out, this is the period in which one can talk about the emergence of an *orthodoxy* in economics, an unprecedented development compared to the pluralism of previous decades.[16]

Of course, despite the general acceptance of GE, economists were not blind to its severe limitations, foremost among them being the assumption of perfect contingent markets for all future goods and services. Indeed, GE only makes sense if agents are assumed to be able to trade not just current goods but also future goods, each of them characterized by two attributes: the instant in time that the actual trade is to take place and the state of the world that will prevail at that instant. In that context, therefore, the assumption of contingent markets implied that each agent is in the position to fully specify the future trades she will wish to carry out at every conceivable state of the world.

To non-economists, the assumption of contingent markets may sound absurd. To economists trained in neoclassical microeconomics, however, it merely meant an extension of the perfect knowledge assumption, which they had learned to accept as an analytically legitimate conceptualization of how markets actually work. Of course, this could not mean that it would be unquestioningly accepted. Rather, it was precisely because the assumption of contingent markets constituted an extension of the postulate of perfect knowledge that economists were prompted to address the acquisition of knowledge as a legitimate problem of economic inquiry.

In this part I will examine two important works of the early 1960s in this vein.[17] The first, which initiated a strand in economic theory known as 'the economics of information' is George Stigler's (1961) paper by the same title. Stigler's conceptual innovation is to treat knowledge as a commodity. In the context of GE theory, the ingenuity of this innovation is that, by treating knowledge as a commodity, Stigler manages two things: first, he fleshes out, as it were, the model's contingent markets by giving them an object to trade in today, rather than at some distant date in the future. Secondly, by describing knowledge as a marketable commodity he can proceed to analyze its provision with the well established tools of microeconomics. There is a further implication, which is of great interest for what I am going to discuss later in this chapter. The fact that knowledge is viewed as a commodity allows Stigler to treat it as something external to the agent, which the latter neither produces nor can in any way affect through her action. There is no better illustration that Stigler indeed has this view from the fact that, although he begins the paper by using the terms 'knowledge' and 'information' interchangeably, he goes on to focus on *information*.

Stigler maintains that the framework he is proposing can, in principle, cover all kinds of information. However, he chooses to focus on just one such type: information on prices. He begins his analysis by postulating a pre-equilibrium situation, in which no uniform price for a specific commodity exists. This implies the existence of price dispersion, which is only another way of describing the ignorance that agents face. Thus, rational agents have an incentive to try to get informed about the prices offered, through a process that Stigler describes as *search*. By searching for prices, the agent achieves two things: first, she increases the stock of knowledge in her possession and, second, she reduces the price dispersion in the market.

However, search itself has a cost, therefore the agent will engage in it only to the extent that the expected benefits – that is the possibility of discovering a lower price for the commodity – are greater than the search–cost itself. On these grounds, Stigler maintains that agents will engage in search up to the point that marginal benefit equals marginal cost. The reaffirmation of the marginal equilibrium condition has a further important implication: agents will never be perfectly informed and, thus, some dispersion will always remain. However, the remaining dispersion will be itself optimal, in the sense that agents have rationally decided not to expend any resources in order to reduce it further.

Only a year after the publication of Stigler's paper, Kenneth Arrow's 'Economic Welfare and the Allocation of Resources for Invention' (1962a) appeared. The central issue, of course, is again knowledge. Unlike Stigler, however, who focused on the information conveyed by prices, Arrow concentrates on the creation of new knowledge, through the process that the term 'invention' usually describes. Importantly, therefore, and in contrast to Stigler, Arrow focuses in the production rather the reception of knowledge.[18]

Arrow makes no reference to Stigler (1961). However, one cannot but feel that his paper constitutes a direct critique of Stigler, as it aims to refute the latter's central idea: that information can be treated just like any other good or service. Against this view, Arrow puts forth three interrelated arguments. The first is that the benefits that ensue from a piece of information are independent of the costs that its reproduction entails. Thus, it is virtually impossible for the seller to recover the full costs of its production, since the buyer can reproduce and distribute it at low cost. On these grounds, the value of a piece of information will always be much higher than the payment that its original seller will be able to command. The seller will, therefore, always be in a disadvantage that can only partially be protected through legal means – for example patents, license contracts, etc.

Arrow's second argument is that information is a peculiar kind of commodity also in another sense: even after its sale, it never leaves the property of its original owner. Obviously, it is now the buyer of the information that is placed at a disadvantage, for she pays for a commodity without being able to exercise a full property right over it. Again, one can think of a whole array of legal means through which the buyer may attempt to restrict the original owner's right of use of the specific information. However, given the peculiar nature of information as a commodity, such protection can never be absolute. On the other hand, the fact remains that the buyer's incentives are significantly distorted and, as a consequence, she will wish to pay less than the actual value of the information to her.

Arrow's third argument focuses again on the peculiar nature of information as a commodity. Price theory teaches that a buyer will be willing to pay for a good at a price equal to the marginal utility she expects to enjoy from its consumption. Implicit in this is the assumption that the buyer can fully ascertain her marginal utility, for only if that is the case will she be in a position to know what she wishes to pay. However, the paradox of information as a commodity is that one cannot know the utility derivable from it unless she already possesses it; but in that case why buy it in the first place?[19] On the basis of these arguments, Arrow concludes that the costs of producing new knowledge in an uncertain context – through research – are subject to high inappropriabilities, the consequence being that outlays in R&D will tend to be lower than the social optimum.[20]

Stigler and Arrow, therefore, offer two opposing views on the essence and the role of information. The former insists on the commodity-like character of information, and thus describes its provision as an entirely market outcome. In contrast, by denying the commodity character of information, Arrow sees its provision as subject to market failure. However, the differences between the two contributions are much deeper than that. For Stigler, the commodity character of information implies a view of the latter as an unambiguous signal, which says the same thing to all its recipients. In this context, the only difference between agents arises from differences in their expected utilities from the same bit of information, which accounts for the different costs they are willing to incur in order to obtain it. By contrast, we find in Arrow one of the first instances in which the *identity* of the parties exchanging information matters. This is already obvious in the first two of his arguments, as it is clear that it is important both to the seller and to the buyer of information to know what the other party will do with it after the completion of the exchange. Therefore, it is easily understood why Arrow's contribution is generally recognized as having introduced a much richer conception of knowledge in economics.

THE CONSOLIDATION OF THE DISTINCTION BETWEEN INFORMATION AND KNOWLEDGE: RATIONAL EXPECTATIONS AND ENDOGENOUS GROWTH THEORIES

The 1970s has been the decade of the revolt against Keynesianism both at the theoretical as well as at the policy level. In the former, the revolt has taken the form of the demand to produce solid 'microfoundations' for macroeconomic analysis. Milton Friedman had pioneered the critique of Keynesianism in the previous two decades;[21] however, it was in the 1970s that the most devastating assault on Keynesian theory gained wide appeal under the label of New Classical Economics (NCE). Importantly for our task here, the issue of the acquisition of knowledge lay at the foundation of that paradigm.

NCE assumes that agents respond to changes in relative prices. But in order to be able to make sense of the chaos that these changes signify, the agent is also assumed to continuously compare them to changes in the general price level. Thus, relative prices and the general price level constitute the major sources of information, on the basis of which the agent decides her action.[22] However, the actions of agents are always directed at the future, so they are determined by the expectations agents form on the basis of the knowledge they obtain from price signals. It is here that NCE introduces its greatest theoretical innovation: the assumption of *rational expectations*.[23]

In its strongest version, the assumption of rational expectations postulates that the subjective probability an agent assigns to a future contingency matches exactly the objective probability distribution.[24] Thus the agent discounts accurately any future eventuality. In the weaker version, agents are thought of as responding to external events on the basis of a 'theory', which, given their experience with the functioning of the economy in the past, allows them to predict correctly the outcome of any disturbance.[25] Obviously, in both its versions the rational expectations hypothesis amounts to a complete reaffirmation of the perfect knowledge postulate. The knowledge possessed by agents is thus described as perfect in a dual sense: first, agents are supposed to have access to and, thus, to know perfectly the information contained in relative prices and in a set of macroeconomic indices (inflation, unemployment, interest rates, etc.); second, their cognitive abilities are such that allow them to process this information in the same way as all other agents and, thus, come to identical conclusions regarding the future.

The high point of NCE was the period that followed the stagflation of the mid 1970s, a period in which the demand for macroeconomic stabilization was the order of the day. The 1980s and especially the 1990s, however, brought forth a new demand: the explanation of long-term growth. The fact that this was a period of rapid and radical technological development – mainly in the area of Information and Telecommunication Technologies – meant that this development had to be taken seriously into consideration as one of the determinants of growth.[26] The new stream of research did exactly this, by treating the production of new technological knowledge as an endogenous creation of the system and has thus come to be known as Endogenous Growth Theories.

In order to endogenize technological change, various models proposed in the context of this stream lift some of the key conditions for the existence of perfect competition; the model proposed by Grossman and Helpman (1991), for example, postulates monopolistic competition, while OECD (1992) assumes the existence of increasing returns. Technological change itself is viewed as the result of investment in knowledge creation, either by the private sector – firms' R&D outlays and individual investment in human capital – or by the public sector – investment in education and research infrastructure. But what is it exactly that this investment is expended on? Most models assume that these outlays buy new knowledge, which is thought of as new codified and entirely appropriable information (Lipsey, 1999, p. 13). However, a part of endogenous growth models (Romer, 1990; Aghion and Howitt, 1992) stress the inappropiable character of knowledge and describe new technological knowledge as the creation of a quasi-common (that is social) pool of usable information.

In terms of the problem of knowledge that interests us here, NCE and Endogenous Growth Theories seem merely to reproduce the dominant view of knowledge and information as I described it in the introduction. In NCE we find a strong – albeit implicit – recognition of the importance of prior knowledge, for agents are thought of, in effect, as already possessing *the* true model of the economy, so that they can instantly calculate the effects of any exogenous disturbance. Therefore, agents can be described as behaving in a context of perfect knowledge, for the simple reason that the theory has *a priori* assumed that they possess this all-powerful prior knowledge. By contrast, Endogenous Growth Theories treat knowledge as something augmentable through conscious – and, of course, rational – investment decisions. So what the models endogenize is, in effect, the creation of new knowledge. Again, however, this new knowledge is thought of as a stock of codified information, which is accessible and which, most importantly, has the same meaning for all.

INFORMATION ASYMMETRIES AND THE CONCEPT OF CONTRACT: THE RETURN OF OPPORTUNISM

The 1970s witnessed another major conceptual innovation, this time in micro-theory. The Arrow-Debreu model assumed that agents possess identical information about the current and the future states of the economy. Uncertainty could and has been introduced in such models but the assumption of identical information was retained in a sense, as agents were described as being identically uncertain about future contingencies. The conceptual innovation, to which I referred, constituted a clear break with this tradition, as it introduced the concept of *asymmetric* information. Models were now constructed that assumed that agents possess different sets of information, which were not mutually revealed in the course of their market dealings. In fact, the asymmetry of information prompted agents to act in ways that led to serious market imperfections.[27] The fact that agents know different things prompts each one of them to try to outguess the others. Thus, rather than being depicted as typical price-takers, agents are now thought of as behaving *strategically*. In fact, the 1970s saw the wide adoption by economists of a methodology that allowed the analysis of strategic behavior: game theory.

Clearly, the introduction of the concept of asymmetric information marks a significant break with established micro-theory, as it implies an idea about information as independent of prices. Information is now perceived as an integral part of the agent's initial endowments, which she is in a position to manipulate strategically. However, unlike other kinds of endowments, non-disclosure constitutes the essence of its effective exercise.[28] Therefore, not only have agents no incentive to reveal this personally held information, but they also have an incentive to act upon it in ways that promote their own self interest against that of others, that is to act *opportunistically*.

On these grounds, the relevant literature usually distinguishes between two categories of information asymmetries, although not all theorists agree on the criteria for the distinction. I follow here Makowski and Ostroy (2001), who propose distinguishing between: (a) asymmetries arising from *privacy* of information and (b) asymmetries arising from *delivery* problems. The first category refers to information that is privately held by the parties and that is not revealed in the course of their market dealings. The second category refers to information asymmetries between two agents that arise from the fact that the first does not know how the second will act in a specific situation, that is what she will actually 'deliver'.

Both categories of asymmetric information pose formidable problems for market efficiency. The latter depends on the coordinated action of agents; however, the existence of asymmetric information implies that the prices that are formed in markets characterized by asymmetric information cannot be considered as safe signals for optimization. Therefore, the attainment of efficiency now requires the curbing of the potential for opportunistic behavior that information asymmetries create. Of course, the solution to the problem could not be sought in the formation of prices, so theorists had to look for other ways in which rational agents could be thought of as solving the problem of opportunism. Thus they focused on the concept of *contracts*: the instrument through which agents choose to configure their dealings.

Contracts have traditionally been invoked in economics to refer to the legal means and the legal form through which agents shape their exchanges of property rights over goods and services. They could be explicit or implicit, the latter assumed to govern even the simplest transactions. Contracts were mainly thought as ensuring that the parties will behave in the agreed manner thus, implicitly, the underlying idea was that of commonly held knowledge, on the basis of which the parties agreed on joint future actions, and on sanctions in case of breaching. However, the possibility of opportunistic behavior by the contracting parties now led to a major reconsideration of the notion of contracts in a double sense. First, contracts should now be viewed as specifically aiming to curb opportunism, in situations characterized by significant information asymmetries. Second, to the extent that such asymmetries characterized typical situations among transacting parties, contracts were now viewed as giving rise to the creation of stable institutions.

Opportunism was therefore staging a dramatic come-back in economics, based on the notion of asymmetric information. However, there was another development, which was potentially even more devastating for the standard paradigm based on perfect knowledge, that had been going on for some time. That was the strand of 'behavioral economics' and especially Herbert Simon's concept of *bounded rationality*.[29] Simon assumed that agents are intendedly rational but only limited so, that is there are limits to their capacity to learn and to process all available information in order to make rational decisions. As a consequence, agents should be assumed to make decisions on the basis of procedural rules that aim at economizing on rationality.[30] However, although the concept of bounded rationality had been introduced in the 1950s, its appeal to economists began to be important much later, as well see below.

OPPORTUNISM, CONTRACTS AND ORGANIZATIONS

These new developments inspired a novel strand of theorizing that explicitly addressed the phenomenon of economic institutions and especially economic organization, which is usually described as the contractual theories of economic organization or, more generally, as New Institutional Economics. Although this strand is made up of various streams of approaches to the study of organizations and institutions, there exist some common unifying principles that allow us to treat it as a unique paradigm. First, the concept of contract constitutes the ultimate unit of analysis, as it is assumed that it is the instrument through which agents attempt to structure their relations in ways that curb opportunism. Second, the possibility of opportunistic behavior by the parties is believed to spring, first and foremost, from information asymmetries. Third, the process of contracting among agents tends to establish stable organizations or institutions, in the sense that whole classes of institutions emerge that aim at mitigating the problem of information asymmetries in specific kinds of contexts. Understandably, the institution-organization that has attracted the highest interest of economists working in that paradigm is the business firm and other forms of business organizations.

The fact that contractual theories of economic organization begin with the assumption of the existence of various sorts of information asymmetries means that they can be usefully categorized into two streams, each stemming from the two kinds of asymmetries according to Makowski and Ostroy (2001) that we mentioned above: (a) asymmetries arising from privacy and (b) asymmetries arising from delivery problems. The first stream includes transaction cost economics and the theory of incomplete contracts, while the second is comprised of agency theory and the view of the firm as a nexus of contracts. We will now briefly review these approaches to economic organization and discuss the specific way in which they treat the problem of knowledge.

For transaction cost economics (Coase, 1937; Williamson, 1975, 1985a), a 'fundamental transformation' in contractual relations occurs as soon as two parties agree on a contract that will guide their cooperation for a period of time in the future. Even if the pre-contract situation were one of perfect competition, the post-contract situation is transformed into one of bilateral monopoly. Thus, each party faces a potential hazard from the possibility that the other party will act opportunistically *ex post*.[31] It is here that the concept of bounded rationality comes to the fore: opportunism is a problem because, given bounded rationality, agents cannot structure contracts *ex ante* in order to curb opportunism. Obviously, the problem here springs from the private knowledge – of special importance here is private knowledge obtained during contract execution – through which each party will try to take advantage of any post-contractual contingency not explicitly addressed in the contract.[32] The possibility of opportunism is, of course, a major source of transaction costs, as each party will have to take it into consideration when contemplating to enter a long-term contractual relation. To avoid this cost, agents opt for a special kind of contract that establishes a hierarchical relation between them, thereby replacing a market transaction with a relation of fiat. Thus we have the emergence of the classical capitalist firm as an institution.

The theory of incomplete contracts (Grossman and Hart, 1986; Hart, 1995) focuses on ownership of specific resources – rather on transactions – which is defined by Hart (1995) as the 'residual control rights' over assets. The importance of ownership stems from the fact that any long-term contract will be inevitably incomplete, in that it will never be possible to foresee all future contingencies. This incompleteness makes it necessary that the original contract setting up a firm assigns ownership rights to the party that is most likely to make the necessary investment to enhance the profitability of the organization as a whole. Obviously, this will be the party that has the private knowledge about how best to pursue the joint effort. Therefore, both for transaction costs economics as well as for the incomplete contracts theory of the firm, it is privately-held knowledge that explains the emergence of the firm as an organization and the organizational forms that it takes in various contexts.

The second stream of contractual theories put 'delivery problems' at center stage. Agency theory (Ross, 1973; Jensen and Meckling, 1976) is one such approach that conceptualizes the principal-agent relation. In that context, a principal is supposed to delegate a task to an agent to carry out on the former's behalf. The principal is assumed to be unable to tightly monitor the agent's work, so she has to assess the latter's performance. However, it is difficult for the principal to judge whether the agent's performance reflects her actual conduct or is a matter of sheer luck. On these grounds, agency theory purports to construct models that devise efficient incentives structures *ex ante*, thus making the agent behave in the principal's best interest. Again, it is obvious that the principal-agent problem arises from the information asymmetries that characterize the knowledge sets of each of the two parties. However, in this case, what the principal wants to know is not the information the agent holds initially but, rather, the actual performance that the agent will ultimately deliver.

The 'nexus of contracts' view of the firm (Alchian and Demsetz, 1972) falls also into the category of delivery problems arising from asymmetric information. The problem here arises from the fact that, in the context of team production, where metering each agent's performance is costly, every agent has an incentive to free-ride on the efforts of other team members. Again, what is at issue is the actual performance that each team member will ultimately deliver, regardless of the initial knowledge with which she enters the employment contract. The solution to this information asymmetry is the contractual arrangement of the monitoring function, whereby one agent is assigned the responsibility (and, thus, the cost) of monitoring the performance of all others, in return for being recognized as the sole residual claimant of team production. Again, we have here an account of the emergence of the classic capitalist firm.

The above account shows that contractual theories of economic organization introduce into the analysis one attribute of knowledge that had not appeared in economics since the calculation debate: that it is liable to be treated opportunistically. We argue that this has become possible because these theories have focused on contracts as the units of analysis, rather than on price formation in markets. By focusing on interpersonal contracts, they inevitably had to transcend the view of prices as the sole bearers of information and to look deeper into the incentives that shape the intentions of agents to enter into contracts.

FROM CONTRACTS TO CAPABILITIES: THE CENTRALITY OF KNOWLEDGE

The proponents of contractual theories of economic organization – and of New Institutional Economics more generally[33] – pride themselves on the fact that their paradigm studies economic organization with the well established tools of neoclassical microeconomics. This may add rigor to the analysis but, at the same time, it imposes on it the strict static outlook of that paradigm. On these grounds, Foss (1998, pp. 182-3) stresses three limitations of contractual analyses: (a) an implicit assumption that alternatives are given, thus depicting agents as having to choose among a very clearly defined set of contractual alternatives; (b) a suppression of process, which implies that the optimal solution to the contract-design problem continues to be optimal throughout contract execution; (c) a set of strong knowledge assumptions, thus leaving no room for theory to conceptualize the discovery of new knowledge by agents. Importantly, all three drawbacks that Foss describes revolve around the issue of knowledge. The first implies a view of knowledge as information that is already available to agents. The second suppresses time as an essential aspect of the analysis, implying that agents do not learn anything during the execution of the contract. Finally, the third blocks any understanding of the discovery of new knowledge by agents.

And yet, contractual theories of economic organization brought along two novel ideas, thus opening a research path that attempts to break loose of the constraints that these drawbacks represent. The first idea is that, rather than viewing the firm as a mere transformer of inputs into outputs, it was now recognized that economic theory could seek to explain the relations between its constituent elements. The second idea is that, by focusing on the concept of interpersonal contracts rather than merely on market-mediated relations, it was now possible to extend the analysis to the study of a wide range of hybrid forms of economic organization like firm alliances, networks and clusters. This line of research allowed the abandonment of the view of competition as the sole determinant of inter-firm relations, along the lines that Richardson (1972) had suggested.

This new line of research has developed in many directions, has focused on a wide variety of organizational aspects, and has thus come to be described under various labels: Resource-Based View of the Firm, Evolutionary Theory, Knowledge-Based Theory of the Firm, to name only a few. However, in spite of the diversity of these approaches, what arguably unifies this stream of research into one distinct paradigm is the centrality of the concept of *knowledge,* which, as we will argue below, acquires the fullest recognition of its complexity in economics.

A full reference to this already vast literature is not possible here.

However, the distinctiveness of the treatment of knowledge in the context of this paradigm was already evident in the two contributions that are generally recognized as having laid its foundations: Penrose (1959) and Nelson and Winter (1982). Penrose (1959) is generally recognized as the initiator of the Resource-Based View of the Firm, as she was the first economist to describe the firm as a bundle of resources. But her greater contribution was the distinction between the resources available to the firm and the services that the firm can draw from them. In her view, there is not a one-to-one relation between the two concepts, which means that the firm can obtain different services from different combinations of its resources. But in this context, what is inside the firm becomes an object of discovery by the firm's management, as the services obtainable from different combinations of resources are not immediately available but something for the management to discover. Clearly, Penrose provides a forceful argument for the importance of learning by doing and of the sources of innovation in the modern firm.

Nelson and Winter (1982) are generally recognized as the initiators of modern evolutionary economics. Their greatest contribution is the introduction of the concept of *routines*. Routines are products of human interaction within the firm; however, they are mostly spontaneous growths of interactions, in the sense that they have not been designed by any single or collective will. As such, routines constitute a type of knowledge that is characterized by two major attributes: it has a large part that it is *tacit*, while at the same time it is *social*, in the sense that the knowledge represented by routines is not held by individual agents but it is shared by all the human constituents of the firm. In fact, the tacit knowledge embedded in routines actually transcends the knowledge set of the members of the firm, so that this knowledge remains embedded in the routines even when the members of the firm change.

In a sense, routines represent the memory of the organization, or the 'cognitive commonality' shared by all its constituents (Witt, 1998, 2000). They have been shaped by the history of the organization and, in turn, they shape its future as they determine the mode in which a specific organization will react to unexpected change, or will attempt to bring about change through innovation. In other words, the concept of routines captures both the prior knowledge of the organization as well as the direction of the learning processes that it tends to activate. On top of the firm's routines sit the *competencies* or *capabilities* (Teece and Pisano 1994) of this organization, which determine what the firm can do, and how effectively, thus constituting the major foundation of competitive advantage. Because they are built on routines, competencies are characterized by the same attributes of knowledge acquisition, management and creation, as routines. As Malerba and Orsenigo (2000, p. 311) maintain, 'the notion of competencies constitutes a key concept ... precisely because it aims at capturing the ways through which agents structure their knowledge and manage the interactions between differentiated fragments of information, knowledge codified in different codes and tacit knowledge'.

THE FUTURE OF KNOWLEDGE IN ECONOMICS

Let us sum up our discussion. The issue of knowledge has been at the core of economic theory for the whole of 20th century economics. However, for the schools of thought that have constituted the mainstream in various periods of the past century, knowledge has been consistently reduced to information: perfectly codifiable – and decodifiable – signals that mean the same things to all market participants. In a sense, information was thought of as something very much like – and, sometimes, actually equivalent to – prices. Thus the agent was and still is conceived as a passive information-taker, quite in line with the agent as price-taker view of orthodox theory. In such a context, the identity of the agent that actually receives the information does not matter, again in line with the receiver of a price signal. To the extent that knowledge is addressed as something distinct from information in this framework, it is usually viewed as a stock of information that has been created historically, and which agents can rationally choose to augment through conscious investment decisions.

However, this unanimity on the treatment of knowledge and information begins to crack as theory attempts to address information asymmetries and the potential for opportunistic behavior that this introduces. We have seen that it is for this reason that theory focuses on contracts as the institutional tool through which agents attempt to structure their dealings in order to curb the potential of opportunism. Economic institutions, such as the business firm and other forms of economic organizations, are thought of as emerging webs of interpersonal contracts. However, agents are still treated as information-takers, in the sense that they are described as choosing among clearly known contractual alternatives and as not learning anything new during contract execution. In other words, agents are still depicted as *passive* respondents to changes in their environment rather than as being able to effect change through their *creative* behavior. Finally, we have seen that any attempt to perceive agents and the organizations they constitute as creative actors inevitably leads to a deeper understanding of the issue of knowledge, and especially it introduces the tacit dimension for a part of individually held but also collective – that is social – knowledge.

It seems, therefore, that we have come full circle to where we started from, that is the debate about the feasibility of socialism. For we have seen that it has taken more than half a century for economics to deal in a rigorous manner with the two novel ideas that were first voiced during the debate: opportunism and tacit knowledge. However, whereas opportunism is here to stay, the concept of tacit knowledge, although influential, has a much more uncertain future, because of the far-reaching consequences for mainstream economics that its wide adoption would entail. For if part of the knowledge required for – and produced by – economic action is of tacit character, the belief in rational action as optimization within given and known constraints must be greatly qualified. There is too much at stake both for the supporters of the idea of tacit knowledge as well as for the skeptics. The former have to seek to define the distinction between codifiable and uncodifiable knowledge more rigorously, turning to other sciences for assistance if need be, like Ancori et al. (2000) who ground their argument for tacit knowledge in epistemology or Nightingale (2003) who seeks help from evolutionary biology. The skeptics, quite predictably, question the validity of the distinction on the basis of sound mainstream economics principles. Thus, Foss (2003) wonders about the consistency of the concept of tacit knowledge with methodological individualism, while Cowan et al. (2000) insist that all knowledge is in principle codifiable and, thus, that whether a part of knowledge will indeed be codified or not is a question for cost-benefit analysis. Importantly, a corollary of the latter view is that the growth of information and communication technologies reduces the cost of codification, thus tending to increase the volume of codified knowledge at the expense of knowledge that remains uncodified. Interestingly, almost forty years after Oscar Lange's (1967) famous remark, the electronic computer comes again to the rescue; this time though not of socialism but of mainstream economics.

NOTES

[1] A similar distinction between knowledge and information has been introduced by Hanappi (1988), who treats the former as a stock and the latter as a flow entity.

[2] Hodgson, of course, follows here Polanyi's (1967, p. 4) famous remark that 'we can know more than we can tell'.

[3] Usually referred to as the 'Marshallian scissors', after Alfred Marshall (1890).

[4] And, of course, the intentions are themselves reflections of the agents' preferences.

[5] Arguably, the problem of knowledge begins to appear here, as the assumption of profit maximization is based on the idea that the firm *knows* the prices of inputs, the available technologies, the prices of outputs, and so on.

[6] See also Weintraub (1979, pp. 141-154).

[7] A full list of the conditions for perfect competition can be already found in Frank Knight (1921). However, it is interesting to note that Knight proposed that long list of conditions because he wanted to focus on what happens in the event that some of them – importantly, the

perfect knowledge assumption — cease to hold. By contrast, later theorists, for example Stigler (1957), took Knight's list as the final word on the issue, that is as describing a real state towards which the market always converges. For the history of the concept of competition see McNulty (1967, 1968).

[8] Hicks (1939) is a major milestone in that development.

[9] This was the case in the interwar years with the work of Robinson (1933/1979) and Chamberlin (1933/1962), on 'imperfect' and 'monopolistic' competition respectively.

[10] See Shackle (1972/1992, p. 83) for a critique.

[11] See Ioannides (2000) for a survey of the debate.

[12] The *ex post* nature of the CPB's intervention would, supposedly, avoid the problems of the mathematical solution, which attempted to affect price setting *ex ante*. Interestingly, Lange (1967) continued to defend the practicability of his model even much later, claiming that the electronic computer would make the calculations necessary for solving it much easier.

[13] Interestingly, Mises' initial argument made no reference to the problem of knowledge, other than reconfirming the neoclassical view of equilibrium prices as bearers of 'correct' information.

[14] However, for the profession at large, the neoclassical socialists had won the debate, as Bergson (1948) declared.

[15] See Keynes (1936/1973, Chs 5 and, especially, 12).

[16] Arrow and Debreu (1954) was recognized as the Bible of the GE paradigm.

[17] Stigler (1961) and Arrow (1962a).

[18] It must be noted that, implicitly, Arrow deals only with codifiable knowledge. However, as we will see below, Arrow (1962b) was one of the pioneers in introducing learning and, with it, the tacit dimension of knowledge in economic theory.

[19] One can find a similar argument in the most prominent member of the modern Austrian school of economics (Kirzner 1973).

[20] In fact, Arrow's arguments on knowledge have furnished an influential argument for the public funding of research, in most of the relevant literature. An earlier statement to this effect can be found in Nelson (1959).

[21] With his 'permanent income hypothesis' (Friedman 1957) and, especially, his attack (1968) on the Phillips curve.

[22] See Lucas (1977, pp. 232-3) and Kyun (1988, p. 4).

[23] First introduced by Muth (1961).

[24] See Lucas (1977, p. 233).

[25] See Lucas (1979, p. 213) for the distinction between the strong and the weak versions of rational expectations.

[26] In contrast to the approach to growth that was dominant in the 1950s, when technology was considered to be entirely exogenous — the famous Solow's residual. See Solow (1957).

[27] Akerlof (1970) is generally recognized as having initiated this stream of research. Other important contributions to this stream of research are Holmström and Myerson (1983), Milgrom and Roberts (1982) and, of course, more recent work by Joseph Stiglitz.

[28] Recall Arrow's ideas on information as a commodity that we discussed in the previous section.

[29] See Simon (1957) and Newell and Simon (1972).

[30] Importantly, Simon (1951) was one of the first economists to introduce the idea that contracts serve to structure relations between agents that give rise to institutions, in his work on the labor contract.

[31] Williamson (1985a, p. 175) defines opportunism as 'self interest seeking with guile'.

[32] Williamson assumes bounded rationality, which explains why it is not possible to address every possible contingency *ex ante*.

[33] See how this paradigm is described by three of its main protagonists: Coase (1984), North (1986), Williamson (1985b).

REFERENCES

Aghion, P. and P. Howitt (1992), 'A Model of Growth through Creative Destruction', *Econometrica*, Vol. 60 (2): 323-51.

Akerlof, G. (1970), 'The Market for Lemons: Quality, Uncertainty and Market Mechanism', *Quarterly Journal of Economics,* August, 488-500.

Alchian, A.A. and H. Demsetz (1972), 'Production, Information Costs, and Economic Organisation', *American Economic Review*, Vol. 62: 777-95.

Ancori, B., A. Bureth and P. Cohendet (2000), 'The Economics of Knowledge: The Debate about Codification and Tacit Knowledge', *Industrial and Corporate Change*, Vol. 9: 255-88.

Arrow, K.J. (1959), 'Toward a Theory of Price Adjustment', in M. Abramovitz et al. (eds), *The Allocation of Economic Resources*, Stanford: Stanford University Press.

Arrow, K.J. (1962a), 'Economic Welfare and the Allocation of Resources to Invention', in R.R. Nelson (ed.), *The Rate and Direction of Inventive Activity: Economic and Social Factors*, Princeton, NJ: Princeton University Press.

Arrow, K.J. (1962b), 'The Economic Implications of Learning by Doing', *Review of Economic Studies*, Vol. 29: 155-73.

Arrow, K.J. and G. Debreu (1954), 'Existence of an Equilibrium for a Competitive Economy', *Econometrica*, Vol. 22: 265-90.

Bergson, A. (1948), 'Socialism', in Ellis, H.S. (ed.), (1949), *A Survey of Contemporary Economics*, New York: Blakiston.

Chamberlin, E.H. (1933/1962), *The Theory of Monopolistic Competition*, Cambridge: Harvard University Press.

Coase, R.H. (1937), 'The Nature of the Firm', *Economica*, Vol. 4: 386-405.

Coase, R.H. (1984), 'The New Institutional Economics', *Journal of Institutional and Theoretical Economics*, Vol. 140: 229-31.

Cowan, R., P.A. David and D. Foray (2000), 'The Explicit Economics of Knowledge Codification and Tacitness', *Industrial and Corporate Change*, Vol. 9: 211-54.

Dickinson, H.D. (1933), 'Price Formation in a Socialist Community', *Economic Journal*, Vol. 43: 237-50.

Dickinson, H.D. (1939), *Economics of Socialism*, London: Oxford University Press.

Durbin, E.F.M. (1936), 'Economic Calculus in a Planned Economy', *Economic Journal*, Vol. 46: 676-90.

Edgeworth, F.Y. (1881/1932), *Mathematical Psychics*, London: London School Reprint.

Foss, N.J. (1998), 'Austrian Insights and the Theory of the Firm', *Advances in Austrian Economics*, Vol. 4: 175-98.

Foss, N.J. (2003), 'Bounded Rationality and Tacit Knowledge in the Organizational Capabilities Approach: An Assessment and Re-evaluation', *Industrial and Corporate Change*, Vol. 12: 185-202.

Friedman, M. (1957), *The Theory of the Consumption Function*, Princeton, NJ: Princeton University Press.

Friedman, M. (1968), 'The Role of Monetary Theory', *American Economic Review*, Vol. 58, 1-17.

Grossman, S.J. and O.D. Hart (1986), 'The Costs and Benefits of Ownership', *Journal of Political Economy*, Vol. XCIV: 671-719.

Grossman, G. and E. Helpman, (1991), *Innovation and Growth in the Global Economy*, Cambridge, MA: MIT Press.

Hanappi G. and Th. Grechenig (1988), 'There is no Homunculus, a Critique of A.I.

Fundamentals', Contribution to the EMCSR 88, April 1988 in Vienna, in *Cybernetics and Systems* (edited by Robert Trappl), 1988, Reidel Publishers.

Hart, O. (1995), *Firms, Contracts and Financial Structure*, Oxford: Clarendon Press.

Hayek, F.A. (1935), 'The Present State of the Debate', in *Hayek (1935/1975)*.

Hayek, F.A. (ed.) (1935/1975), *Collectivist Economic Planning*, London: G. Routledge & Sons.

Hayek, F.A. (1940), 'Socialist Calculation III', in Hayek (1949).

Hayek, F.A. (1949), *Individualism and Economic Order*, London: Routledge & Kegan Paul.

Hayek, F.A. (1963), 'Rules, Perception and Inteligibility', in Hayek (1967).

Hayek, F.A. (1967), *Studies in Philosophy, Politics and Economics*, London: Routledge & Kegan Paul.

Hicks, J. (1937), 'Mr. Keynes and the "Classics": A Suggested Interpretation', *Econometrica*, Vol. 5, 147-59.

Hicks, J. (1939), *Value and Capital*, Oxford: Oxford University Press.

Hodgson, G.M. (1999), *Economics and Utopia: Why the Learning Economy is not the End of History*, London: Routledge.

Holmström, B. and R. Myerson (1983), 'Efficient and Durable Decision Rules with Incomplete Information', *Econometrica*, Vol. 51: 1799-1820.

Jensen, M.C. and W.H. Meckling (1976), 'Theory of the Firm: Managerial Behavior, Agency Costs, and Ownership Structure', *Journal of Financial Economics*, 305-60.

Ioannides, S. (2000), 'Austrian Economics, Socialism and Impure Forms of Economic Organisation', *Review of Political Economy*, Vol. 12: 45-71.

Ioannides, S. (2005), 'Information and Knowledge in 20th Century Economics: From Prices, to Contracts, to Organizations', in G. Kouzelis, M. Pournari, M. Stoeppler and V. Tselfes (eds), *Knowledge in the New Technologies*, Frankfurt: Peter Lang.

Keynes, J.M. (1936/1973), *The General Theory of Employment, Interest and Money*, London: Macmillan.

Kirzner, I.M. (1973), *Competition and Entrepreneurship*, Chicago: University of Chicago Press.

Knight, F.H. (1921), *Risk Uncertainty and Profit*, Chicago: University of Chicago Press.

Kyun, K. (1988), *Equilibrium Business Cycle Theory in Historical Perspective*, Cambridge: Cambridge University Press.

Lange, O. (1938), 'On the Economic Theory of Socialism', in B.E. Lippincott (ed.), *On the Economic Theory of Socialism*, New York: McGraw Hill.

Lange, O. (1967), 'The Computer and the Market', in C. Feinstein (ed.), *Capitalism, Socialism and Economic Growth*, Cambridge: Cambridge University Press.

Lerner, A.P. (1934-5), 'Economic Theory and Socialist Economy', *Review of Economic Studies*, Vol. 2: 51-61.

Lerner, A.P. (1937), 'Statics and Dynamics in Socialist Economics', *Economic Journal*, Vol. 47: 253-70.

Lipsey, R. (1999), 'Some implications of endogenous technological change for technology policies in developing countries', paper presented in the workshop, *The Political Economy of Technology in Developing Countries*, Brighton, 8-9 October, INTECII–UNU.

Lucas, R.E. Jr. (1977), 'Understanding Business Cycles', in Lucas (1981).

Lucas, R.E. Jr. (1979), 'An Equilibrium Model of Business Cycle', in Lucas (1981).

Lucas, R.E. Jr. (1981), *Studies in Business Cycle Theory*, Cambridge, MA: The MIT

Press.

Makowski, L. and J.M. Ostroy (2001), 'Perfect Competition and the Creativity of the Market', *Journal of Economic Literature*, Vol. 34: 479-535.

Malerba, F. and L. Orsenigo (2000), 'Knowledge, Innovative Activities and Industrial Evolution', *Industrial and Corporate Change*, Vol. 9: 289-314.

Marshall, A. (1890), *The Principles of Economics*, London: Macmillan.

McNulty, P.J. (1967), 'A Note on the History of Perfect Competition', *Journal of Political Economy*, Vol. 75: 395-9.

McNulty, P.J. (1968), 'Economic Theory and the Meaning of Competition', *Quarterly Journal of Economics*, Vol. 82: 639-56.

Milgrom, P. and Roberts, J. (1982), 'Limit Pricing and Entry under Incomplete Information: An Equilibrium Analysis', *Econometrica*, Vol. 50: 443-59.

Mises, L. von (1920), 'Economic Calculation in the Socialist Commonwealth', in Hayek (1935).

Muth, J.F. (1961), 'Rational Expectations and the Theory of Price Movements', *Econometrica*, Vol. 29: 315-35.

Nelson, R.R. (1959), 'The Simple Economics of Basic Scientific Research', *Journal of Political Economy*, Vol. 67: 297-306.

Nelson, R.R. and S.G. Winter (1982), *An Evolutionary Theory of Economic Change*, Cambridge, MA: Harvard University Press.

Newell, A. and H.A. Simon (1972), *Human Problem Solving*, Englewood Cliffs, NJ: Prentice-Hall.

Nightingale, P. (2003), 'If Nelson and Winter are Only Half Right about Tacit Knowledge, Which Half? A Searlean Critique of "Codification"', *Industrial and Corporate Change*, Vol. 12: 149-184.

North, D.C. (1986), 'The New Institutional Economics', *Journal of Institutional and Theoretical Economics*, Vol. 142: 230-37.

O'Driscoll, G.P. Jr. and M.J. Rizzo (1985), *The Economics of Time and Ignorance*, Oxford: Blackwell.

OECD (1992), *Technology and the Economy: the key relationships*, Paris: OECD.

Penrose, E.T. (1959), *The Theory of the Growth of the Firm*, Oxford: Oxford University Press.

Polanyi, M. (1967), *The Tacit Dimension*, London: Routledge and Kegan Paul.

Richardson, G.B. (1972), 'The Organisation of Industry', *Economic Journal*, Vol. 82: 883-96.

Robinson, J. (1933/1979), *The Economics of Imperfect Competition*, London: Macmillan.

Romer, P. (1990), 'Endogenous Technological Change', *Journal of Political Economy*, Vol. 98, October: 71-102.

Ross, S.A. (1973), 'The Economic Theory of Agency: The Principal's Problem', *American Economic Review*, Vol. 63: 134-9.

Shackle, G.L.S. (1972/1992), *Epistemics and Economics: A Critique of Economic Doctrines*, New Brunswick, New Jersey: Transaction Publishers.

Simon, H.A. (1951), 'A Formal Theory of the Employment Relation', *Econometrica*, Vol. 19: 293-305.

Simon, H.A. (1957), *Models of Man*, New York: Wiley.

Solow, R.M. (1957), 'Technical Change and the Aggregate Production Function', *The Review of Economics and Statistics*, Vol. 39: 312-20.

Stigler, G.J. (1957), 'Perfect Competition Historically Contemplated', *Journal of Political Economy*, Vol. 65: 1-17.

Stigler, G.J. (1961), 'The Economics of Information', *Journal of Political Economy*, Vol. 69: 213-25.

Teece, D.J. and G. Pisano (1994), 'The Dynamic Capabilities of Firms: An Introduction', *Industrial and Corporate Change*, Vol. 3: 537-56.

Vaughn, K.I. (1980), 'Economic Calculation under Socialism', *Economic Inquiry*, Vol. 18: 535-54.

Walras, L. (1874/1954), *Elements of Pure Economics*, New York: Augustus Kelley.

Weintraub, E.R. (1979), *Microfoundations: The Compatibility of Microeconomics and Macroeconomics*, Cambridge: Cambridge University Press.

Williamson, O.E. (1975), *Markets and Hierarchies: Analysis and Anti-trust Implications*, New York: Free Press.

Williamson, O.E. (1985a), *The Economic Institutions of Capitalism*, New York: Free Press.

Williamson, O.E. (1985b), 'Reflections on the New Institutional Economics', *Journal of Institutional and Theoretical Economics*, Vol. 141: 187-95.

Witt, U. (1998), 'Imagination and Leadership: The Neglected Dimension of an Evolutionary Theory of the Firm', *Journal of Economic Behavior and Organization*, Vol. 35: 161-77.

Witt, U. (2000), 'Changing Cognitive Frames – Changing Organizational Forms: An Entrepreneurial Theory of Organizational Development', *Industrial and Corporate Change*, Vol. 9 (4): 733-55.

Index

Agarwal, R. et al. 66
Aghion, P. and P. Howitt 220
Albarracin, D. et al. 101
Alchian, A. 18, 183
Alchian, A. and H. Demsetz 224
Ancori, B. et al. 228
Andersen, E. 20, 193, 195–6
Anderson, J. 103, 104, 116
Anderson, P. and M. Tushman 193, 194, 196
Angresano, J. 82
Argandona, A. 116
Argyrous, G. and R. Sethi 81
Arrow, K. 168, 189, 212, 217, 220
Arthur, W. 22, 30, 90
Astley, W. 193

Baaij, M. 197
Baldwin, W. and J. Scott 30
Bandura, A. 102, 105, 109
Barnard, C. 38
Barnett, W. 193, 196
Barnett, W. and R. Burgelman 181
Becker, G. 115
Becker, M. and N. Lazaric 55
Bellets, M. and F. Sosthe 82
Berger, Sebastian 79–96
Bergson, A. 229
Bertalanffy, L. von 83, 84
Bhaskar, R. 83
Binder, Martin 97–120
Binmore, K. 10
Blaug, M. 123
Blume, L. and D. Easley 21
Boeddrich, H.-J. 187–8
Boschma, R. and R. Wenting 67
bounded rationality
    and evolutionary economics 26, 27

and individualism 132
    and knowledge 222, 223
Bowles, S. 97, 98, 106, 109–10
Bowles, S. and H. Gintis 43, 115
Boyd, R. and P. Richerson 30, 49, 116
Brazeal, D. and T. Herbert 187
Brenner, T. 21
Brock, W. and D. Evans 186
Buenstorf, Guido 14, 59–78
Buss, D. 50

Campbell, D. 13, 14, 37, 43, 52, 56, 184, 189
Cantner, U. et al. 67
capitalism *see* economic liberalization
Carabelli, A. 150
Carlton, D. 67
Carree, M. and A. Thurik 186
Castells, M. 200
Chandler, A. 183
Chattoe, E. 21
Christensen, C. 191
Cialdini, R. and M. Trost 116
Clark, A. 136, 138
Clower, R. 172
Coase, R. 87, 223
Cohen, W. and D. Levinthal 202
Colander, D. and H. Landreth 167
competition
    and evolutionary economics 61
    and industrial evolution 194–6
    market, and innovation 62, 65, 66
    market, and supply-side bias 61–2
    perfect 212
    resource, of firms 43, 44, 51–2, 53, 226
consumer protection, and industrial
    evolution 193, 194

244   *Index*

and firms 39, 52, 53, 61, 62, 63–4,
    66, 226–7
and knowledge 226
Rumelt, R. 181, 183
Runde, J. and S. Mizuhara 150

Sachs, S. 196
Samuelson, L. 10, 167, 168, 170, 171
Sandelin, B. 81
Savage, L. 148, 156–8, 159
Schaper, M. and T. Volery 186, 187
Schlicht, E. 143, 185, 193, 201
Schroedinger, E. 84
Schumpeter, J. 2, 14, 15, 17–19, 20,
    21–2, 25, 26, 27–8, 60, 91, 186,
    189, 193, 195–6
Schuster, P. and K. Sigmund 10
Schwefel, H.-P. 21
Searle, J. 144, 161
Shackle, G. 229
Shimp, T. et al. 103
Silva, S. and A. Teixeira 9
Silverberg, G. and B. Verspagen 185
Simon, H. 1, 19, 50, 126, 132, 229
Simons, K. 66, 67, 195, 196
Skinner, B. 56, 104
Skott, P. 81
Sleeper, S. 61, 65, 66
Smith, A. 43, 200
Sober, E. and D. Wilson 42
social organization
    centre-periphery approach 83
    and division of labor 43
    and dominance hierarchies 48, 50,
        52
    economic and social dimension,
        distinction between 48, 49
    evolution of 189–90
    evolutionary view of
        socio-economic behavior and
        Darwinism 35–58
    and group membership 48, 49–50,
        52
    and hierarchical power 50, 52
    individualism and social identity
        134, 135, 136
    and knowledge growth 190
    and market exchange 48, 49, 51, 52

Open-Systems Approach (OSA),
    institutional dimension of
    societal organisations 85–6
peer pressure 48, 49, 52
and perceived characteristics
    189–90
population ecology 27, 191, 192,
    193, 194, 198
social economic policy towards
    individualism 139–40
social evolution model 191–2
social evolution and strategy 192–9
social systems theory and knowledge
    159–60
'socialist calculation' debate of
    1930s 213–14
socio-economic selection
    environment of firms 50–53, 87
socio-economic selection
    mechanisms 48–50
survival instincts 48, 49
see also individualism
Stacey, R. 196
Stahlberg, D. and D. Frey 112
Steppacher, R. 80, 83, 85
Sternberg, R. et al. 189
Stigler, G. 115, 216–17, 218, 229
Stoelhorst, J.W. 35–58
strategy
    and evolutionary game theory
        182–3, 191
    evolutionary learning perspective
        181–208
    and industrial evolution 192–4,
        196–9, 200
    research 183
Stroebe, W. and K. Jonas 108, 112,
    113
Stuart, E. et al. 103
Sugden, R. 116

technology
    change and innovation 26, 27
    choice and societal and
        environmental objectives 88
    institutions and technology,
        co-evolution of 20–21, 26, 27
    technical knowledge, and